Memphis Innovations

People, Ideas, and Innovations That Changed Our World

By Richard Raichelson
with Donna West

Original Photography by API Photography / Bill Carrier and Robert W. Dye

ISBN: 0-9767330-0-5 (hardcover)
ISBN: 0-9767330-1-3 (softcover)

Publisher: Bob Snodgrass
Editor: Mark Potter
Art Direction & Design: Lisa Wayland
Editor of Profiles: Deborah Morehead
Project Coordinator: Vickie Bishop
Photography Coordinator: Richard Raichelson
Publishing Consultant: Frank Armato and Scott Voorhees
Design Assistance: Christy Douglass

Attention schools and businesses: Power House books are available at quantity discounts with bulk purchases for education, business, or sales promotional use.

Every effort was made to ensure accuracy of the information herein. However, the authors and publisher are not responsible for any errors or omissions which might have occurred. Photos were provided from a variety of sources. Every reasonable attempt was made to give proper photo credit. If there are any errors, please notify the publisher and corrections will be made in subsequent editions.

© 2006 Power House, Inc.

Beverly Timmons Bluff City Graphics Books
Printed in China.

Overland Park, KS 66210

Memphis Innovations

Development of MEMPHIS INNOVATIONS has itself been a highly complex and entrepreneurial venture. It involved research, interviews, and cooperation of those who are pictured and profiled and, in the case of deceased business leaders, their families. More than 1,000 individuals were considered for inclusion in this publication. About 250 were actively researched. Only 50 could be selected. The editors understand that many business leaders worthy of inclusion must wait for the next edition.

It is impossible to name everyone who contributed to this book and to thank them properly. Everyone who played a role in the research, writing, photography, and production of MEMPHIS INNOVATIONS displayed a sincere interest in the education of students in Memphis and Shelby County.

The Publisher

Table of Contents

Preface   3
Dedication to Junior Achievement   page   10
Memphis A City of Culture, Enrichment, and Innovation   page 12
Biographies:

IN HONOR OF THE ENTREPRENEURS

Entrepreneurship has characterized America for more than 200 years. Some call it "the great American dream." It has been the constant of our nation despite technological, social, and governmental changes.

The dream persists, whether the next great idea involves music, transportation, a more comfortable hotel, medicine, or a device to prolong life. This book is not only about the past. It is intended to provide inspiration and a roadmap for the next generation of entrepreneurs.

Memphis has a long and distinguished history of entrepreneurship. MEMPHIS INNOVATIONS has biographies of fifty individuals who have changed the way we live in our community, and for that matter, the world.

Dedication to Junior Achievement Volunteers

MEMPHIS INNOVATIONS is dedicated to the 8,700 individuals who each year volunteer their time, expertise, and resources to the Junior Achievement programs and students in the schools of Memphis and Shelby County. The book is no less dedicated to business leaders and organizations that provide generous, ongoing support to perpetuate the creativity, innovation, and business climate of Greater Memphis, making it a unique and vibrant area.

Junior Achievement has an outstanding, active 40-person board of directors. An additional 60 community leaders are involved in the organization's fund-raising. Junior Achievement's education programs are made possible by 267 business volunteers, 940 college and university students, and 1,200 parents who regularly contribute their time and knowledge to educating future business leaders. The organization is supported by 5,000 individuals who participate in its annual bowling tournament and 1,200 volunteers who participate in the annual 5K run.

Last year, more than 50,000 Memphis and Shelby County elementary and high school students began to learn the skills, risks, and obligations that form the foundation of success, entrepreneurship, and innovations in the business world. We all will benefit from continuation of the spirit of business leadership and prosperity.

Today, the Junior Achievement program reaches a worldwide audience, accommodating nearly six million students of all ages in 99 countries. Junior Achievement now provides 20 programs for students in 145 U.S. locations.

Kemmons Wilson, founder of Holiday Inns, grew one of the greatest hospitality organizations in the world. His legacy started from a single popcorn machine, shown above and culminated with his donation of the Kemmons Wilson School of Hospitality and Resort Management at the University of Memphis (pictured on the following page). His example sets the standard for entrepreneurship and Jr. Achievement students and volunteers. He was inducted into the Junior Achievement National Business Hall of Fame in 1982.

Kemmons Wilson School of Hospitality & Resort Management, University of Memphis (photo by Robert W. Dye).

Memphis
A City of Culture, Enrichment, and Innovation

"History is neither more or less than biography on a large scale."
-- Lamartine

The Hub of the Mid-South

In the period of 1848-50, when almost the entire railroad track lay east of the Mississippi River, the country was abuzz with talk of a transcontinental railroad that would tie the nation together. Cities like St. Louis, Memphis, Vicksburg, and New Orleans were excited about the prospects of being chosen as one of the main eastern terminals. Memphis did not have an elaborate railroad system at the time, but Memphians envisioned their city's strategic location as a logical choice for a gateway to the Pacific.

At a Memphis railroad convention in 1849, Lieutenant Matthew F. Maury recommended Memphis. Lt. Maury was a distinguished naval scientist and a Memphis booster. He pointed out that the city was located halfway between Lake Michigan and the Gulf of Mexico, and its climate was more suitable than those in northern cities. Maury also said if the railroad went through Texas, it would open up trade with Mexico. In 1841, Maury successfully convinced U.S. Congress to build a Navy yard in Memphis. Memphians became excited as they envisioned prosperity through trade and business, along with additional economic benefits from a major population increase. Memphians underwrote the extension of the Memphis & Charleston Railroad, hoping to gain recognition as the portal to the West. The Civil War interrupted plans for railroad construction through Memphis. Eventually, the Transcontinental Railroad was established much further north and Memphis was left out.

The Mississippi River looks like a paved highway as it sweeps south underneath the Harahan, Great, and I-55 bridges. In the distance is the state of Mississippi, just below the Memphis border (photo by API Photographers, Inc.).

Located in the South Main Art District, the Central Train Station was built in 1914. To the left is the Arcade Restaurant, one of Memphis' longest operating eateries (photo by API Photographers, Inc.).

Nevertheless, Maury's plea represented an early argument for Memphis as a distribution center through which goods and people would flow. Memphis' status as a key location for distribution was attained during the late 1800s by the city's powerful cotton industry. It solidified in the 20th century due to a transportation system that consisted of an array of highways, railroads, and air traffic extending out like spokes on a wheel. All of this growth and activity was borne from the fact that numerous businesses relocated or built plants in Memphis because of its central geographical location. Memphis is still referred to as "the nation's distribution center," which can best be seen in the FedEx system developed by Fred Smith. FedEx brings packages to Memphis before they are sorted and flown to various destinations around the world.

On another level, in accordance with its large population, Memphis is the hub of the Mid-South. The Mid-South is a region that extends in an outward radius from the city by about 100 to 150 miles. Memphis is the cultural and economic kingpin of the region, as displayed by its variety of museums, art galleries, theaters, concert halls, parks, sports facilities, and medical and financial systems. Memphis' cultural influence also results in a diverse number of corporations, high tourism, and in the attitude of its people.

Because of its central role in the Mid-South, Memphis is a desirable location and a good place to develop entrepreneurial ideas. In this short history of the Bluff City, the groundwork is laid for 50 Memphians who set in motion innovations that positively influenced Memphis and our world.

Starting from Lake Itasca, Minnesota, the Mississippi River meanders 2,340 miles downstream to its outlet in the Gulf of Mexico. Memphis lies about two-thirds of the way downstream, perched high above the river on a bluff. It is one of four such bluffs along the river between Cairo and Vicksburg, and all are located in Tennessee within a 60-mile distance of one another. The land on which Memphis sits was part of the Chickasaw Indian Nation. The Chickasaw Nation used the location as a trading post, which showed an early sign of the river's mercantile value. The Memphis region was also a strategic location because of its elevation above the Mississippi and relative protection from the perils of floods.

In 1818, generals Andrew Jackson and Isaac Shelby struck a deal with the Chickasaw Nation and purchased several million acres of land for the United States in an agreement named the Chickasaw Cession. A portion of this land included the Chickasaw Bluff, the place where Memphis was founded. The Rice Grant, which consisted of 5,000 acres of land in Shelby County, was owned jointly by John Overton, James Winchester, and Andrew Jackson. The three instructed their agents to design and lay out a community in 1819.

The history of entrepreneurship in Memphis began with those three proprietors, but none of them ever lived in the city. The people of the community were the real developers because they recognized the area's value and stayed to form something out of nothing despite tough times. They built houses for their families and for future Memphians. These pioneers did all they could to promote the city up and down the Mississippi River, and they did their best to develop businesses. The Lawrences, Rawlings, Bettises, and Carrs were among Memphis' first entrepreneurs. They set the forces in motion and laid the groundwork for the city's future.

At first, Memphis was slow to grow, perhaps because it was a lawless town that was made unapproachable by flatboatmen. These individualistic, rough-house types served a purpose in supplying goods to the fledgling town, but on their own hell-raising terms. Finally, in 1842, the city put an end to their defiance. Everything began to change. The city grew more rapidly and the Mississippi River, with its new riverboat inhabitants, became its lifeline.

High on the Memphis bluff overlooking the Mississippi River, cotton is hauled down the bluff so it can be loaded onto riverboats (photo Illustrated London News, July 2, 1853, courtesy of the Memphis Room, Memphis Library and Information Center).

VIEW OF MEMPHIS, TENNESSEE.

The Majestic Mississippi

Many people in Memphis refer to the Mississippi River as if it were part of their soul, and with good reason. The river was significant in city commerce in the 19th century, but it also dug deeply within the psyche of Memphians.

From the 1840s on into the first two decades of the 20th century, riverboats were important in carrying goods to and from Memphis. Riverboats became less important when railroads began their upward spiral after the Civil War. Today, the barge has taken on the role that riverboats once held, while airplanes and trucking lines dominate the railroad industry.

Memphis may have felt comfortable sitting atop a bluff high above the river, but that didn't settle the stomachs of those in the delta. The Mississippi River, paradoxically loved and hated by all who knew her, had its own mind and seemed like an invincible being. The river seemed to make decisions about the lives of people and animals, the geographical makeup of the land through which it cut, and the success rate of local economies. Flooding was a major problem in the Mid-South until the 1930s. The river was difficult to navigate, which required immense skill and a detailed knowledge of its shifting patterns, not to mention guts. The grandfather of FedEx founder Fred Smith was a riverboat captain who could have probably enlightened us. Many were frustrated with the river, as one person exclaimed it was "too thick to drink and too thin to plow."

Even so, the river prevailed in Memphians by means of literature, story, and song. Memphis author George W. Lee wrote about the river, roustabouts, and Beale Street, which is the center for African-Americans in Memphis. People told stories about gamblers and other characters who traveled on riverboats or relaxed on the riverfront. Tales were told about Apple Annie, Sam's Catfish Stand, and Suzette's Boarding House and Drink Emporium, which was just up from the landing on Beale Street.

Huge barges have replaced the riverboat in the transportation of goods and agricultural products on the Mississippi River (photo by API Photographers, Inc.).

Songs were part of roustabouts' routine work as they struggled, pushing huge bales of cotton along the levee. Jazz bands provided entertainment aboard local showboats as they made excursions to St. Louis and Helena. Blues musicians entertained as well, on cobblestones and sometimes on riverboats.

Today, Memphians still celebrate the river. "Memphis in May" packs Tom Lee Park to the Mississippi during its music and barbecue festivals, and with the Sunset Symphony. Residents of Harbor Town can see the river swirling downstream from their porches, or as they jog along the river walk. So, too, can homesteaders in the South Bluffs and those in Riverbluff condominiums. In July and August, WEVL FM-90, Memphis' individualistic radio station, holds its "Blues on the Bluff" concert on the grounds of the National Ornamental Metal Museum, high above one of the most beautiful spots on the river.

Many years ago the city's expansion was all eastward, away from downtown and the river. Now, the trend has almost reversed, thanks to the provision of housing by Henry Turley and Jack Belz, and the establishment of many key downtown attractions. For the majority of people, the Mississippi River remains a main component of life in Memphis.

Cotton, Memphis' most important economic resource of the 19th century, was not a significant part of the economy until the riverboat became more prevalent in the late 1830s. Because of its close proximity to Arkansas and the rich bottomlands of the Mississippi Delta, Memphis laid claim to the title of being the "biggest inland cotton market in the world" in the 1850s. In the 20th century, the name was changed to the "largest spot cotton market in the world." Front Street, known as "cotton row," was overrun by cotton factors that elbowed for room within its few blocks. A short jaunt from Front was the levee, where splendid riverboats crowded the cobblestones to gobble up cotton bales. When cotton was plentiful, boats were overloaded, and sometimes they sank.

Jim Lee Sr., a highly experienced 300-pound riverboatman who kept people spellbound with his stories, founded the Lee Steamboat Company line in Memphis during the 1860s. Lee favored short runs and became wealthy hauling cotton from Friars Point, Mississippi to Memphis. His sons, Jim Lee Jr., and Stacker Lee were also captains. There were about 14 boats in the Lee line, many named after Lee's children and grandchildren. The last of his boats, "Harry Lee," was sold in 1930.

By the latter part of the 19th century, cotton factors dominated the business climate of Memphis and the Mid-South. They not only owned all the cotton firms, but controlled the wholesale and retail grocery companies, banks, and the insurance industry. Most of them also had large real estate holdings. Many financial institutions were formed to fund the cotton industry, such as the National Bank of Commerce, which was founded in 1873. Also during the year of 1873, the Memphis Cotton Exchange was organized as a place where businessmen could gather to discuss prices and talk about markets. The cotton factor helped Memphis become one of the largest cotton markets and a distribution center for groceries and provisions. Most of the prominent Memphis families involved with cotton continued their influence well into the 20th century. Napoleon Hill was one of the wealthiest Memphians, and was a cotton factor, banker, and financier. Hill owned cotton warehouses and large tracts of real estate. Dunavant Enterprises, an entrepreneur featured in this book, is tied to the cotton economy. Other important families who had an influence in the industry include those of Fontaine, Mallory, Neely, Norfleet, Fargason, and Treadwell, among others.

Cobblestones comprising the Memphis riverfront landing were laid beginning in the late 1850s. Their iron rings, used to tie off steamboats, are no longer used by newer touring riverboats (photo by Robert W. Dye).

The modern term "agribusiness" has always defined the Memphis economy, even in the 19th century. Despite the fact that Memphis has made many attempts to diversify its industrial output, agriculture has remained dominant. Other businesses came and went, but agribusiness stayed. Cotton, and later soybeans and rice, have helped sustain the economy.

During the late 19th and early 20th centuries, cottonseed oil manufacturing plants, cotton compress businesses, and cotton-filled warehouses

Cotton factor offices were mainly on Front Street, but these were on Howard's Row, now part of Union Avenue. The building in the foreground, 45-47 Union, was built in 1843 (photo by Dorothea Lange, 1937, Library of Congress, Prints & Photographs Division, FSA-OWI Collection, courtesy of Memphis Archives).

were important to Memphis. Many companies came to Memphis because of its central geographical location, agricultural proximity to Mississippi and Arkansas, and pure artesian water system. Orgill Brothers, established by William Orgill in 1847 to supply the needs of frontier life, is the oldest family-owned business in Memphis. The wholesale and retail hardware business equipped travelers going west and sold cotton presses and other farming equipment to cotton planters in the Mid-South.

After World War II, International Harvester opened a plant to manufacture cotton pickers because of Memphis' proximity to the delta. Kellogg established a Memphis plant to be near the Arkansas rice fields, and to reduce its shipping costs to southern markets. Willard Sparks, one of the innovators in this book, was an important figure in selling grain to Russia when he worked for Cook Industries, which was one of the country's largest agribusinesses.

Similarly, Memphis' role as the "world's largest mule market" was tied to its agricultural roots. Thousands were corralled in several city stockyards, and then auctioned to supply farmers' needs. When tractors were readily available in the 1950s, mule traffic practically ceased.

By the turn of the century, timber was brought to Memphis from huge hardwood forests in the delta and in Arkansas. The wood was processed in one of numerous mills. Memphis gained a reputation as a manufacturing center for furniture and hardwood flooring. At one time, E.L. Bruce was the world's largest producer of hardwood flooring. Hence, Memphis earned the nicknames "world's largest hardwood market" and "the hardwood flooring capital of the world." When wood was commonly used in automobiles, such as for wheels, several such companies came to operate in Memphis. The businesses folded soon thereafter when cars began to have all-steel bodies.

After World War II, much of the economic diversity in Memphis was the handiwork of a number of entrepreneurs featured in this book. They recognized a potential need and literally carved a mountain out of a mole hill. For instance, in 1951 Kemmons Wilson concluded that the motel business was the "greatest untouched industry in the world." Not long after, Wilson became "The Nation's Innkeeper." Fred Smith built FedEx on a centralized distribution plan, while Ira Lipman and Guardsmark gave corporations a sense of confidence by providing the best security possible. The Welcome Wagon Empire, built by Thomas Briggs, led a local businessman to quip, "You have the most remarkable business. Every year you give away $10 million worth of gifts and get paid for doing it." Briggs' concept was the ultimate in hospitality, a perfect reflection of his character and personality. And then there was James K. Dobbs, who, being a gregarious type, offered to help an ill airplane stewardess distribute food during a flight. Dobbs said the food was "awful looking... I was pretty sick myself when I got through." He thought he could do better so he developed an airline catering business, which is still in operation.

Other than cotton, real estate, and human traffic, the railroad attracted the most entrepreneurs before the Civil War. Two railroad barons were especially prominent. Robertson Topp was president of the Memphis & Ohio Railroad. He was a member of the Tennessee Whig party, and responsible for the development of south Memphis where Beale Street is located. Robert C. Brinkley developed the Memphis & Charleston Railroad. Brinkley also built the original Peabody Hotel, and was president of Planters Bank in Memphis.

Memphis lacked a bridge over the Mississippi River until 1892, and had to ferry trains across by means of boats. The entire exercise was inconvenient to say the least. For more than 30 years, until the 1880s, the same six railroad companies served Memphis. By the time the Great Bridge was built, the city had 13 railroads, which brought additional economic benefits. For four days Memphians celebrated the only bridge south of St. Louis. At the time, it was the third largest in the world. In 1916 the Harahan Bridge, which carried both rail and automotive traffic, was built just 200 feet north of the first one.

As trains became more important for transportation, they began to take over the major portion of cotton transportation. By the 1880s, more than 80 percent of cotton shipments were by railroad.

The gateway to the West. Construction of the Memphis Bridge, or Great Bridge, began in 1888 and was completed in 1892 for the Kansas City, Fort Scott & Memphis Railroad. When the Frisco Railroad bought the line in 1903, its name was changed to the Frisco Bridge. It is flanked on its right by the Harahan Bridge and on its left by the Memphis and Arkansas Bridge (photo by Robert W. Dye).

The Harahan Bridge was named after James T. Harahan, a former president of the Illinois Central Railroad. When it was built in 1916, the bridge carried both automobiles and trains (photo by Robert W. Dye).

In the 19th century, riverboats played a prominent role in immigration by transporting people up the Mississippi from New Orleans. They also carried people down from the upper stretches of the Mississippi, and from the East via the Ohio River. The Irish were the first big wave of immigrants, coming to the United States in the 1840s because of the potato famine. They were followed by the Germans. Each of these groups had various social orders, and they were important additions to Memphis' economy. German Jews, such as merchants Lowenstein and Seessel, also added considerably to the society of Memphis.

In the mid-1800s, the bulk of Memphis' Irish population resided in north Memphis – the Pinch area, which contained some of the poorest sections in the city. "Pinch" (or, "Pinchgut") may have referred to irregular eating habits, or the inability of male adults to afford drinks at local saloons. Other neighborhoods in north Memphis were just as colorful: Goat Hill (Irish town), Darby Town, Scotland, Happy Hollow, Bear Wallow, and many others.

There were a few free people of color in the city prior to the Civil War. After the Battle of Memphis on June 6, 1862, when Memphis was occupied by Federal forces, contraband came into the city by the thousands. Several thousand African-American Union troops were stationed at Fort Pickering. When the war ended, many stayed. Although African-Americans resided throughout the city, the Beale Street area was becoming the predominant black community by the 1870s. This community soon had its own newspapers, churches, social organizations, and professionals. Robert Church Sr., who was born a slave, was an important contributor to Memphis. He became a significant figure in the area's development, and his story can be read in this book.
During the 1890s there was a significant

migration from north Mississippi to Memphis, especially among the African-American population. Memphians joked that Mississippi's greatest export was people to Memphis. One immigrant was Edward H. Crump, deemed the undisputed king of Memphis politics for 40 years. Crump arrived from Holly Springs, Mississippi in 1894 with 25 cents in his pocket.

Following the Civil War on into the 20th century, there were a significant amount of Italian immigrants, and lesser numbers of Chinese, Greek, French, and other immigrants. The family Jack Belz – one of our entrepreneurs - immigrated to Memphis in the early part of the 20th century. During this period, the areas around Pinch and Beale Street remained multicultural, even though the former was regarded as a Jewish community and the latter as a black community.

At the end of the Vietnam War, there was a significant immigration of Vietnamese and other Asians. The city is even more diverse today with the arrival of the Japanese, Koreans, and others. Hispanics are the most recent immigrants to come to Memphis.

Among the 50 entrepreneurs listed in this book, half were born in Memphis. Of the others, about half were from the Mid-South region.

The Island Queen chugs along to dock at the levee, passing Mud Island on its left. The open-air amphitheater – used for concerts – can be seen on Mud Island with the Hernando DeSoto Bridge hovering in the background (photo by API Photographers, Inc.).

In the 1870s, Memphis suffered through three yellow fever epidemics that crippled the city. The worst was in 1878. The details of the epidemic can be read in the section on Robert Church Sr., who lived through its devastation. This resulted in Memphis losing its charter, becoming a taxing district of the state. A great deal of criticism was leveled at the city for unsanitary conditions. Many citizens left, selling their property for next to nothing. It was a horrible time in Memphis' history. In 1880 a sewer system was finally put in place. This was a step forward, but the city didn't completely cover up the Bayou Gayoso until 1916. It backed up whenever the Mississippi River rose, causing all kinds of havoc.

Amid tragic deaths, the heroic side of Memphis mounted. The Howard Association of Memphis was comprised of ordinary citizens who stayed to help fight the scourge, despite losing several of its members. Several religious leaders, physicians, and even wealthy funeral directors George and Theodore Holst died while helping others. And without the efforts of the Zouave Guard and McClellan Guard, two black militias, the city would have folded from disorder.

Dr. Richard B. Maury, a relative of Lieutenant Matthew Maury, opened his medical practice in Memphis in 1867. He became west Tennessee's first representative on the state board of health. Dr. Maury criticized his adopted city about its lack of sanitary practices. One of his important contributions was in helping create a city hospital system. He opened the first infirmary for women, where nurses trained. He also started the Lucy Brinkley Hospital in the late 1880s.

By 1900, Memphis had three hospitals: the Lucy Brinkley, St. Joseph's, and the Memphis City Hospital. The stage was set for its reputation as one of the largest medical centers in the world. In 1911 Baptist Memorial Hospital was built, and the University of Tennessee Medical School moved from Nashville and merged with the Memphis College of Physicians and Surgeons. In 1918 the Lucy Brinkley Hospital became the Methodist Hospital.

Dr. Willis C. Campbell and Dr. John Shea, whose biographies appear in this book, were among those who helped Memphis attain its high status in the medical field. A number of related industries grew as well, from Plough pharmaceuticals to several orthopedic products such as Sofamor Danek and Wright Manufacturing. Finally, the birth of St. Jude Hospital is a story combining human triumph with medical excellence.

From left to right, Baptist Memorial Hospital (to be replaced by the UT–Baptist Research Park shown on page 21), St. Francis Hosptial, and Methodist University Hospital, make up part of Memphis' medical complex (photo by API Photographers, Inc., and Robert W. Dye).

An architectural model of the UT-Baptist Research Park which will replace Baptist Memorial Hospital (photo by API Photographers, Inc.).

The gold dome shines in the sunlight at St. Jude Children's Research Hospital (photo by Robert W. Dye)

Memphis music is comparable with the 19th century cotton industry as a significant contributor to the Memphis economy. Nothing tops it as a tourist attraction. Memphis is known as the "home of the blues" and the "birthplace of rock 'n' roll." Its primary contributions to music history include blues, rockabilly, and soul genres.

Beale Street is one of the top tourist attractions in the city. It provides a historic atmosphere mixed with wall to wall clubs. Robert Church Sr. and his son, Robert Church Jr., ran their business from an office on Beale Street. They also rubbed elbows with W.C. Handy, known as the "Father of the Blues." Handy Park was named after him in 1931, and the Memphis Handy Awards are given to celebrate and honor blues artists. When B.B. King first came to Memphis in 1946, he played in the park for tips.

Graceland and Sun Studios each salute Memphis rock 'n' roll. Elvis' life is eulogized each year on his birthday and death anniversary with ceremonies on the grounds at Graceland. Elvis' house can be toured to see how he lived and to view the incredible number of awards he received. Sun Studio is where Elvis, under the supervision of Sam Phillips, recorded "That's All Right Mama," a recording that initiated his metamorphosis into a cultural icon.

The Stax Museum of American Soul Music was rebuilt to match the original theater where Stax Records was founded. The structure is well designed, with loads of video footage, display cases, and original recording equipment. It is highlighted by Isaac Hayes' fancy "Superfly" automobile. Next to the museum is a music academy, which is a state-of-the-art teaching facility for school children.

The smaller building on the left was Sam Phillips' Memphis Recording Service, better known as "Sun Studio," the birthplace of rock 'n' roll (photo by Robert W. Dye).

The Gibson Guitar Factory is located one block from Beale Street, and conducts tours of its manufacturing plant. The importance of Memphis music is also noted through the local chapter of the National Academy of Recording Arts and Sciences, an organization responsible for the Grammy Awards.

Sun and Stax represent only two of more than 400 labels recorded in Memphis. Memphis as a recording site dates back to the 1920s, when the old Ellis Auditorium and other places were used for field recordings by northern companies. Pepper Records, Hi, American Sound Studio, Fernwood, Phillips, Sonic, and Ardent represent some of the independent recording companies that appeared after World War II. Most of them are no longer in business, but many new ones have launched, including Inside Sounds, Ecko, Easley, Cotton Row, and Ebony.

The Smithsonian Rock 'n' Soul Museum is located in the FedEx Forum complex. It was designed and produced by the Smithsonian Institution and became the organization's first exhibit to be permanently established outside of Washington. It displays all aspects of Memphis music and the city's socio-cultural roots.

Memphis' Rock 'n' Soul Museum is housed in the FedEx Forum, and is the first exhibit produced by the Smithsonian Institution to be permanently established outside of Washington (photo by Robert W. Dye).

On April 7, 1968, mourners held a 40-minute memorial service for Dr. King at the Lorraine Motel (photo from Special Collections Department, University of Memphis Libraries).

Civil rights is an attempt by a people to gain their place in a social system. In the old South, segregation continued as it had prior to World War II. During the 1950s, the Memphis African-American population began voter registration drives in an attempt to elect more black candidates. The black community had several successes, but none like the success achieved by Harold Ford Sr., who was elected to the Tennessee legislature and then as a member of U.S. Congress.

With the U.S. Supreme Court decision in the 1954 case Brown v. the Board of Education of Topeka, Kansas, the door was open for desegregation in all public facilities and schools. Through court orders beginning in the late 1950s, the local NAACP was able to desegregate all restaurants and theaters, as well as other public facilities including zoos and public libraries. Dr. Vasco and Maxine Smith were important civil rights figures, as was Judge Benjamin Hooks, who became the first African-American appointed to a judgeship in Tennessee. Each of these heroes can be read about in this book.

The toughest fight was in desegregating schools. The struggle finally paid off at the University of Memphis in 1959. In response to a 1960 court order filed by Benjamin Hooks and

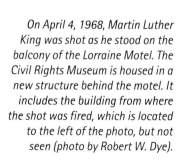

On April 4, 1968, Martin Luther King was shot as he stood on the balcony of the Lorraine Motel. The Civil Rights Museum is housed in a new structure behind the motel. It includes the building from where the shot was fired, which is located to the left of the photo, but not seen (photo by Robert W. Dye).

nonviolent methods, contrary to other areas in the South. But the assassination of Martin Luther King Jr. was another matter. He came to Memphis to help African-American garbage men in their sanitation strike against the city. On April 4, 1968, Martin Luther King was shot as he stood on the balcony outside his room at the Lorraine Motel. In 1991 the motel became part of the National Civil Rights Museum, which was organized to honor King and the Civil Rights Movement, as well as promote human rights around the world. It is a unique facility and one that attracts tourists far and wide.

Thurgood Marshall, city schools began integrating in 1961. The school system acted slowly, however, and full desegregation did not occur until several years later. When Dr. Willie Herenton became superintendent of public schools, he was faced with unifying a school district that had major problems with white flight due to the federal busing mandate. Herenton's life is also highlighted in this book.

Usually, white people in Memphis reacted to desegregation by

On April 8, 1968, 19,000 marched from Clayborn Temple to City Hall for a three-hour eulogy in honor of Martin Luther King (photo from Special Collections Department, University of Memphis Libraries).

A city's value is often determined by its recreational and educational amenities. Memphis has a wealth of places and institutions that serve to satisfy the needs of a diverse, cosmopolitan population. Several entrepreneurs who are mentioned in this book have donated to the city's universities and colleges, especially to the University of Memphis. Many have provided funds for a number of Memphis sports facilities such as FedEx Forum, AutoZone Park, and the Racquet Club. The FedEx St. Jude Classic golf tournament takes place each year at Southwind.

A carriage ambles past the Gibson Guitar Factory toward FedEx Forum, home to Memphis' NBA team, the Grizzlies, and to the Rock "n" Soul Museum (photo by Robert W. Dye).

At the turn of the last century, Memphis was lacking in many amenities, notably a highly developed park system. In 1901 the Overton Park land was purchased from the Overton family, who helped found Memphis. Zoo construction began in 1905 in the northern portion of the park, and it later expanded. The Brooks Memorial Arts Gallery opened in 1916, and additions were completed in 1989. The Overton Park Shell was the spot where

Memphis' Open Air Theater entertained audiences with Broadway shows and opera. Elvis performed there in July, 1954.

The Memphis Botanic Garden, located in Audubon Park, contains several specialty gardens. It added a very popular summer concert series to its event list in 2001. The Parkways, which began in 1904, extends all around the city. It combines beautiful landscaping with a superb highway system.

Shelby Farms is comprised of 4,400 acres of land that was once used for the Shelby County Penal Farm. It has been a recreational center for a number of years. Balloon races and equestrian events are held there. It is home to Ducks Unlimited and Agricenter International, built in 1985.

The Pink Palace Museum, Memphis' history museum, opened in 1930. Originally, it was the home of Clarence Saunders, a grocery baron and the designer of self-serve Piggly Wiggly stores. In 1977 a new section was added to the museum. This was followed by the construction of an IMAX Theater, the Bodine Exhibit Hall, and the Sharpe Planetarium in the 1990s. The

Clarence Saunders' palatial home, which he never lived in, became the Pink Palace Museum in 1930. It is Memphis' history museum, containing exhibits on anything from African-American culture to technology (photo by Robert W. Dye).

Pink Palace Museum is now an umbrella organization that includes the Lichterman Nature Center and the Mallory-Neely House and Magevney House.

Dixon Gardens, founded in 1976, includes the original home of the Dixon family. Its art gallery specializes in impressionist and post-impressionist paintings and decorative arts. Mud Island's River Park is a combination park and museum containing Mississippi River memorabilia. One of Mud Island's highlights is the RiverWalk, a scale model of the river from Cairo to the Gulf of Mexico. Other Memphis museums include the Fire Museum, Children's Museum, National Ornamental Metal Museum, Peabody Place Museum, Center for Southern Folklore, Memphis Police Museum, and W.C. Handy Museum. In addition, the Cotton Museum will open in 2005.

The Fairgrounds were built in 1912 on the site of Montgomery Park, a location that was initially used for horse racing. It is home to the Mid-South Fair, the Liberty Bowl, Mid-South Coliseum, and Tim McCarver Stadium.

Memphis also has its share of theaters. The various theaters present plays, concerts, and special events. The theaters include Playhouse on the Square, Circuit Playhouse, Theater Memphis, Germantown Performing Arts Centre, and the

The Pyramid, Memphis' unique entertainment facility, stands against the skyline with Harbor Town nestled at its feet (photo by API Photographers, Inc.).

The Orpehum Theater was built in 1928 and completely rennovated in 1984 to its original architectural splendor. The Orpheum is host to several touring national theatrical groups each year (photo by Robert W. Dye).

Orpheum Theater. The Orpheum is housed in a completely renovated theater from 1928. It hosts Broadway shows and other events. The Cannon Center for the Performing Arts opened in 2003 on the site of the old Ellis Auditorium, next to the Memphis Cook Convention Center. It is home to the Memphis Symphony Orchestra and presents ballet and opera concerts.

The South Main Arts District is host to Memphis' art community, and includes about 40 galleries sandwiched between Vance and the Central Train Station. Brenda Joysmith, featured in this book, operates Joysmith Galleries in the district. Other art galleries are located on Marshall Street near Sun Studio, and further east. The Memphis College of Art is located in Overton Park.

After the success of the Ramses the Great exhibition, WONDERS was established in 1989. Included in WONDERS' 12 presentations are "Titanic," "Catherine the Great," "Napoleon," "Imperial Tombs of China," "CZARS," and most recently, "The Art of the Motorcycle." WONDERS is located in the Pyramid, which has given Memphis such a unique and distinguishing skyline, beckoning all to visit and discover its riches.

"The Golden Age is not in the past, but in the future...."
-- E.H. Chapin

The preceding history places Memphis in perspective and points to a rich and viable tradition of entrepreneurship that has existed for more than 175 years. The city has had a remarkable number of innovators, which is a tribute to its citizens.

Memphis' location has certainly been a drawing card. Over the years, the city's government leaders, financial executives, bank employees, and other businessmen have supported entrepreneurship. On another level, according to Fred Smith, "Memphis is a very open and casual society. It is not judgmental. It's a place where new ideas and new people seem to be welcomed."

Memphians point toward their high quality of life and a wide range of social and cultural opportunities. Citizens say their city exemplifies an admirable environment and a place where families can feel confident raising their children. The city offers a multitude of attractions and amenities for people of all ages, including sports teams, museums, parks, and concert halls. It also maintains a reasonable cost of living index and provides adequate employment opportunities.

One of the teams at the Memphis in May Barbecue Festival (photo by API Photographers, Inc.).

Many of Memphis' cultural, social, and charitable organizations were funded and/or supported by several entrepreneurs in this book. The philosophy of giving back to the community has existed in Memphis since the 19th century. Their generosity reinforces and strengthens the community by drawing others into the city. For example, the University of Memphis has constructed institutes, teaching facilities, and conference centers from funds donated by Avron Fogelman, Fred Smith, Willard Sparks, and Kemmons Wilson.

Where is Memphis' future for entrepreneurship? Perhaps it is in the artificial intelligence and nanomaterials research that is conducted at the University of Memphis FedEx Institute of Technologies. Maybe it rests with the new Memphis Business Activity Survey, which tracks the amount of goods flowing through Memphis to determine the health of the national economy. Memphis' future for entrepreneurship may lie in the hands of Pact, founded four years ago by several youth who want to become city leaders. Perhaps it rests in the creative minds of Junior Achievement students at Exchange City. Or, maybe the source for future entrepreneurs will be found in all of these sectors and more.

This book highlights 50 Memphis innovators who have shaped our world. The story is not complete and certainly does not end here, however. Memphis can only look ahead to its next generation of great innovators. In turn, these fledging innovators can look forward to working in a nourishing environment of people who support their endeavors.

The Riverwalk on Mud Island is one of Memphis' hidden secrets. It is a scale model of the lower Mississippi River, and includes city maps, naturally-occurring river features, and bridges. The photo shows Memphis (photo by Robert W. Dye).

It is true that entrepreneurship is a spirit. It requires a vision, an idea, and a will to take risks and to overcome obstacles and naysayers.

James L. Barksdale
Barksdale Management Corporation

"It's frustrating when you look at the statistics...the best way to attack a tremendous problem like illiteracy is to attack it at the source.... This is a problem that needs action now, and we want to make sure that these young children become successful readers and lifelong learners. "
--James L. Barksdale

James L. Barksdale was born in Jackson, Mississippi. After graduating from the University of Mississippi with a degree in business administration, he joined IBM as a salesman. Later, at Cook Industries in Memphis, he became the company's chief information officer.

In 1979, he joined FedEx. Here he spent 13 fruitful years. He began as senior vice president of data systems before being promoted to executive vice president and chief operating officer. During his stay with FedEx, Barksdale helped to steer the company from a revenue of $1 billion to $7.7 billion per year. Gerry Roche, head of Heidrick & Struggles, a New York executive search firm, called him "one of the finest operating executives in the world, having achieved extraordinary results in building a complex, far-flung multi-unit organization."

Barksdale left FedEx in the later part of 1991 to become the president and chief operating officer of McCaw Cellular Communications, developers of Cellular One. From 1992 to September 1994 when it was acquired by AT&T Wireless Services, Barksdale helped to build the company into a multi-billion dollar enterprise.

From January 1995 to March 1999, when it was acquired by AOL, Barksdale was president and CEO of Netscape. One of his main interests was to develop software to help businesses attain success on the Internet. During his stay at Netscape, alumni groups from Stanford and Harvard business schools honored the company with the "Entrepreneurial Company of the Year" award in 1997. *Computer Reseller News* named him "#1 Executive of the Year," while *PC Magazine* labeled him "Person of the Year." At the 1997 European Technology Roundtable Exhibition Conference in Budapest, he received the "Executive of the Year" award.

Barksdale has served on the boards of Time Warner, Federal Express, Mayo Foundation, The Fund for the Capitol Visitor Center, Sun Microsystems, Inc., and TechNet. He was appointed by President George W. Bush to the President's Foreign Intelligence Advisory Board. Along with co-chair Zoe Baird, Barksdale serves on the Markle Foundation Task Force on National Security in the Information Age.

In April 1999, after he left Netscape, Barksdale became president and CEO of the Barksdale Management Corporation, a philanthropic investment company, and relocated to Silicon Valley, California. He also co-founded The Barksdale Group, which advises growing companies about Internet services.

Jim and Sally Barksdale have made sizeable donations to the University of Mississippi. They also have provided for scholarships to African-American students at the university's Jackson medical school, and to the University of Mississippi Foundation. For his work in education, Barksdale received the NetDay Hero Award from the state of Mississippi.

Barksdale hoped that his donation to fight illiteracy in Mississippi would serve as an inspiration to other philanthropic organizations. He commented that those with wealth, who lacked a productive use for it should consider a similar program. The Barksdales, whose net worth approaches $1 billion, plan on donating all of it before they die.

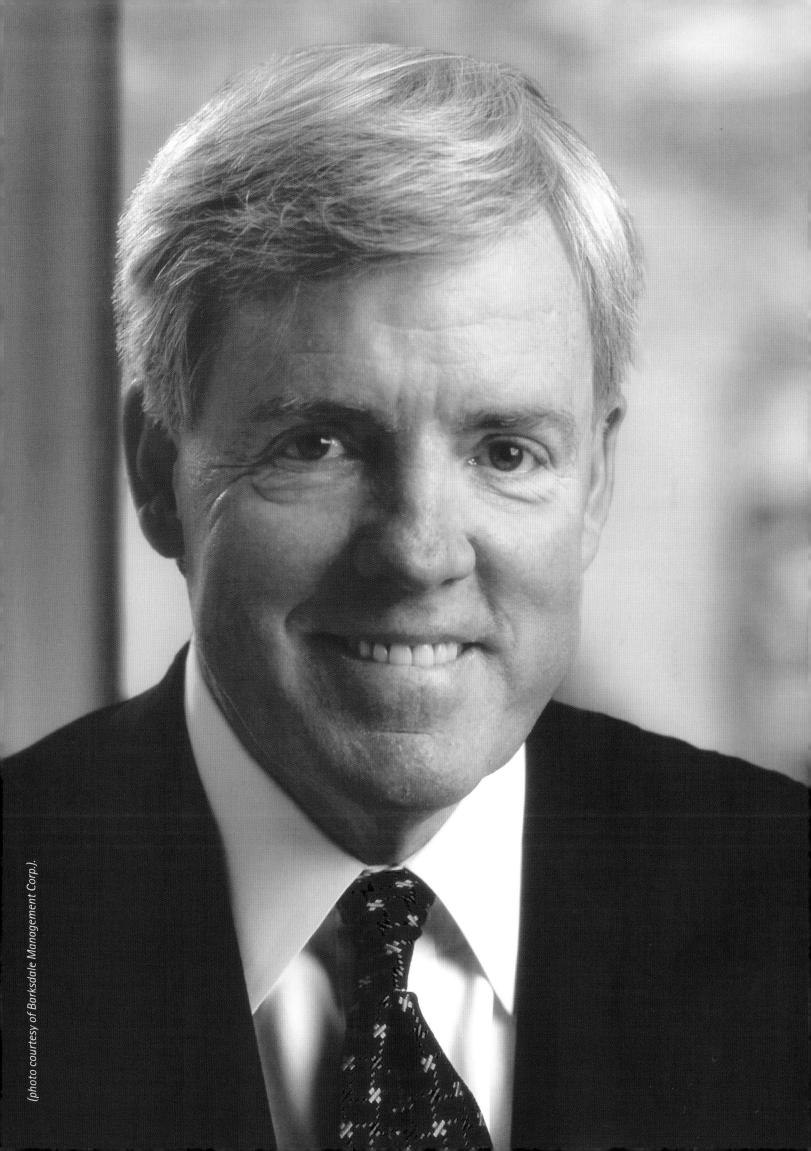

L.D. Beard
Sofamor Danek Group, Inc.

"Entrepreneurship is the only true creator of wealth, therefore of jobs, because the basis of entrepreneurship is the creation of customers willing to pay for a new technology, a new product, or a new service."
-- L.D. Beard

L.D. Beard's modest upbringing gave him the incentive to improve his financial and community standing. Beard is responsible for Danek's growth into a world-class company, which is no small feat. His company's growth also blends in with his vision that "entrepreneurship is the backbone of any successful socioeconomic system."

L.D. Beard initially worked for the Memphis-based Richards Manufacturing Company. A man named Don Richards started Richards Manufacturing in 1934 in a basement garage on Madison Street. At that time, Richards Manufacturing made basic splints and belts. Then, in 1956, the company manufactured the first middle ear implant, which was designed by Dr. John J. Shea Jr. Beard, however, did not join the company until four years later, in 1960. Of the many posts Beard held, one was chief executive officer. To help potential executives, Beard arranged for them to take a educational course at company expense. Richards Manufacturing is now part of Smith & Nephew, a global medical devices company developing innovative products that help people regain their lives.

Beard and a group of investors bought Warsaw Orthopedics, a privately held company in Warsaw, Indiana. Beard left Richards Manufacturing to become president and director of Warsaw Orthopedics in 1983. The company moved its executive offices to Memphis and eventually changed its name to "Danek." In 1993 Danek purchased a French company named Sofamor, Inc. to become the Sofamor Danek Group, Inc. Under Beard's guidance, Sofamor Danek became a world leader as a supplier of products in the treatment of degenerative conditions, deformities, tumors, neurological disorders, and spinal injuries.

Sofamor Danek's products fall into three categories: implants, minimally invasive systems that use optical and computer technologies, and biologicals. The company has obtained several hundred patents and continues to work closely with surgeons in the research and development of new products.

Sofamor Danek received accolades from *Forbes, Fortune,* and *Inc.* magazines as one of the best small companies. The company has spread its domain over the entirety of Europe and Asia, and it has maintained subsidiaries in several countries.

In 1999, Medtronic, a Minneapolis-based company, purchased the Sofamor Danek Group. It is now called the "Medtronic Sofamor Danek Company." L.D. Beard remained on the company's board until the transition was complete.

In 1998, a year before Medtronic's purchase, Beard became a director of EagleVision, Inc. Beard's experience in the development, design, and marketing of new medical products was highly welcomed. Dr. Jerre M. Freeman founded EagleVision, as well as Memphis Eye and Cataract Associates. Among other procedures, Dr. Jerre specialized in cataract surgery and intraocular lens implant surgery.

Along with serving as director of EagleVision, Beard also serves on the boards of trustees for the Orthopedic Research and Educational Foundation and Risk Assessment Systems, Inc.

"The first advice that I would give to anyone planning to start a business is to learn every single thing they can about that business. In all probability they are not inventing something new, but rather trying to do something better than has been done in the past. That gives them the benefit of studying what has been done, and making certain they have the opportunity to improve a business and make real economic success and a personal success out of it.... You must keep your eye on the target and be willing to persevere, and not become frustrated if it is not easy. To be successful requires enormous effort and a willingness to accomplish the believable."
-- Jack A. Belz

"The most important priorities in my life are my family, religion, and business," Jack Belz said. "They are interrelated and always have been in my vision of life." Belz's statement is the only way to fully understand the philosophy that drives Belz Enterprises.

Many people refer to Jack Belz as the person who revitalized Memphis' downtown area because of his purchase of The Peabody Hotel, which reopened in 1981 after renovations were completed. This beautiful building, constructed in 1925, became a Memphis institution over the years. Belz received advice in 1975 to let the hotel be torn down for use as a parking lot by the Greyhound bus terminal, but Belz and his family had a different thought in mind. They envisioned that if restored, The Peabody Hotel could jumpstart a downtown revitalization. After analyzing the task and considering his options, Belz decided to take the giant financial risk. His reasons to embark upon such an endeavor may have included his aesthetics for beautiful architecture and antiques, his support for traditions, and his fond family memories at the hotel. In fact, Belz was married there in 1948. Nevertheless, his decision to rebuild The Peabody Hotel greatly propelled a renewed interest in downtown Memphis.

Ever since the formation of Belz Enterprises, the company has been a family affair. Jack Belz claimed that his father, Philip, was the primary individual who exerted the most influence on him. From his father's teachings, Belz learned the old ways of forging deals. By shaking hands and looking people in the eyes, they formed bonds of trust between businessmen and customers alike.

Philip Belz was born in 1904 in Lancut, Galacia, located within the old Austro-Hungarian empire. After Philip's father immigrated to Memphis, he sent for his family. Philip went into business, and by the 1940s he was manufacturing furniture, as well as dabbling in the construction industry. Jack Belz attended Massachusetts Institute of Technology, where he concentrated on architecture, business, and construction. When he returned home in 1948, Jack Belz decided to go into the construction business full-time. Soon after, he partnered with his father under the banner "Belz Enterprises." Eventually, his two brothers also joined the company.

Belz Enterprises, Inc. is now one of the South's largest real estate developers of both commercial and industrial properties. It owns, develops, and manages factory outlet malls, apartments, residential developments, warehouses, retail centers, land, and hotels in Memphis and elsewhere. The company built some of the first shopping malls in Memphis, namely Northgate and Southgate. Belz Enterprises, in partnership with Kemmons Wilson, developed the first factory outlet mall in the United States in 1979. The next year Belz Enterprises, in partnership with two other companies, opened the Rivergate Industrial Port, which was the largest privately developed enterprise of its type in the country.

Many of Belz Enterprises' developments sprang from Jack Belz's vision for downtown Memphis. "Downtown Memphis is a perfect example of recycling existing properties into new and exciting usages and models," Belz once said. The resurgence of the city started with The Peabody Hotel, which serves as an anchor for Belz's

vision. Renovations and expansion then spread to the development of residences in Harbor Town and South Bluffs, as well as Uptown, a 1,000-unit residential area north of St. Jude. Belz Enterprises accomplished these housing developments in partnership with the Henry Turley Company. Perhaps the blockbuster of them all, however, is Peabody Place, which is considered to be the largest mixed-use development in the United States. It includes office buildings, shops, restaurants, theaters, parking garages, the Gayoso House, and the Peabody Place Museum. The Peabody Place Museum houses part of Jack Belz's personal collection of Chinese art.

While writing checks for charities and volunteering to help good causes are necessary and truly appreciated, individuals are needed to direct monetary donations and determine their uses. This job is for business-savvy innovators and people with vision. The vision of Belz Enterprises can be seen in the Memphis skyline.

The Belz family prides itself in ensuring that Memphis remains one of the "belles of the South," and a place in where anyone would want to live. Memphis' revitalization is proof of a true American success story, and it demonstrates that hard work combined with an entrepreneurial spirit ultimately pays off.

As he received an award for Outstanding Community Salesman in 1971, Belz said, "In my religion, a man is taught that he must always give more to his community than he takes from it." Belz has received innumerable awards as a result of his service to the Jewish community, such as the B'nai B'rith National Humanitarian Award. He was a founding member of the Tennessee Holocaust Commission, and he has been involved in various civic affairs. Belz's commitment to family and religion, his work ethic, and his vision for Memphis continue to serve as an example for youth.

Peabody Place contains retail stores, movie theaters, parking facilities, and restaurants, one of which is Isaac Hayes' Music-Food-Passion (photo by Robert W. Dye).

It started during the early 1930s when Frank Schutt, Peabody manager, put his live decoy ducks in the fountain. Now, the public eagerly awaits the coming and going of the ducks as they march to and from the fountain on a red carpet to their quarters atop of the hotel (photo by Robert W. Dye).

The beautiful Peabody Hotel was originally opened in 1925. After being renovated during the 1970s, it reopened in 1981 to become the stimulus for downtown revitalization (Photo by API Photographers, Inc.).

J. Bayard Boyle, Jr.
Boyle Investment Company

"Entrepreneurship...involves a lot of determination to overcome obstacles and a lot of imagination.... The most successful usually come up with a new idea that is marketable or figure out a better way of doing something that everybody else has overlooked. The best are good at figuring how to get people to work together and who is best at doing what. They are good at motivating teams, creating excitement about achieving a goal, and at selling their ideas within and outside the company."
-- J. Bayard Boyle, Jr.

Boyle Investment Company, a real estate business, was founded in 1933 by three brothers: Bayard, Snowden, and Charles Boyle. Their father, Edward Boyle, developed the beautiful Belvedere Boulevard in 1906. This street, cutting from Union to Central, is notable for its gracious homes, attractive landscaping, and tree-lined promenade. The Boyle family descended from John Overton, who helped found the city of Memphis alongside Andrew Jackson and James Winchester in 1819.

In the 1930s, Boyle Investment Company mainly managed foreclosed property for the New York Life Insurance Company. But, following World War II, Boyle began to finance new residential properties in addition to commercial and industrial properties. The company then expanded its interests to include mortgages and insurance, and later developed its first housing subdivision.

Bayard Boyle, Sr. was the genius of the three brothers. He had a knack for figuring out which properties were the best for investment. J. Bayard Boyle, Jr. pointed out that his father "was always researching, planning and predicting" – a basic approach to real estate investment that has stayed with the company. A good example of the company's foresight was the development of the property at the Poplar and I-240 corridor during the 1970s. Today, this area sits in the heart of Memphis' population base and includes the Regalia Shopping Center and Ridgeway Center.

Beginning in the 1960s, the Boyle Investment Company became known as a star in the residential development arena. Its communities were known for their desirable areas, sculpted layouts, and unique design.

Some of Boyle's most innovative developments were areas combining both commercial and residential usage, such as Schilling Farms, a well-planned development in Collierville. This community resembles a town within a town, as it blends residential properties with businesses and office buildings. By the 1970s, Boyle became known as the originator of Memphis office parks. The huge Ridgeway Center, for example, houses the Morgan Keegan Building. Also, Humphreys Center in East Memphis is a mixed-use development with a beautiful tree-lined boulevard.

Boyle Investment Company is truly a family owned business. J. Bayard Boyle, Jr. joined the company in 1960 and became president in 1971. In 1985, he became chairman of the board. His close partner and brother-in-law, Henry W. Morgan, joined the company in 1965. Morgan's father was a commercial banker and his uncle led Boyle's insurance division. After working his way through the ranks, Morgan became President, a position he still occupies. He works in tandem with Bayard Boyle to oversee the company and its development. Both have worked hard to maintain the integrity of the company and foster the type of civic care that Boyle Investment Company promotes. The fourth generation is represented by Paul Boyle, Henry Morgan, Jr., and Bayard Morgan.

If one were to take a map of Memphis and color in the areas that the Boyle Investment Company has developed, one would realize what an innovative and progress-driven company Boyle truly is. Boyle Investment Company has been creating, developing, and enhancing Memphis since its birth.

Thomas W. Briggs
Welcome Wagon

"Someone once said that every business is the length and shadow of a man, and if there was ever an individual who typified this remark, it was Tom Briggs. In the development of Welcome Wagon worldwide, he left his footprints in many towns and all states of the United States, and many foreign countries. It is a great thing to take nothing and make something of it."
-- Abe Plough, commenting on the death of Thomas Briggs, 1964

It was in 1928 that Thomas Briggs conceived of the idea for Welcome Wagon. While visiting big companies with frequent personnel changes, Briggs wondered whether people who moved to new locations were adjusting. He overheard some friends talking about someone who had to restart his social life. Briggs recalled the old-time practice of the Conestoga Wagons, which provided aid in the form of fresh water and food to travelers making long journeys across the country. The wagons also helped people carry important items with them on their way to a new life. This concept inspired Thomas Briggs to begin Welcome Wagon.

Born in 1886 on a farm near Memphis, Briggs was the oldest of 11 children. His father, originally from Arkansas, was a dairy and cotton farmer who moved his family first to Mississippi and then to Tennessee. Thomas Briggs had a brief stint on the vaudeville stage. Under the name Briggs and Skinner, his act consisted of magic and hypnotism. Briggs partnered with his father-in-law to sell advertising to newspapers. Eventually, the business was renamed Thomas W. Briggs Co. In 1920, Briggs published two books in collaboration with *Commercial Appeal* editor C.P.J. Mooney: *The Mid-South and its Builders* and *Distinguished Folks*.

The Great Depression was a tough time to launch a business, but Briggs started Welcome Wagon. The idea was to have people greet new home owners and welcome them into the community. Wagon workers provided newcomers with gifts from local merchants and information regarding civic happenings. In the beginning, the company employed men to sell the idea to merchants, but over time, all of the salesmen were replaced by women. Women also took staff positions as supervisors and executives.

Welcome Wagon started in Memphis, but soon spread to Nashville, then the Midwest and Canada, and finally to New York. Beginning in 1949, Briggs began his expansion of Welcome Wagon to Europe. Just a year before his death in 1964, he visited the South Seas and South America for the same purpose. During the 1950s, Welcome Wagon had two office buildings. Its office on Fifth Avenue in New York City was 19 stories. Its Memphis office was located on the corner of Court and Second Street, facing Court Square.

Thomas Briggs was also a philanthropist. Prior to his death, he organized the Thomas W. Briggs Foundation. The foundation sponsors the Excellence in Teaching Award at the University of Memphis and the city wide Community Service Award. Briggs also gave freely to a variety of charities and organizations such as Goodfellows.

Like most great ideas, Welcome Wagon was emulated by an organization called Getting to Know You. In 1988 the two merged under the more popular Welcome Wagon name. In 2001 Welcome Wagon became part of a larger organization, Homestore. Today, more than 75 million families have been made to feel a little more comfortable in their new surroundings - even new presidents moving into the White House. Welcome Wagon adapted to fit modern times and now welcomes new people to the community via mail and the Internet.

When Thomas Briggs died March 2, 1964, Lady Bird Johnson, the wife of President Lyndon Johnson, wrote a letter to the company in New York. She summarized the feelings of many with her words: "The president and I were sad to learn of the passing of Mr. Briggs. The wonderful work he initiated will continue through the years to serve as a tribute to his concern and compassionate understanding for his fellow man and a better way of life."

Dr. Stanley J. Buckman
Buckman Laboratories

"The customer is most important. We need to be effectively engaged on the front line, actively involved in satisfying the needs of our customers. We have to be so tuned into our customers that we anticipate what they need. If an employee is not effectively engaged with the customer, why are they employed?"
-- Robert H. Buckman, son of Dr. Stanley Buckman

For solutions to emerge in times of need, people must learn to think outside the lines. Dr. Stanley Buckman realized this truth, allowing him to become a national authority on wood preservation.

Buckman received his Ph.D. in biochemistry in 1933 from the University of Minnesota. Buckman co-founded Central Laboratories, a lab that developed decay-resistant wood for military defense purposes during World War II. In 1945 Buckman founded Buckman Laboratories, which debuted with the production of microbiocide BMS-11, a product used for reducing slimes in paper machine systems. The company's work with chemicals for paper products made it a leader in its industry.

Though Dr. Buckman was heavily involved in his business, his primary love was in the research and development arena. Pursuing solutions to problems intrigued him. His name remains on most of Buckman Laboratories' initial patents as either the inventor or a co-inventor. Buckman also authored 26 scientific articles.

Dr. Buckman's wife, Mertie Willigar Buckman, was perhaps one of Memphis' greatest philanthropists. Following her parents' deaths in her teenage years, Mertie earned a master's degree in education with the help of her aunt and uncle. Since that time, thousands of children and people of all ages have benefited from her generous endowments of millions of dollars to schools and universities. She and Dr. Buckman had two sons, John and Robert. When Dr. Buckman passed away in 1978, Robert took over the company and carried on his parents' traditions of discovery, invention, and philanthropy. He also followed his mother's quest for excellence in education.

Robert Buckman's management style was quite different than that of his father. Before his death, Dr. Buckman oversaw every detail of the company's procedure. Robert, in contrast, wanted individuals to have the power to make decisions. "I realized that if I can give everybody complete access to information about the company, then I don't have to tell them what to do all the time," Robert said. "The organization starts moving forward on its own initiative." This mindset fostered an increase in communication, influence, and efficiency in the workplace. Robert's influence spread with his involvement in the White River Institute in Vail, which exists to examine new ideas, create communication, and share knowledge about personal development. After 22 years, Robert Buckman retired as the president and CEO of Buckman Laboratories, but he still serves on the board of directors for Bulab Holdings, Inc., the parent company of Buckman Laboratories. Steven Buckman is the current president and CEO of Bulab Holdings and Katherine Buckman Davis is its chairperson.

The philosophy of Buckman Laboratories has always been to provide solutions for its customers' problems. From its humble beginnings of four employees working in a small house, the company has grown immensely. Today, Buckman Laboratories is internationally focused, employing more than 1,300 people and producing more than 500 different products in over 70 countries. While Buckman Laboratories' innovative approach to problem solving has allowed the company to overcome many challenges, its greatest pride may be in its concern for the environment.

Buckman Laboratories is a leader in the chemical industry and has set the standard for controlling environmental hazards, reducing emissions, and increasing productivity.

Dr. Willis C. Campbell
Campbell Clinic

"Campbell Clinic's values are derived from its heritage. Originating from that heritage are the values of humanity, compassion, mercy, fairness, and justice, and a dedication to providing the most advanced orthopaedic care through highly skilled physicians and active programs in research and education."
-- Campbell Clinic Mission Statement

The Campbell Clinic has a history that is quickly approaching the 100-year mark. Founded in 1909 by Dr. Willis C. Campbell, the clinic introduced the Department of Orthopaedic Surgery a year later at the University of Tennessee in Memphis. Fourteen years after that, the university established the first orthopaedic residency program. The program started with four doctors, and since then the number of residents has grown to eight times its original amount. Today, the Campbell Clinic is responsible for giving the world more than 300 orthopaedic surgeons.

Dr. Campbell had great aspirations for his little clinic, and he was able to watch it blossom into a world leader in orthopaedic surgery. In 1933, he established the American Academy of Orthopaedic Surgeons, becoming its first president. Campbell Clinic physicians also make up the faculty at the University of Tennessee Department of Orthopaedics. They are responsible for updating *Campbell's Operative Orthopaedics*, which is commonly accepted as one of the field's staple textbooks and has been printed in four different languages.

The clinic itself has earned a worldwide reputation in pediatric orthopaedics, joint replacement, and surgery of the hand, hip, foot, knee, shoulder, and spine. Regarding sports medicine, Campbell physicians work as team doctors for several high schools and all of the local universities, as well as the Memphis Grizzlies and the Memphis Redbirds.

Dr. Campbell himself brought a very prestigious background to the program. Though he was born in Jackson, Mississippi and received his medical degree from the University of Virginia, he decided to begin his practice in Memphis. Campbell initially specialized in general surgery, anesthesia, and pediatrics. He left his practice to travel to London and Vienna for a formal study of orthopaedics. Returning to the states, he continued his studies at clinics in New York and Boston. Upon returning to Memphis in 1909, the Campbell Clinic was born.

Dr. Campbell authored several books, including *Orthopaedics of Childhood, Injuries and Surgical Diseases of the Joints,* and the aforementioned *Campbell's Operative Orthopaedics.* He was one of the first to employ sulfanilamide in the treatment of bone diseases, as well as use certain innovative surgical procedures.

Dr. Campbell believed that all crippled patients could be healed through orthopaedic surgery. Many afflicted people who once believed their immobility to be permanent now found themselves able to walk and run due to Dr. Campbell's intervention. In 1919, he and his colleagues founded the first Crippled Children's Hospital. He also founded the Crippled Adults Hospital through the cooperation of Rotary Club. Dr. Campbell and his associates saw the need for indigent care. Today, Campbell Clinic doctors commit at least 10 percent of their time to care for the needy at the Regional Center of Memphis, LeBonheur Children's Hospital, St. Jude Children's Research Hospital, and Baptist Memorial Hospital.

Dr. Willis Campbell died in 1941. In his honor, the Campbell Foundation was formed to continue Dr. Campbell's desire to educate and forge new directions in orthopaedic care. Many people owe their ability to fully function to this unassuming doctor. Dr. Campbell truly set the highest standards in teaching, research, and patient care. Campbell physicians continue to lecture at the University of Tennessee, as well as across the United States and the world.

Dixie Carter
Singer, Actor

"When I was 7, my brother and sister and I were taken to Jackson, Tennessee (to) have our tonsils out. (The doctor) mutilated my throat. After that operation, the right side of my throat was solid scar tissue and I was told that I would never be a great singer. But I couldn't stop. And it's a miracle that I've been able to sing the way that I have. But I do – because it was just in me. It was in my heart to sing."
-- Dixie Carter

Southern charm, grace, elegance, and a slow, smooth country drawl – all of these attributes describe Dixie Carter, one of Memphis' favorite daughters. The middle of three children, Carter was born and raised in McLemoresville, Tennessee, in an atmosphere of sociability and music. Her father was a shop owner who ran several small stores.

As a young child, Carter had aspirations of becoming an opera singer, but at the age of 7, she suffered from the misfortune of a botched tonsillectomy. Having her throat scarred nearly squelched her dream. Carter pressed forward in her musical aspirations, however, and learned to play the piano, trumpet, and harmonica. She pursued vocal studies and became recognized for her proficiency in opera and dance. Her compact disc *Dixie Carter Sings John Wallowitch Live at the Carlyle* was released in 1991. The album, compiled from her cabaret act at New York's Café Carlyle, includes songs and comedy.

Dixie Carter's abilities apparently have no limit. Valedictorian of her senior class, her college success was all but guaranteed. She graduated from the University of Memphis with a degree in English, but found that she had a true love for the stage. Carter's professional stage debut was in a local production of *Carousel* at the Front Street Theater in 1960. Three years later, she moved on to the glitter of New York City, where she landed a large role in Joseph Papp's production of Shakespeare's *A Winter's Tale*.

When she moved, her career took several twists and turns. Instead of remaining with Papp, she left to join a musical theater program at Lincoln Center, supervised by Richard Rodgers. After that, Dixie worked with Madeline Kahn and Lily Tomlin in cabaret revues staged by Julius Monk at the Downstairs nightclub. Carter turned down an offer for a part in the film *That's No Way to Treat a Lady*. In 1967 Carter married Arthur Carter, publisher of the *New York Observer*. They had two daughters, Ginna and Mary Dixie. Carter's two daughters quickly became the center of her life, and she focused her attention on raising them for the next eight years.

When Carter was 35, she desired to return to her life as a performer, but no agents would consider her. Undaunted, she refused to give up. She was given solid roles in the musicals *Pal Joey* and *Sextet*, and then found fame as an actress in TV sitcoms. Her most prolific role was as Julia Sugarbaker on the show *Designing Women*, which debuted in 1986. Sugarbaker's character was portrayed as a soft-spoken and eloquent, yet dogmatic and zany, southern woman.

Since the conclusion of *Designing Women* in 1993, Carter has been involved in a plethora of activities. She played the role of her idol, Maria Callas, in Terrance McNally's play *Master Class*. She also made guest appearances in other TV series, produced TV specials and two fitness videos, wrote a book, traveled the concert and cabaret circuit, and spoke all over the country on various topics. In addition, Carter signed on as a member of the President's Committee for the Arts and Humanities.

Despite her health scare when she was a child, Carter did not cave in to defeat. She overcame adversity and continued her dream as a stage performer. From her motivation came an incredibly versatile entertainer who had success as a singer, actress, and comedian. She and her husband, Hal Holbrook, have been married since 1984 and live in Los Angeles. Though she resides far away from her hometown, Carter still makes it a priority to return to her southern roots in McLemoresville, Tennessee.

(photo courtesy Memphis Symphony)

Robert R. Church Sr.
R.R. Church & Son, Real Estate Developer

"...Mr. R.R. Church is strictly a self-made man. He was not nursed in the lap of luxury. His colossal fortune is not an inheritance, but is the result of indomitable pluck, grit, and business foresight coupled with remarkable judgment. He has always known the value of a dollar...yet he has always been generous and liberal in all worthy causes."
-- Memphis Conservator, 1908

On November 19, 1902, President Theodore Roosevelt visited Memphis to honor General Luke E. Wright, a native Memphian. Wright returned home from the Philippines, where he was a commissioner. One of his receptions was held at Church's Park and Auditorium on Beale Street, right in the heart of a predominantly African-American community. The auditorium was built in 1899 to hold 2,300 people. Its maximum occupancy level did not stop more than 3,000 admirers from packing in to see and hear Roosevelt, Wright, and other dignitaries. The individual who was responsible for the park and auditorium's construction was Robert R. Church Sr., reputed to be the wealthiest black man in the South.

Robert Church's wealth seemed to be completely at odds with his background. He was born a slave in 1839 to Captain Charles B. Church, a white steamboat captain, and his black seamstress named Emmeline. Emmeline died when her son was 12 years old. Robert worked on his father's boats as a cabin boy, and later as a steward. While working as a steward, Robert learned the ways of the wealthy and how to provide the ultimate in customer service.

Around the year 1865, Robert Church quit his river jobs and opened a saloon at 29 Monroe St. At various times throughout the years, Church owned multiple saloons, a saloon/billiard parlor, a well-appointed hotel, and a restaurant. He mainly focused on real estate, however. All the money he earned went into buying buildings and land. By 1908 he owned more than 100 buildings in Memphis, plus scores more in other cities. It was estimated that he collected $3,000 in monthly rent, a huge sum at the time.

Being an amateur architect and civil engineer, Church supervised the construction of several of his buildings. One example of this is Church's Park and Auditorium, which was built to satisfy an urgent need of a civic center for the black community. The auditorium was well-built with all the proper amenities on six acres of land. It had beautiful walkways, a playground, a gazebo with a bandstand, and free-roaming peacocks. Church's Park and Auditorium became a center of activity for the African-American community. Travelling entertainment companies, conventions, and speakers were booked. W.C. Handy's Orchestra frequently played in its gazebo.

During the 1870s, Memphis was struck with three yellow fever epidemics, the worst taking place in 1878. Nearly 25,000 people fled the city, many of whom never returned. Of those remaining, 5,150 died. The bulk of the surviving population consisted of poor white people and a large majority of the African-American community, including Robert Church. Since many people tried to leave the city and sell their property, real estate values tumbled. Church purchased sizable tracts of land, adding significantly to his holdings. Because of its smaller population base and an increased debt, the city went bankrupt. It lost its corporate charter in 1879 and became a taxing district of the state. But in 1881, the city issued municipal bonds in an attempt to regain its charter. Robert Church was the first person to purchase a bond for $1,000.

In 1906 Church founded the Solvent Savings Bank and Trust Company, the first black-owned bank in Memphis. He became its president, and he also was a company director. A couple years later, Beale Street Baptist Church was facing foreclosure. The Solvent Savings Bank paid off creditors to save the church for its members. This historic church dates back to 1868 and still stands on Beale Street.

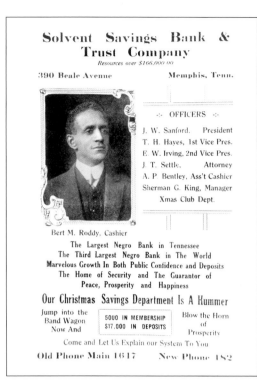

The Solvent Savings Bank and Trust Company was founded by Robert Church in 1906. It was the first bank owned by African-Americans in the city and the second oldest in Tennessee (photo from Arcadia Archives).

President Theodore Roosevelt and his entourage to visit Church's Auditorium in 1902. Locally, he was instrumental in helping African-Americans find jobs in the school system and in the post office.

In this day and age, an enterprising young black man who has aspirations of gaining wealth is not an impossible dream. During the late 1800s, however, this feat was practically unattainable. The fact that a black man who was born a slave could amass wealth and become such a great community leader during that particular time period is staggering. It is even more impressive to learn that Robert Church is not best remembered for his riches or his great business mindset, but rather his generous spirit and philanthropic deeds.

Though Church had political aspirations, he was never elected to office. However, he was a delegate to the 1900 Republican National Convention, which nominated soon-to-be President William McKinley. Church was influential in helping a couple of black Memphians be appointed to federal positions. His connections were vital in paving the way for

Church was honored in 1984 by the Chamber of Commerce as one of Memphis' pioneer businessmen. The Mid-South Minority Business Council gives an annual award in his honor to an outstanding African-American businessman. Nearly 100 years after his death, Robert Church continues to provide inspiration.

Robert R. Church Sr. built Church Auditorium and Park in 1899 to fill a need in the African-American community. The original structure was demolished and a new one constructed in the 1920s, facing Beale Street (photo from, Memphis Room, Memphis Library and Information Center).

Beale Street looking west in the pawn shop district, 1950. In the middle of the left side is Schwab's, a Memphis institution, which has been in business at this location since 1912 (photo by Don Newman, courtesy of API Photographers, Inc.).

Between Second and Third, Beale Street has a number of music clubs. Blues legend B.B. King performs at his club a couple times a year (photo by API Photographers, Inc.).

Majorie Coleman
Coleman-Etter, Fontaine Realtors

"Real estate is a field women can do well in. Women are on an equal footing with men, if they are willing to work. Salespeople are totally self-employed, even when they're with a firm, and can set their own hours.... It isn't a 'fun job' because the responsibility is terrific. When you sell a home, you're handling the largest investment most people make in their lifetimes. Contracts must be properly written, and clients must be protected in all aspects."
-- Majorie Coleman

In today's world of real estate, it is probably more common to have a female realtor than a male agent. This was not always the case, however. Men dominated the industry in its early days, but Majorie Coleman helped reverse the trend when she and Fran Etter opened the first female-owned real estate company in 1951 in Memphis. At the time, there were only 30 female sales agents in the entire city. Twenty-five years later, 88 of the 390 Memphis firms were owned by women. Coleman and Etter's daring move paid off, forever changing the world of real estate in Memphis.

It is strange how some businesses are created. In the case of Coleman and Etter, they claimed that they "stumbled" into the business 20 years after college. After the two graduated as classmates from Southwestern (now, Rhodes College), Etter became society editor of the *Commercial Appeal*, while Coleman became assistant society editor for the *Memphis Press-Scimitar*. Coleman worked for her mother, who was the publication's editor.

Coleman and Etter's paths frequently crossed for a number of reasons throughout the 1930s-40s. Then in 1951, the duo reconnected at a debutante tea, the type of event they both covered for the society page. The *Commercial Appeal* had an article on a woman realtor who made a big sale. Coleman looked at Etter and said, "Let's go into that business." On the same day, Coleman's aunt mentioned that her husband and a friend were preparing to develop an area by Coro Lake on Highway 61. The locale developed into a subdivision of custom built homes and lodges. Coleman and Etter handled the sales, emphasizing the neighborhood's scenic view.

Coleman and Etter rented a one-room office on Jefferson and attended the University of Tennessee at night to get real estate licenses. When the subdivision was ready, they sold 30 homes in one week. It took them a year to sell all the area's properties. The partners then decided to become full-time residential realtors. To establish themselves in the business, they sometimes worked 70 hours a week, including nights and weekends. But all their hard work paid off. By 1976, both of them were members of the Memphis Board of Realtors' Million Dollar Sales Club.

In 1985, they welcomed a new partner, Taylor Fontaine, who became the president and broker just two years later. Coleman-Etter Fontaine Realtors is now one of the top five real estate companies in Memphis, despite the fact that they have chosen to remain small and "family-like." The company now employs more than 40 agents and has listings in cities around the state. New leadership has helped take the company into the technological age, and they now boast the latest in virtual marketing, web management, and bookkeeping.

Majorie Coleman and Fran Etter followed P.T. Barnum's advice: "Whatever you do, do it with all your might. Work at it, early and late, in season and out of season, not leaving a stone unturned, and never deferring for a single hour that which can be done just as well now." Coleman and Etter's accomplishment of opening their own company in a competitive, male-dominated profession was certainly a remarkable challenge. They described it as a spur-of-the-moment idea, given impetus by the success of one female sales agent. "If she can do it, so can we," they thought. And they certainly did do it, but bigger and better.

Edward W. "Ned" Cook
Cook Industries, Memphis-Shelby County Airport Authority

"Ned Cook has been the airport of the city of Memphis. I've never seen him on the street or anywhere that he isn't talking about the airport and what it has done. People talk about it all over the world, the beauty of it and the utility of it"

--former Mayor Wyeth Chandler

According to Airports Council International statistics in 2003, Memphis had earned the Number 1 ranking for the 12th-straight year by passing along over 3.3 million metric tons of cargo. This reality stemmed from the vision of Edward Willlingham "Ned" Cook.

He used his influence as the first chairman of the Memphis - Shelby County Airport Authority to recruit a professional staff that lured not only Federal Express – an upstart shipping company from Little Rock, Arkansas – but laid the groundwork to lure Northwest Airlines as well. Since that decision was made, Federal Express and Northwest Airlines have gone on to assist in making Memphis International Airport a worldwide leader in air cargo shipping.

He took his 14-year tenure at the head of this organization very seriously, and considered his role in building Memphis into the worldwide air cargo leader the most important of his civic activities. Upon Ned's passing in 2001 at the age of 78, it was pointed out that one in five Shelby Countians worked for a business connected to the busy airport. This is attributed to Ned Cook.

The path Cook had taken to that point is marked with success. He was born in Memphis on June 19th, 1922; the only son of WWI flying ace Gen. Everett Cook and his wife, Phoebe.

After attending Pentecost-Garrison for grade school, Hotchkiss for high school, and Yale for college, Ned followed in his father's footsteps by serving in the Air

Force during WWII. His 54 missions earned him the Distinguished Flying Cross, the Bronze Star, and the Air Medal with six oak leaf clusters. That also earned him the rank of major.

Upon his return from the war, Cook teamed up with his father at his Memphis cotton firm, Cook & Co. There were about 30 employees at this point. After learning the business, Ned took the initiative in 1963 to expand into grains as well – mostly soybeans. Things really took off then, and the new Cook Industries were able to acquire E.L. Bruce Lumber Co. (including Terminix) and Riverside Chemical Co., among others. By 1975, Ned was chairman of the board of Cook Industries, with sales of nearly $460 million and 5,500 workers employed worldwide.

Cook was named National Agri Marketing Association's "Marketing Man of the Year" in 1975 after he became the first man in U.S. history to sell a significant quantity of American soybeans to Russia. His activities included three terms on the Shelby County Quarterly Court (now known as the County Commission).

He spearheaded the creation of the Memphis Cook Convention Center in 1974, naming it after his father. Much later, in 1988, Ned helped make the Memphis Wonders cultural exhibits series a reality.

James Kirby Dobbs
Dobbs International Services, Inc.

*"If your food is better than anything else in town, the public will come to eat with you.
That's the secret of our success."*
-- James Kirby Dobbs, 1949

In 1984 Dobbs Houses, Inc. divided into three components. One of these components was an airline catering division named Dobbs International Services, Inc. Its birth resulted from the foresight of two men: James Kirby Dobbs and Horace Hobson Hull. Dobbs and Hull had opposite personalities, but they attained success nonetheless. Dobbs was outgoing, amicable, a super salesman, and a constant source of ideas. Hull was rather quiet, analytical, very precise, and careful about wild business ventures. *The Saturday Evening Post* described Hull as "a rock on the Maine coast," and Dobbs like "a California sunset." Hull had an engineering degree, while Dobbs dropped out of school. Even so, the two relied on each other as business partners.

The duo's association dates back to 1921, when they both worked for the Fisher Automobile Agency in Memphis. Fisher loaned them money to start their own agency. The Hull-Dobbs Ford Company became the largest Ford dealership in the world. It was located just south of The Peabody Hotel in the block that is now covered by Peabody Place. Hull and Dobbs also ventured into the oil drilling business, and they established a Chicago-based finance company named Dobbs Investment.

In 1934 Dobbs and Hull decided to branch into the restaurant business. One of the policies the partners instituted was a profit-splitting plan, which was a way of increasing employee motivation and productivity. This incentive program returned a percentage of company profits to its workers – the higher the profits, the higher the sharing.

One day in 1941, Dobbs was on board an airliner over Texas. When the flight attendant was too ill to serve dinner, Dobbs volunteered his services. After looking at the airline's food, he was convinced he could do better in providing decent meals. After returning, he purchased a restaurant in Memphis' airport. He added a fast food service, which consisted of a 12-stool counter. This was the same type of installation in his other small restaurants. Dobbs also instituted an auto-cashier system in which customers were able to pay for their purchases. In addition, the company prepared box lunches for departing flights.

In 1946 Dobbs Houses, Inc. was born. By 1947 the company was packaging meals for 16 airlines at 23 airports. Its first catering kitchen was in Memphis. After Dobbs was unable to obtain a contract for Atlanta's airport in 1946, his company built its first independent kitchen exclusively for Delta airlines.

Hull was never fully enamored by the restaurant/catering business. It was James K. Dobbs who relentlessly pursued it. He constantly flew to check in on his restaurants and work out the kinks in his catering business. Many times he ended up serving customers at his small coffee shops. Dobbs tried to improve the quality of airline food by personally testing it and using different recipes. He insisted on high quality, fresh food.

If nothing else, James Kirby Dobbs focused his attention on his employees. He believed a profit-sharing plan would help them as well as himself. He also demanded the best from his workers and acted accordingly to set the proper standard. He wrote personal letters to his stockholders, describing the company's state of affairs. One such letter ended with the following statement: "My salary remains the same as it was, and I do not want a raise. I would like to tell you about my grandchildren, but I know you are all too busy to hear about them." The Dobbs approach was personal, friendly, and open, which produced a very effective management style.

Lewis R. Donelson III
Attorney and Community Leader

"Entrepreneurship understands that there are some absolute values in society and that success and failure are the result of individual actions, not occasioned by the errors and frailties of society."
-- Lewis R. Donelson III

During the Crump era of politics, Memphis was in one of its most politically charged episodes. Edward H. Crump ran for mayor of Memphis in 1909 in support of a five-person city commission, as opposed to an elected city council. On January 1, 1910, after Crump won the election, the city commission took power. It was in effect until 1967, the year in which Memphis' first city council was established. A young attorney named Lewis Donelson was elected as one of the city's first councilmen.

Donelson worked his way through school on a work-study program. He graduated with distinction in 1938 from what is now Rhodes College. From there he went on to receive his law degree from Georgetown University in 1941. Forty years after receiving his original degree from Rhodes, his alma mater awarded him with an honorary doctorate.

Alongside Ben C. Adams, Donelson founded the law firm Donelson & Adams in 1954. Since that time, Donelson & Adams merged with eight other firms to form a new firm called Baker, Donelson, Bearman, Caldwell, & Berkowitz, of which Donelson is a senior partner. Currently, it is one of the largest law firms in the country with public policy and international advisors in 10 U.S. cities, as well as Beijing, China. The firm also has more than 400 lawyers. Of this number, 72 are listed in *Best Lawyers in America* guide for 2005-06. Donelson, who specializes in corporate and tax law, has appeared in the guide for 20 or more years, and he continues to be included.

Many in Donelson's firm are highly respected attorneys who have served in a variety of high profile positions and government departments, including the following: Chief of Staff to the President of the United States; U.S. Secretary of State; U.S. Senator and Congressman; and U.S. Ambassador. The firm represents clients on a worldwide spectrum, and its lawyers help a network of 10,000 attorneys in providing legal advice to various countries.

Donelson took his lawyer skills into the political arena. He was a financial and issues advisor for Tennessee Governor Lamar Alexander. He was a delegate for the Tennessee Constitutional Convention from 1979-81, and he also participated as a delegate at the Republican National Convention in 1964 and 1968. In addition, Donelson served as a member of the Platform Committee in 1988.

Over the past few years, through litigation, Donelson has sought to increase state funding for rural schools. Representing a group of 77 rural school districts, he successfully forced the state of Tennessee to distribute funds more evenly. In this regard, both poor and well-to-do school districts are given an adequate opportunity to provide students with excellent educations. Because of his expertise in this area, Donelson was elected to the Rural School and Community Trust's board of trustees in February 2002.

A recipient of numerous awards and recognitions, Lewis R. Donelson III continues to focus on how he can make a difference in the Memphis community.

William B. Dunavant Jr.
Dunavant Enterprises, Inc.

"I fell in love with the cotton business. It's a moment business and I'm a moment man. You're selling one minute and buying the next.... Flexibility has been the key - changing not with, but ahead of the times."
-- William B. Dunavant Jr.

Front Street in Memphis has been known as "Cotton Row" since the 19th century. On the street, rows of three-story buildings stand like monuments of the cotton business, referred to at one time as the lifeblood of the Memphis economy. In 1929, another business took root at 112 Front St. The business was named T.J. White & Co., of which William Buchanan Dunavant Sr. was a partner. Woodson Thomas Knight, Dunavant Sr.'s father-in-law, owned large cotton acreage near Tunica, Mississippi. Dunavant Sr., along with William P. Dunavant and Nathan Bedford Forrest, founded the Memphis & Selma Railroad. It was later renamed the Frisco Railroad, and it was used almost exclusively to haul cotton.

Despite the difficulties fostered by the depression, Memphis still remained the world's largest interior market for cotton. T.J. White & Co. survived the depression and became known for its good reputation and stability. After World War II, the company handled between 75,000 and 80,000 bales. It had its best seasons in the early 1950s and late 1960s. T.J. White & Co. handled more than 100,000 bales during those years despite overseas cotton production and competition from synthetic fibers.

William B. Dunavant Jr., who was commonly referred to as "Billy," joined the company in 1952 when he was enrolled at the University of Memphis. Dunavant Jr. became a full partner of T.J. White & Co. in 1956. After T.J. White retired in 1960 and Dunavant Sr. died the next year, Dunavant Jr. gained full control of the company, renaming it W.B. Dunavant & Co. In 1971 he moved his offices from the traditional folds of Front Street to a modern building on New Getwell Road. With a new location came a final name change: Dunavant Enterprises, Inc.

Dunavant Jr. was more aggressive than most of the other Front Street residents. He took proactive steps toward increasing revenue by cutting overhead costs and increasing volume. With regard to the latter, his company was one of the first to use "forward contracting," a marketing concept in which a farmer agrees to a price for his entire acreage prior to planting. Dunavant's risk-taking approach led to an increased volume that topped out at 300,000 bales in the 1960s and skyrocketed to one million in the 1970s.

Part of Dunavant Enterprises' increase in volume was a result of Dunavant's foresight in developing links to foreign markets. He currently has offices in Europe, Asia, Central America, South America, and Australia. The Australian market is a main competitor of the United States. Beginning in 1972, Dunavant Enterprises participated in the sale of U.S. cotton to China. In 1990 the company supplied nearly all of its 1.2 million bales to China, a transaction recorded as the largest sale of U.S. cotton in history at the time. Because of his experience with foreign markets, Dunavant was elected president of Cotton Council International in 2002.

Since it first began business, Dunavant Enterprises has continued its steady growth upward. Although most of the company's focus is on cotton, Dunavant Enterprises includes warehouses, a truck brokerage company, real estate investments, a commodities corporation, a coal company, a poultry farm, a computer software development, and the Racquet Club of Memphis. In 1987 Dunavant purchased Producers Cotton Oil Company, which made Dunavant Enterprises the largest ginner of cotton in the world.

Dunavant Enterprises has received numerous accolades for its success as a private company. *Forbes Magazine* has consistently ranked it as one of the best small companies in America. With yearly revenues in excess of $1 billion, Dunavant Enterprises has been listed in *Forbes'* 400 largest private companies since 1989. The *Memphis Business Journal* ranks it as the largest

private company in Memphis based on its four million bales of cotton handled annually in the U.S. and overseas markets.

There is a reason for the success of Dunavant Enterprises. One of the company's greatest assets has been its commitment to service. There are few, if any, cotton merchants in the world with the access and ability to transport as many bales as Dunavant Enterprises. Currently owning warehouses from Memphis to Moree, Australia, the company has the capability to warehouse 1.5 million bales per year.

Dunavant's sense of commitment extends to several community interests, such as LeBonheur Children's Hospital, Memphis Young Life, and the Boy Scouts of America. He has received awards from Civitan Clubs of Greater Memphis, the National Conference of Christians and Jews, and the City of Hope, among others. The Master of Free Enterprise Award from Junior Achievement was given to him in 1985.

Dunavant is an avid sportsman, especially tennis and hunting. He is a conservationist and has contributed to such groups as Ducks Unlimited. His interest in sports also reveals itself at the professional level. In 1984 he brought the Memphis Showboats, a member of the ill-fated United States Football League, to the city. If the price was right, Dunavant would have done the same with the San Antonio Spurs in 1988. In 1974, he built the Racquet Club, a state of the art tennis facility. The complex is the home of the world's oldest indoor tennis tournament, which is one of the city's major annual sporting events.

One of the reasons why William B. Dunavant Jr. has become involved with professional sports is to promote Memphis. He has spoken of his commitment to the city and to its people. Though few have matched Dunavant's loyalty to a city, his greatest sense of commitment is to his family. He said, "I wanted to build this (Dunavant Enterprises) for my children."

A Cotton Classing room from 1939 where the purpose is to determine the quality of cotton samples with regard to color, leaf, fiber length and strength, among other factors (photo by Marion Post Wolcott, Library of Congress, Prints and Photographs Division, FSA-OWI Collection, Courtesy of Memphis Archives).

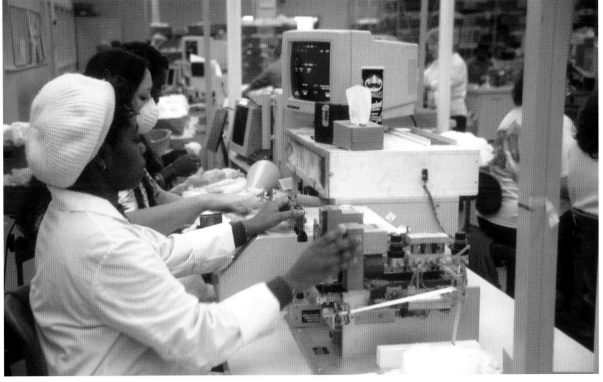

Modern technology has replaced older analytical techniques in assessing the quality of cotton (photo courtesy of Cotton Council).

Avron B. Fogelman
Fogelman Properties, Inc.

"Never consider a person's economic or social position in evaluating his or her ability."
-- Avron B. Fogelman's motto

Fogelman Properties, Inc. began from a company that was founded by Morris S. Fogelman. Morris came to the United States from a small town near Warsaw, Poland, when he was 11 years old. In 1928, he graduated from Central High School in Memphis and joined a respected realtor and mortgage company named Marx and Bensdorf. Initially an office boy, Morris worked hard and became manager of the mortgage servicing department. In 1941, he established his own real estate business, Fogelman & Co., in a one-room office at 127 Madison Avenue.

Avron Fogelman, Morris' son, also went to Central High School. After graduating in 1958, he attended Tulane University. In 1963 he enrolled in the University of Memphis Law School. He then joined his brother and father at Fogelman & Co. At the time, the company primarily dealt with single homes and insurance. When Avron came aboard, he helped establish a development and property management group called Fogelman Management Corporation. With Avron as president, the group that initially focused on the Memphis market, quickly expanded to numerous cities in the south, southeast, midwest and Atlantic Coastal regions of the country. Now called Fogelman Properties, the company is one of the largest of its type in the nation, owning and managing well over 15,000 apartment units.

Avron Fogelman has supported Memphis sports at the professional and university levels for more than 30 years. Writers have called Fogelman the father of professional sports in Memphis. In the early 1970s, he was president of the Memphis Pros basketball team, part of the American Basketball Association. In 1978 Fogelman brought baseball back to Memphis as owner of the class AA Memphis Chicks. During the same year, he purchased the Memphis Rogues soccer team, a team that went on to play in the championship. He was also part owner of the World Football League's Memphis Grizzlies. Then in 1983, he bought the Kansas City Royals baseball team, a team that went on to win the 1985 World Series under the leadership of Hall of Famer George Brett. In 1999, he was inducted into the "Tennessee Sports Hall of Fame".

Of all of his interests, Fogelman has focused primarily on education. He is convinced that students should be given every possible opportunity to succeed. Since 1981, Fogelman Properties has sponsored Richland Elementary School, funding such programs as Arts in the Schools. In 1987 he launched the Avron B. Fogelman Scholars Program to help disadvantaged students who wish to attend the University of Memphis. Fogelman also served on the Tennessee State Board of Education. In 1998, he was elected in to the public schools "Hall of Fame".

Mr. Fogelman has received the highest award from the National Conference of Christians and Jews and, from 1980 to 1988, was the chairman of the Shelby County Planning Commission. He then served as the first chairman of the Memphis and Shelby County Sports Authority. His awards include the Master of Free Enterprise Award, the Big Brothers Big Sisters Man of the Year Award, Philanthropist of the Year, and Civitan "Citizen of the year".

In addition to supporting sports programs at the University of Memphis, Avron Fogelman and his brother Robert endowed the Morris S. Fogelman Chair of Excellence in the school of business. For this and other contributions, the University of Memphis named its college of business and economics the Fogelman College. In 1980, the Fogelman Executive Center, which was also funded by The Fogelman Family, opened in 1986. In 1988, the Tennessee State Legislature and the U.S. Department of Transportation name the interstate in Memphis the Avron B. Fogelman Expressway.

Avron is now retired and two of his sons, Richard and Mark Fogelman, third generation family members, now operate Fogelman Properties. The company continues to function with professionalism and support public education. The company's tremendous generosity is a testament to Avron's belief that his own success in business and civic responsibilities had its foundation in Memphis city schools.

Shelby Foote
Historian and Novelist

"I think that everything you do helps you to write if you're a writer. Adversity and success both contribute largely to making you what you are. If you don't experience either one of those, you're being deprived of something."
-- Shelby Foote

Like Memphis, Greenville, Mississippi is a cotton town, albeit much smaller in stature. In 1916, Shelby Foote was born there to Shelby Dade and Lillian Rosenstock Foote. The Foote family tree is intertwined with the state of Mississippi's history, particularly within the town of Greenville.

Shelby Foote's great grandfather, attorney Hezekiah William Foote, was a successful planter. After the Civil War, he became a circuit court judge. Hugar Lee Foote, Shelby Foote's grandfather, was born in 1855. Hugar proved to be a successful businessman and manager. He also prospered as a statesman, first becoming a sheriff, and then a senator. Hugar's son, Shelby Dade, was the novelist's father. Shelby Foote and his family moved into a 30-room mansion, which was the inspirational setting for most of Foote's novels. With the Mississippi Delta as his backdrop, he provided a sense of place for his readers which drew upon his personal experiences.

When Shelby Foote spoke of adversity, he referred to his family and the tragedy they suffered. With a family background of great wealth and such prestige, where could any hardship lie? His grandfather, Hugar Lee Foote, lost his fortune through gambling. On Shelby Foote's mother's side, Morris Rosenstock was wiped out by the 1921 depression. According to Shelby, "They barely had the money at their deaths to pay for the shovel that buried them." The writer used his family's deprivation as a theme in his books.

With the family fortune gone, Shelby Foote's father got a job working for Armour Meats. But he died tragically of septicemia in Mobile, Alabama, when Shelby was only 5 years old. His mother never remarried. An only child, Shelby Foote was frequently alone. For him, loneliness was an advantage. It allowed him to take time to read and reflect on his life.

School was not a priority for young Foote. He made adequate grades, but he preferred reading instead of the chosen curriculum. *The Bobbsey Twins* and *Tarzan* were among the first books he enjoyed reading, along with other typical childhood material. But then Foote was given a copy of *David Copperfield*, which had an extraordinary influence on him.

Everyone can point to at least one person who has significantly influenced their life. Foote was primarily influenced by William Alexander Percy, who was a lawyer, poet, and philosopher. In Percy's home, Foote met writers Sherwood Anderson and Langston Hughes. He was stimulated to read the works of James Joyce, Marcel Proust, Thomas Mann, and William Faulkner. Foote also met William Percy's cousin, Walker Percy, who was an important author in his own right. Foote and Walker Percy quickly became best friends.

For Shelby Foote, his poetic writings served as a springboard into writing prose. In fact, every writer he knew did likewise. Interestingly, William Faulkner viewed himself as an unsuccessful poet.

In 1935, Foote found himself at the University of North Carolina, where he rarely attended any classes, except those in English and history. He loved the university's extensive library, and he spent nearly all of his time there. Foote took the opportunity to write short stories and book reviews for the school's magazine, *Carolina Magazine*. In 1937, he returned to Greenville and attempted to write his first novel, *Tournament*. The book focused on his grandfather's successes and failures. The novel's final publication did not occur until 1949.

World War II interrupted Foote's life, as it did for so many. He joined the Mississippi National Guard.

Following the war, he wrote stories for the Associated Press. He married and divorced. After his first novel, he published several others: *Follow Me Down* (1950), *Love in a Dry Season* (1951), *Shiloh* (1952), and *Jordan Country* (1954). Another novel, *September, September*, appeared in 1978.

In December, 1953, Shelby Foote decided to start life anew, so he moved to Memphis. In Memphis, he created his greatest work, a three-volume set on the Civil War. The project took him nearly 20 years to complete. He said he wrote slowly, perhaps writing no more than 500 or 600 words a day. The three Civil War volumes contained around 1.5 million words. For his efforts, he earned a Pulitzer Prize nomination, and many people deemed the work as one of the most important of its time. The *Modern Library* ranked it No. 15 out of the top 100 books of the century. Time-Life Books released a 14-volume edition of the masterpiece, further touting its importance. Also, Ken Burns decided to produce the work in an 11 hour PBS documentary.

Shelby Foote started out as an author and became a celebrity. He was the subject of magazine articles and the recipient of fan-mail. He was invited to deliver speeches and give interviews. As a result of his publicity, people had a renewed interest in reading Foote's novels. Many have refered to him as one of the greatest Civil War historians.

THE CIVIL WAR IN AMERICA: DESTRUCTION OF THE CONFEDERATE FLOTILLA OFF MEMPHIS—FROM A SKETCH BY OUR SPECIAL ARTIST.—SEE PAGE 84.

THE ILLUSTRATED LONDON NEWS

On June 6, 1862, the Federal fleet under the command of Captain Charles Davis approached Memphis with five ironclads and 19 rams. Commodore J.E. Montgomery blocked the way south to Vicksburg with only eight converted river steamboats. As 10,000 Memphians watched, the battle ended in 90 minutes with a total defeat of the Confederate forces. Only one ship escaped, but Memphis remained in the hands of Federal forces until the end of the war (photo from Illustrated London News, July 19, 1862, courtesy of the Memphis Room, Memphis Library and Information Center).

Foote holds his novel, September, September, *written in 1978, against a backdrop of a Civil War cap and a shelf of miscellaneous books (photo from Memphis Room, Memphis Library and Information Center).*

The Hunt-Phelan Mansion on Beale Street was appropriated by General Ulysses S. Grant as his headquarters in 1862. As shown in this 1865 photo, it was later used as a soldiers home (photo from the Tennessee State Library and Archives, courtesy of Memphis Archives).

Harold E. Ford Sr.
U.S. Congressman, Politician

"(A substantial number of black voters follow my suggestions because) I think I have responded to the issues in such a way that my views on politics are listened to."
-- Harold E. Ford Sr.

Harold Ford Sr. was born into Newton and Vera Ford's large family of eight sons and four daughters. Newton founded the N.J. Ford and Sons funeral home in 1932, soon after he graduated from Manassas High School. He learned the business from his father, who also operated his own funeral home. Education was highly valued in the Ford family. Each of Newton and Vera's children graduated from Nashville's Tennessee State University. Harold Ford received his mortuary science degree from John Gupton College in 1968. Then, in 1982, he earned an MBA degree from Howard University.

In 1969, Harold Ford became vice president of his father's funeral home, a post he still holds to this day. At age 25 in 1970, he was elected as one of the youngest members of the Tennessee House of Representatives, and one of the few African-Americans to serve in that assembly. In 1972, he served as a delegate to the Democratic state and national conventions.

1972 was also an important year in revamping the Eighth Congressional District. The redistricting resulted in a larger African-American population. Ford decided to run for U.S. Congress and try to overtake the incumbent. In 1974, Ford waged a tough campaign, soliciting heavily among the black population. In the end, he won the election and became the first African-American from Tennessee to be elected to U.S. Congress. He continued to be re-elected, winning handily after the district was changed to the Ninth Congressional District in the 1980s. Ford served in the position for 22 years.

The 1974 election gave the Ford camp even more political leverage. Beginning in 1970, he developed a grass-roots organization that became the only one in the city to yield a 40,000-voter block. Candidates competed for Ford's support. From his standpoint, the publicity helped promote his views. His volunteers organized voter registration drives, contacted voters in person and by telephone, and encouraged voters to go to the precincts on Election Day. Ford also printed a "Ford ballot," which listed candidates he supported. His endorsement was good for thousands of votes, and was often enough to influence elections at the city, county, or state level.

Among the many committees on which he participated, Congressman Ford served as chair of the Ways and Means Subcommittee on Public Assistance and Unemployment. Throughout the 1980s, he supported social welfare programs at a time when the Reagan administration attempted to dissolve them. Ford argued for reformed social welfare programs and improved job training.

Ford was also concerned about issues of health care and child welfare. He felt negligent parents should be forced to pay child support. For this, Ford was named Child Advocate of the Year in 1987 by the Child Welfare League of America. On another level, Ford supported the Earned Income Tax Credit for the working poor because he thought it provided incentive for single parents and poor families to continue working.

The aforementioned issues were each important in Ford's home district of Memphis. In fact, Congressman Ford believed his constituents' needs were more important than anything else. In 1978, FedEx Chairman Fred Smith had only positive remarks for Ford. The congressman had been aggressive in passing legislation that allowed companies such as FedEx to increase the size of their aircraft. This saved in the cost of fuel and the number of personnel.

Congressman Ford served until 1996, when his son, Harold E. Ford Jr., was elected to replace him in Washington D.C.

Abe Fortas
Supreme Court Justice

"The law is the witness and external deposit of our moral life.
Its history is the history of the moral development of the race."
-- Oliver Wendell Holmes Jr.

Abe Fortas was born in Memphis in 1910 as the youngest of five children. His parents were among the scores of Jewish immigrants who left Russia and Lithuania for America during the first decade of the 20th century. From such humble beginnings, Abe Fortas became known as an effective and intelligent lawyer, a confidant of President Lyndon B. Johnson, and one of the Supreme Court's most active and influential members. Throughout his life, Fortas believed courts are principal guardians of human liberties.

As a teenager, Fortas played violin in dance bands. As a result, he garnered the nickname "Fiddlin' Abe." But it was his excellent academic standing, not his musical talent, that earned him a scholarship to Southwestern College (now named Rhodes College) in Memphis. He graduated from there in 1930 with honors. At age 20, he received a scholarship to attend Yale Law School. At Yale, he became editor in chief of the Yale Law Journal, and graduated second in his class in 1933.

Fortas became a professor at Yale University, but he divided his teaching with government service in Washington. Throughout the Franklin D. Roosevelt administration, Fortas worked in several areas, including the agricultural department and in public utilities. He became assistant secretary of the interior from 1942-46. He left government service in 1946 to form a private law firm with fellow Yale professor Thurmond Arnold. Later, Paul Porter joined them to create the firm Arnold, Fortas & Porter.

Fortas' connection with Lyndon Baines Johnson started in 1948, when Johnson was accused of voting irregularities during the Texas primary for U.S. Senate. Johnson won by only 87 votes, and his opponent filed a court order to remove Johnson's name from the ballot. Fortas was central in helping reverse the injunction.

Because of this, Johnson regarded Fortas as one of the best lawyers in the country. Fortas was the first person Johnson phoned after President Kennedy's assassination, and Fortas was called upon to organize the Warren Commission. Fortas initially refused a position in President Johnson's administration. Nevertheless, Johnson appointed Fortas to the prestigious position of Supreme Court justice in 1965, thus ensuring the court maintained a liberal majority. In 1969 President Johnson appointed Fortas as chief justice, but political entanglements led to his resignation from the Supreme Court. He then set up another private firm, and he practiced law until his death in 1982.

For most of his life, Fortas helped protect human rights. He fought hard against Roosevelt's Japanese relocation program. His law firm was equally active. During the McCarthy witch hunt era, Fortas and his colleagues defended many whose loyalty was called in question. They also offered free services to those who could not afford legal counsel. In 1954 the court appointed Fortas in Durham v. United States, which resulted in a broader, more scientific view of insanity. In another ground-breaking case, he gave up his salary to defend a destitute man from Florida for breaking and entering (Gideon v. Wainwright, 1962). Fortas appealed the case to the U.S. Supreme Court, which voted unanimously to have states provide free legal counsel to the indigent in every criminal trial. As a Supreme Court Justice, Fortas broke the tie which produced The Miranda Decision and was active in protecting individual rights in privacy and juvenile court cases.

Fortas could not explain where or when he developed an interest in civil rights. He thought it may have come from his college days, and was a result of thinking or reading about human rights issues. Whatever influenced his thinking, it became his life's work.

Thomas M. Garrott
National Commerce Financial

"For an established enterprise to grow and prosper, one must encourage entrepreneurs within the organization to constantly challenge and improve upon what has come within their sphere of influence.... We've found that nothing brings customers to the bank like you truly understanding their needs. You don't convince them of that with catchy slogans. You do it by offering innovative programs and products that serve them like no one ever has before."
-- Thomas M. Garrott

The placement of branch banks with extended hours in grocery stores has served as a great convenience for those who fail to deposit their paycheck before 5 p.m. on Friday. The person responsible for this innovation is Thomas Garrott, one of those rare individuals in the banking industry that loves to think outside the box. Garrott has served as chairman of National Commerce Financial, the parent company of National Bank of Commerce, which has been in business more than 130 years. In 2004, SunTrust Banks, Inc. acquired National Commerce Financial. Garrott is currently a member of the company's board of directors.

Garrott did not start out in banking, however. A native of Mississippi, he graduated from Vanderbilt University and the University of Pennsylvania's Wharton School of Finance. He soon became chief financial officer of Malone & Hyde, a diversified food wholesaler for which he worked 17 years. At Malone & Hyde, he made the connection between banking and business, and he was credited with helping regain its financial prosperity. "Banking is like selling coffee, tea or milk, only more so. It is a commodity business... the only way to separate yourself is by having lower costs than the next guy."

In the early 1980s, National Bank of Commerce had a low return on stockholders' equity compared to other banks in Tennessee. At the time, Garrott served on the board of directors and gained the attention of Board Chairman and CEO Bruce Campbell. Although Campbell recognized that Garrott had no banking experience, he hired him as president. Campbell said Garrott "has shown a keen interest in our company and an exceptional understanding of the financial industry in general."

Garrott's assessment of the bank's operations led to several innovations, each of which originated from the basic premise of providing better services and programs to meet the needs of a busy public. Over the years, the bank has looked at account structures, branch locations, credit programs, and Internet banking so customers can maximize their time. The company's primary approach in customer convenience was to provide extended-hour banking branches in grocery stores.

In 1985, Garrott's bank made an agreement with The Kroger Company to begin placing banks in their stores in Tennessee and surrounding states. National Commerce Financial became the expert on such arrangements, and now operates a consulting business to help banks provide in-store branches for their customers. For a busy country, the opportunity to combine banking with shopping was a bonanza.

Since joining National Bank of Commerce, Thomas Garrott's leadership has placed the bank on firm financial footing. A few years ago, *U.S. Banker*, a financial trade publication, rated National Bank of Commerce as the best performing banking company in the United States. For more than 20 years, the bank's total yearly return on its stock was at 29 percent, which outperformed the S&P 500 index return of 6.82 percent. Wall Street has marveled at the bank's consistent growth in earnings and its high level of shareholder value. In May, 1999, Garrott was named one of the nation's top CEOs by *Chief Executive Magazine*.

William C. Handy
Musician, Composer

"There is something about the (song) "Memphis Blues"…. When I hear it or when I play it, smoke gets in my eyes. There's something beautiful about it. There's something deep in it. And it gave me a name all over the world."
-- W.C. Handy

W.C. Handy, the "Father of the Blues," not only achieved worldwide recognition, but also helped Memphis gain the title "Home of the Blues." Handy and his tunes have become the alma mater for the Beale Street Historic District, one of the top tourist attractions in Memphis.

Handy was born in Florence, Alabama, in 1873. His father, a minister, expected him to follow the same path, but Handy was more interested in popular music. His early musical training took place in Florence's school system. By and large, Handy's parents did not respect musicians, but Handy pursued music anyway.

A turning point for Handy occurred in 1890 when Jim Turner, a Memphis violinist, came to Florence to organize an orchestra. Turner's knowledge of popular dances and songs and his wild stories of Beale Street impressed Handy. Handy took up the cornet and practiced in secret. After he became more proficient on his instrument, he joined Turner's band and continued to play without his parents' knowledge.

A year after leaving Florence, Handy joined the Hampton Cornet Band in 1893 in Evansville, Indiana. Across the Ohio River in Henderson, Kentucky, he received more in-depth musical training. His next big break came in 1896 when he was hired by the world renowned Mahara's Minstrels. Handy became a cornet soloist, and later an orchestra leader. Mahara's Minstrels traveled throughout the United States and Canada, and to Mexico and Cuba. Handy gained professional experience and was introduced to a wide variety of music.

After teaching music at A&M College in Huntsville, Alabama, he became director of a band in Clarksdale,

Mississippi, in 1903. During the same year, Handy heard blues for the first time at the Tutwiler train station. The itinerant musician used a knife to move up and down the strings of his guitar as he sang. Handy's interest was piqued, but he was not completely sold on blues until he noticed the amount of tip money a local blues string band received. He arranged blues songs for his orchestra to play, which increased its popularity.

In 1907, Handy arrived in Memphis, initially teaching music and leading Thornton's Knights of Pythias Band. His arrival brought him close to the world of Beale Street – its glamour, people, clubs, theaters, and music. Handy made Beale Street his home away from home. He spent much of his time at Pee Wee's Saloon, a place where musicians gathered to search for jobs. Then, in 1909, Handy was hired to play for Edward Crump's mayoral campaign, for which he composed the tune *Mr. Crump*. Handy's own Pace and Handy Music Company, located on Beale, published the song in 1912 under the title *Memphis Blues*. Before Handy moved to New York in 1918, he had already composed most of his great blues songs, including *St. Louis Blues, Hesitating Blues, Joe Turner Blues, Yellow Dog Blues*, and *Beale Street Blues*.

With his poise and demeanor, W.C. Handy became an institution. He was offered the best jobs, such as at the swank Alaskan Roof Gardens. Handy was a well-trained musician who saw great potential in blues music. He researched, lectured, wrote articles, and published song books on blues. But most importantly, he was the first main blues composer. Although most of his melodies were taken from folk music, the songs were his arrangements. His tunes became popular around the world. Handy's blues have served as advertisements for Beale Street and Memphis, and for American music.

(photo from Special Collections Department, University of Memphis Libraries).

Isaac Hayes
Musician, Composer, Actor

"In a way, I want to represent blacks in the music field. I try to show that not only can I sing and write music, but also I can be businesslike. I want to show that I'm prosperous so that the black kids in the ghetto that are struggling, just as I did, can reach out and touch me."
-- Isaac Hayes, after winning an Oscar for Shaft, 1972

Born in 1942 in Covington, Tennessee, Isaac Hayes' childhood was a thing of which movies are made. Orphaned as a baby, he and his sister Willette were cared for by their grandparents, who were sharecroppers. The children's grandmother grew and canned vegetables while their grandfather raised farm animals and hunted. Hayes picked cotton and sang and daydreamed in the fields. At an early age, his grandparents taught him to appreciate the simplicity of farm life and the satisfaction gained from hard work.

The family moved to Memphis when Hayes was 7 years old, and his grandfather became ill and passed away four years later. As Hayes grew older, the family fell upon hard times--city life was unfamiliar to them. Hayes was the only man in the immediate family, so he had to bear the responsibility of seeking employment-what ever it took to honorably survive. Hayes loved learning but when he reached puberty, he began to be self concious of not being sharply dressed and dropped out of school without his grandmother's knowledge. She found out about her grandson's secret when a group of teachers from school came to the house. The teachers' words from that day left a life-changing impression on the young boy. "This young man's got too much to offer, and we can't afford to lose him," the teachers said. With much encouragement and support, Hayes re-entered school and continued his job, balancing the two until his graduation.

Hayes joined the school band in junior high so he could have access to instruments, and he regularly stayed late to play the piano. A wino in a cotton field talked him into entering a talent show. When he brought the audience to its feet after singing *Looking Back* by Nat King Cole, he began to realize his potential as a musician.

Hayes earned several music scholarships but turned them down because he wanted to become a performer. He formed a band in high school called "The Missles", playing the alto sax, and piano, as well as singing. After graduation, Hayes continued to work a day job at a meat packing plant while he tried to find the right music connection. Shortly after, he turned all of his energy toward music. With hopes of being offered a recording contract, he brought three different bands into Stax Records on McLemore Avenue in Memphis, but each one was turned away. Finally, Hayes caught his break as a pianist with Floyd Newman in a recording session at Stax. Jim Stewart, the owner, hired Hayes as a session man. At Stax, Hayes and Dave Porter teamed up to become top-tier composers. *Soul Man, Hold On, I'm Coming, When Something is Wrong With My Baby,* and *B-A-B-Y* were a few of the 200 songs they composed and produced. The duo was inducted into the Songwriters Hall of Fame in 2005.

In 1969 Hayes hit it big with his *Hot Buttered Soul* album as it reached No. 1 on the soul and jazz charts. His notoriety grew as his later albums reached the platinum level of $2 million in sales. In 1972 he became the first African-American to receive the Best Musical Score Oscar for his soundtrack to the film *Shaft*, as *Theme From Shaft* hit No. 1. Hayes also won a Golden Globe, two Grammy Awards, the Edison Award, and the Image Award. And in 2002, was inducted into the "Rock and Roll Hall of Fame".

Hayes moved to Atlanta in 1979. He released a few albums in the 1980s-90s, but focused his attention on acting and radio. In 2001, he returned to Memphis and opened a restaurant, *Isaac Hayes-Music Food Passion.*

Isaac Hayes was dubbed "Black Moses" because of his innovative music, enigmatic image, and unpresidented success. Part of his magnificent story came as a result of his teachers' and grandmothers' encouragement. Due to Hayes' motivation, he has become known not only for his work in music, but also his dedication in education, literacy, and teaching initiatives. Hayes is a crusader for children's causes and a King in Ghana, Africa.

Dr. Willie W. Herenton
Educator

"The role of public education is crucial to the future of our country. The reality is, if we fail as a nation to educate all our children, we'll create social and economic problems of immense proportions. There is no way you'll be able to survive in the future without a strong education."
-- Dr. Willie Herenton

Willie Herenton grew up in a tough Memphis neighborhood, where street smarts dominated educational values. When his mother and father separated, he and his sister were raised by their mother and grandmother. Most of the male adults Herenton knew were laborers. This is one reason why his heroes were sports figures, like boxers Joe Louis and Sugar Ray Robinson.

At age 11, Herenton registered in a boxing program at the local YMCA. By the time he graduated from Booker T. Washington High School in 1958, Herenton had won the Tennessee state boxing championship four times. He was offered a boxing scholarship by the University of Wisconsin, but turned it down to go professional. Herenton changed his mind after moving to Chicago, however. One day, he came upon a group of black men waiting for work at a furniture factory. The foreman angrily waved them off because he had nothing for them. At that point, Herenton realized that if he failed at boxing, he may be treated the same way. In response, Herenton decided to pursue a solid education so he could gain necessary skills for success in life.

Herenton returned to LeMoyne College in Memphis, where he graduated with a degree in elementary education in 1963. He received his master's degree in education administration in 1966 from the University of Memphis. Then, in 1971, he received a doctorate from Southern Illinois University and was appointed principal of LaRose Elementary School. From 1973-74, he spent two years studying the Baltimore and Washington school systems on a grant from the Rockefeller Superintendent's Training Program.

On January 1, 1979, Dr. Herenton became the superintendent of Memphis City Schools, inheriting one of the poorest school systems in the country. In 1983, 60 percent of its students were eligible for free or reduced-cost lunches. The Memphis school system had a black population of more than 70 percent because of "white flight." Herenton surprised many community members by coming to grips with education problems. In February, 1981, he proposed a massive plan to save $1.9 million by closing 12 schools, as well as changing school pairings. He canceled 18 bussing assignments that did not affect the court order to achieve racial balance. He restructured the city's school administration by cutting the ratio of district superintendents per school in half. He believed in yearly evaluation plans for both management and teachers, and also helped students increase daily school attendance and their performances on standardized tests. He created optional school programs, which were so popular that parents camped out on the doorstep of the school board to make sure their kids were registered. One of his success stories was his role in improving White Station High School from a second-rate school to one of the best in the city.

Executive Educator named Dr. Herenton as one of the top 100 school administrators, and Rotary Club awarded him with the prestigious Civic Recognition Award. For his services, Herenton also received the Horatio Alger Award. In addition, he was elected to a number of boards, including that of the Holiday Corporation.

Throughout his years as school superintendent, Herenton courted other opportunities, including Tennessee State Commissioner of Education and superintendent of Atlanta's school system. Dr. Herenton's initial aspirations of becoming Memphis' first African-American mayor began in 1981 and became reality in 1992.

Benjamin L. Hooks
Civil Rights Leader, Judge, Clergyman

"I came from Booker T. Washington and in my wildest dreams I never thought I would be a judge in this city. I never thought I would sit on the FCC. I was pushed by my teachers to use my talents. I used my time wisely. I urge you to use your time here wisely."
-- Benjamin L. Hooks, speaking to students at Booker T. Washington High School, Memphis, 1976

A photograph taken during the mid-1930s in the old Hooks Brothers Studio shows a smiling, 10 year-old Benjamin L. Hooks. The picture represents hope for the African-American community in breaking the chains of segregation.

Hooks' grandmother was Julia Britton. She was born in Frankfort, Kentucky, in 1852. Britton was a free black woman and a child prodigy who received training in classical music. She attended Berea College in Kentucky, becoming only the second black woman in the United States to graduate from college. She eventually moved to Memphis and married Charles Hooks. Robert Hooks, one of Julia and Charles' sons, was the father of Ben Hooks. Robert and his brother operated Hooks Brothers Photography studio, one of the oldest African-American businesses in Memphis.

Ben Hooks, a shy student while at Booker T. Washington High School in Memphis, grew up with the dream of one day becoming a Baptist minister. His father discouraged such a profession, however. To please his father, after graduating from high school in 1941, he began preparation for a law degree at LeMoyne College in Memphis. After a stint in the U.S. Army during World War II, Hooks attended DePaul University and graduated with his juris doctorate in 1948. He returned to Memphis and entered private law practice. He also fulfilled his childhood dream and became a minister in 1956, serving at Greater Middle Baptist Church.

With a law degree and a reverend title, Hooks entered the fight for civil rights. He came to despise racial problems as he grew older. He fought for the desegregation of public bathrooms, drinking fountains, and lunch counters. Even when serving his country during World War II, Hooks found himself in the ironic position of guarding Italian prisoners who were allowed to eat in restaurants that barred him. As a young attorney in Memphis, he was forced to withstand racial insults from law clerks. Hooks considered himself lucky to be called "Ben" rather than "boy" in court. As recently as 1990, he and his family were the targets of bombings aimed at civil rights leaders.

In 1965, Hooks was appointed by Governor Frank Clement to fill a vacancy in the Shelby County criminal court. It marked the first time since Reconstruction that a black man held such a position in Tennessee. He was easily re-elected the next year. In 1972, Hooks was appointed by President Richard Nixon to the Federal Communications Commission (FCC), so he and his wife Frances moved to Washington, D.C. He was the first African-American to serve in the agency, and he led the drive to encourage minority ownership of radio and TV stations. Hooks was also executive director of the NAACP from 1977 to 1993.

Benjamin Hooks became a national leader in the fight for equality. His list of awards and accomplishments can fill pages. However, he does not want to be known solely for his fight against racism. Hooks has also fought injustice regarding matters of the environment, health care, and criminal justice. He staunchly supports the philosophy that African-Americans must be held accountable for helping themselves. He has reminded wealthy and middle-class blacks of their responsibilities to their communities. Hooks wants young African-Americans to never take for granted the freedoms they now enjoy – freedoms that their parents and grandparents fought hard to gain.

J.R. "Pitt" Hyde III
AutoZone

"...I grew up watching both my grandfather and father build businesses from the ground up. They took risks that many people considered unwise, and succeeded, despite the odds. I believe my exposure to this type of pioneering mindset from a very young age gave me the drive to try new, unproven ventures. When I start a new venture, I always remember my father's statement: 'No individual ever builds a business. The individual builds an organization and the organization builds the business.'... I think it's important to embrace the risks, responsibilities and rewards of entrepreneurship in order to stimulate constant growth and change in today's business world."
-- J.R. "Pitt" Hyde III

It did not really come as a surprise to anyone that J.R. "Pitt" Hyde became a successful business creator and owner. It was in his blood. He watched both his father and grandfather blaze trails in business, and it just seemed that he was destined to do the same.

After Pitt Hyde graduated from the University of North Carolina in 1965, he joined Malone & Hyde, a wholesale grocery firm founded in Memphis in 1907 by Taylor Malone and Joseph R. Hyde Sr., Pitt's grandfather. Immediately, Pitt Hyde began to expand the domain of Malone & Hyde to include such retail operations as drug stores, sporting goods stores, supermarkets, and auto parts stores. He became CEO of the company and chairman in 1972. During his tenure, annual sales increased from $422.1 million in 1970 to nearly $1.4 billion by 1978. From 1972 to 1982, Pitt Hyde was the youngest chairman of any company listed on the New York Stock Exchange. With annual sales of more than $3 billion in the 1980s, Malone & Hyde became the third largest wholesale food distributor in the United States.

In 1979, Pitt Hyde set up Auto Shack as a division of Malone & Hyde. Its name was later changed to AutoZone. A year before Malone & Hyde was purchased by Fleming Companies, Inc. in 1988, AutoZone became an independent corporation. Hyde served as chairman from 1986 to 1997 and as CEO in 1996. By the time he resigned his managerial positions in 1997, sales had topped $2.7 billion. Today, Hyde remains a member of the company board. In 1999, AutoZone made the Fortune 500 list.

AutoZone developed several business innovations. In 1987, the company introduced WITT II-JR. While the name may sound technical, the invention made life easy for anyone who needed to find a part. Customers simply had to tell employees the make, model, and year of their cars, as well as the needed part, and within a matter of seconds workers were able to electronically locate the part and warranty information. This was a breakthrough for the automotive parts industry, but AutoZone was not done yet.

The company took its auto warranty service a step further and began keeping a database for customers regarding their warranties. To date, AutoZone is still the only auto parts company that offers this service. Additionally, by introducing a satellite system in 1994, the company is now able to broadcast to other AutoZone stores. This allows its stores the ability to request holds and make inquiries for customers who need parts. In 2002, the company developed "hub, feeder, and satellite" stores to streamline operations and save consumers time and money.

One of AutoZone's latest innovations combined its services with the services of two other auto giants - Midas and CarMax. The advancement is really about keeping the customer happy and doing whatever can be done to simplify the tediousness of maintenance and car repair. In 1995, AutoZone established its corporate headquarters in downtown Memphis, overlooking the Mississippi River. It was a significant move that bolstered the growth of the downtown area, which began with the resurgence of The Peabody Hotel and Beale Street.

Hyde became chairman of Malone & Hyde in 1972 at the age of 29. He expanded operations to include grocery stores as shown in the photo (photo from Special Collections Department, University of Memphis Libraries).

"They also ingrained in me one of the responsibilities that goes hand in hand with successful entrepreneurship – reinvesting in your community through charitable and civic support." This is what AutoZone Park and FedEx Forum were all about. The Hyde Family Foundation has shown its community support through the Memphis Biotech Foundation, the J.R. Hyde Chair of Excellence in Rehabilitation Engineering at the University of Tennessee, the Joseph Reeves Hyde Award in Religious Studies at Rhodes College, the National Civil Rights Museum, the Memphis Ballet, and the Brooks Museum of Art, among others.

J.R. "Pitt" Hyde not only followed in the footsteps of his father and grandfather, but expanded upon the business that he inherited. Hyde left a unique imprint on his father's company. AutoZone's motto is also Hyde's philosophy, coined by Doc Crain in 1985. It is taken from the acronym WITTDTJR, which stands for "whatever it takes to do the job right." AutoZone's success directly resulted from realizing this motto.

The downtown's growth followed with Peabody Place, the Gibson Guitar factory, and two important sports complexes that stand only three blocks from each other - AutoZone Park, home of the Memphis Redbirds; and, the Memphis Grizzlies' FedEx Forum. As a board member of FedEx, Hyde backed the construction of FedEx Forum. He also supported the move of Rock 'n' Soul, a museum designed by the Smithsonian Institution, to its current headquarters in the Forum.

Currently, Pitt Hyde is the owner and president of investment company Pittco Holdings, Inc. He is the principal owner of MB Venture Partners, and also the chairman of a biopharmaceutical company named GTx, Inc. Despite his abilities to begin new and successful companies, he dearly remembers what both his father and grandfather taught him.

Contrary to original thinking, AutoZone Park - the home of the Memphis Redbirds baseball team - has been very successful and an important addition to the downtown (photo by Robert W. Dye).

(photo by API Photographers, Inc).

Brenda Joysmith
Artist

*"Art is not a luxury, as many people think; it is a necessity.
It documents history. It helps to educate people and stores knowledge for generations to come."
(The vision of the Joysmith Gallery)
-- Dr. Samella Lewis*

Some children begin their illustrious business careers selling lemonade. Brenda Joysmith, a graduate of Booker T. Washington High School in Memphis, drew portraits of her friends and sold them for a quarter. Though the quarters did not add up enough to pay for college, the budding artist's ability allowed her to obtain a scholarship to the University of Chicago, where she ultimately received a fine arts degree in 1974.

Born into a poor family, Joysmith considered herself rich in terms of family and friends. In a century where many artists focus on negativity, Joysmith sought to capture the positive side of human experience. Her work expresses spiritual warmth and the joys of childhood. Her lifelike pictures form a bond in people's hearts, no matter their childhood experiences.

After Brenda graduated from the University of Chicago, she moved to the San Francisco Bay area. For several years, she experienced ups and downs financially and personally. Joysmith came to grips with her situation and motivated herself to succeed. "I figured out that I was responsible for cultivating a frame of mind where I can be productive," she said. She produced scores of paintings, many of which were sold from her studio in her apartment.

The 1980s were very productive and successful for Joysmith. By 1980, she became a full-time artist with a new studio in her sister's converted garage. With financial support from friends and family, her first portfolio was produced in 1984, titled *Tapestry*. Of the six featured portraits, *Madonna* became Brenda's signature piece. Her client list includes some of the most famous celebrities. Her work has been featured on *The Cosby Show*, *In the Heat of the Night*, and *Lethal Weapon III*, to name a few. She also has illustrated a number of books. Today, many of her works are highly sought after.

A copy of the 1984 *Madonna* limited edition painting sells for more than $4,000. Despite an increased value of many of her paintings, she makes a point of printing copies of her artwork for the general public.

Two of Joysmith's themes are reading and friendship. In her painting *Reading From All Sides* (1988), five small girls read together as they hover over a book. The painting indicates that learning to read is a social experience. Other related works include *Reading and Friendship* (1990), *Storyteller* (1990), and *Ritual of Good Night* (2001).

Joysmith and her husband, Robert Bain, returned to Memphis in 1999 after being gone for 25 years. As she recovered from surgery to remove an orange-sized brain tumor, she found herself wanting to return to her hometown. Joysmith began to realize that she could help other artists. Before long, she was displaying and selling the works of artists around the world. She also opened the Joysmith Gallery in January 2000 at 46 Huling in Memphis' South Main Art District. Joysmith's artwork is also displayed on her website.

Joysmith's work for the art community and her support of the arts is inspirational. She won the Arts and Culture Award in 1997, as well as the Cultural Arts Achievement Award in 1990 from the National Coalition of 100 Black Women. She is active in many charities, and she hosts events at her gallery. Joysmith's art took her from ordinary to extraordinary at a time when women, particularly black women, were not taken seriously in the art world. Her story is uplifting. "To work creatively and sell my work as a successful artist is the fulfillment of a life long ambition," she once said. "Now, the wonderful reception and demand for my work is a new stage, with an exciting complement of rewards and challenges."

Riley "B.B." King
Musician

*"When I sing, I play in my mind. The minute I stop singing orally,
I start to sing by playing (my guitar named) Lucille."*
-- B.B. King

Like many others who ultimately enjoyed success, B.B. King did not have an easy childhood. As a teenager, he was plagued by a stammering that became less noticeable when he gained more self confidence. Riley B. King was born in 1925 on a plantation in Mississippi near the minuscule villages of Berclair and Itta Bena. Indianola and Greenwood were the largest nearby towns. King grew up doing farm work. His mother left his father when he was only 4, and he went to live with his grandmother in the hilly country just east of the Mississippi Delta. Sadly, King's grandmother died when he was 9 years old. He was devastated. She represented an anchor in his life, and he had trouble coping with her passing.

One of the most important influences in King's life and music was Rev. Fair. King worshiped with a Church of God in Christ congregation led by the reverend. King believed Rev. Fair listened to people and tried to understand their problems. Rev. Fair also taught the young man a few guitar chords. King looked up to his minister so much that at one point he considered becoming a preacher. Though he never followed through with his preaching aspirations, King sang in the church choir and was part of a youthful gospel quartet called the Elkhorn Jubilee Singers.

Another of King's musical ventures involved visiting his aunt Mima. Aunt Mima had quite an impressive record collection. She had a load of blues, gospel, and jazz records, and even a Jimmy Rodgers country record. King's cousin, Bukka White, visited the family in Mississippi. By the early 1930s, White was living in Memphis and had already done recording work with a label named Victor. Afterward, he recorded for the Vocalion Record Company. White traveled with his guitar and played for King.

At the age of 12, King bought his own guitar for $15. It was a cherry-red Stella, and it served as his companion. He played it no matter what mood he was in – lonely, depressed, or even happy. He said his guitar gave him a new life. But to his chagrin, someone stole it a year later. King waited a long time before he bought another one. He never got over the loss of his first guitar, and he could hardly believe someone would take something that did not belong to him.

In the late 1930s, King lived with his father. Then, in the early 1940s, he moved in with his cousins near Indianola. While there, he picked cotton at Johnson Barrett's plantation. Although he was too young to get in, he stood outside Johnny Jones' Night Spot in Indianola so he could hear live jazz and blues acts. King also loved to listen to music on radio broadcasts from Nashville, Helena, West Memphis, and Memphis.

King left the plantation twice for Memphis. The first time was in 1946 as a result of wrecking a tractor. He ran away and stayed with his cousin, Bukka White. He returned to the plantation, only to leave again in the fall of 1948, this time for good. He believed Memphis was his best opportunity to make it as a musician. But this time he crossed the bridge from Memphis to West Memphis, Arkansas. His eye was on KWEM radio.

King earned a spot on Sonny Boy Williamson's radio show on KWEM. Then he obtained a regular gig at the 16th Street Bar and Grill. Williamson had double booked himself, and offered King as a replacement. King also heard about Memphis' WDIA radio, the first station in the country to have all-black programming. For a chance to showcase his talent, he took the bus back across the river and walked 20 blocks in the pouring rain with a case-less guitar against his chest. His audition was a success, and he was given a 10 minute spot to advertise Peptikon.

Riley King had arrived. He garnered radio time and maintained a steady gig at a club in West Memphis. On WDIA he became known as the "Beale Street Blues Boy." Eventually, King's nickname was shortened to "Blues Boy," and finally to "B.B."

People often wonder why King named his guitar "Lucille." One night during the winter of 1949, he played in a club in Twist, Arkansas. Two patrons got into a nasty fight, which resulted in a fallen kerosene lamp that set the place on fire. Everyone, including King, rushed out to safety. Once outside, however, he realized he left without his $30 guitar. Without thinking, he rushed back in to get

When W.C. Handy died in 1958, Sunbeam Mitchell changed the name of his club to "Club Handy." King had played in this Beale Street club since the early 1950s.

it, barely escaping with his life. He later discovered the fight started over a woman named Lucille. Since that time, he has named every one of his guitars Lucille.

B.B. King has made his mark on the world of music. He won 13 Grammy Awards. In 1987 he was inducted into the Rock 'n' Roll Hall of Fame and received the NARAS Lifetime Achievement Grammy Award. Over the past several years, King has gained five honorary doctorates. Like Elvis, his honors and awards are too numerous to mention.

In 1991, B.B. King's Blues Club opened on Beale Street. Following its success, others opened around the country, including in Los Angeles and New York's Times Square. King shows no signs of slowing down. Nearing 80, he continues to entertain the world. In 2004, he performed in 126 concerts and shows all over the United States, as well as in Canada.

B.B. King is a testament to the adage "hard work pays off." He rose above the situation in which he was born, and transformed himself into a shining example of success. He is a role model of perseverance. His passion to play from his heart still continues to this day.

King recorded several tunes in Memphis in the early 1950s for RPM, a Los Angeles company. Sixteen Tons, however, was recorded in Los Angeles a few years later (photo from Arcadia Archives).

King is a superb blues guitarist, but never sings at the same time he performs on "Lucille" (photo from Arcadia Archives).

Ira A. Lipman
Guardsmark

"The title 'entrepreneur' should not be restricted to those creative, resourceful people who brainstorm new products or run small, medium, or large companies; it should encompass everybody in America who responds to the free-thinking atmosphere of the American spirit by creating anything."
-- Ira A. Lipman

As a young boy in Little Rock, Arkansas, Ira Lipman worked for his father's small private investigator firm during the summers. His father set him up as a store shopper to buy merchandise to test both cashiers and clerks. In high school, he worked with local newspapers and even helped John Chancellor gather information for Little Rock's school desegregation crisis.

In 1958, Lipman's father moved to Memphis, where he continued his business, Mark Lipman Service, and later moved to the basement of the Dupont Building. It was in this building in 1963 that Ira Lipman founded Guardsmark, which provided guard service to various industries. From the beginning, Guardsmark experienced remarkable growth. As president and chairman of the company, Lipman become a millionaire at age 29. He still holds the company's CEO position to this day.

The one factor that has separated Guardsmark from the competition and turned it into such a lucrative business is the quality of its employees. Many security companies do little or no research on their employees, but Guardsmark's screening process rivals that of the Secret Service. Each Guardsmark applicant is required to fill out a detailed 40-page application. Potential employees must have their education, employment, military, and residential histories reviewed. Guardsmark performs background and police record checks, and the company contacts numerous character references. All potential employees must undergo drug screening in government-approved laboratories that administer extensive 10-panel drug tests. In some instances, polygraph testing is even used to verify the truthfulness of the applicant. Only one in 50 applicants is invited to join the company.

Lipman chooses Guardsmark executives carefully.

Because of their expertise, executives typically remain at the company for years. Many have come over as former police officials, while others have had military backgrounds. Guardsmark hires more retired F.B.I. agents than any other company. The company now has more than 150 offices in the United States, Canada, the United Kingdom, and Puerto Rico, with annual revenues approaching $500 million. A 1992 article in *Time Magazine* dubbed Guardsmark the company "which many security experts consider the best national firm in the business" – quite an accomplishment. Lipman's management style is goal-oriented and fair, yet also demanding and uncompromising on rules and procedures.

Lipman wrote a manual for the U.S. Department of Justice, which was used for its crime prevention efforts. This manual was based on his 1975 book, titled "How to Protect Yourself From Crime." The publication has attracted the attention of both print and television media.

Lipman is internationally recognized for his innovative company standards and the quality of his business. Presently serving as a trustee and member of the Executive Committee of the Simon Wiesenthal Center, Lipman is also widely respected for his work with human rights. He has served as National Chairman of the National Conference of Christians and Jews and became the Honorary Chairman for Life in 1992. In 1997, he helped found the Memphis Shelby Crime Commission. He was also chairman of the National Council on Crime and Delinquency. Guardsmark received the American Business Ethics Award in 1996 and the Corporate Citizenship Award in 2002 from the Committee for Economic Development. Mr. Lipman also received the Stanley C. Pace Award for leadership in ethics in 2002.

Rev. Peter J. Lunati Sr.
Inventor of The Rotary Lift

"I don't intend to preach for a salary as long as I have any income or any way to make a living. I think that is what is wrong with the churches now. They try to go for business too much."
-- Peter J. Lunati

As a soldier in the Air Transportation Corps in France during World War I, Peter J. Lunati learned a great deal about cars and trucks - a skill he took with him into civilian life. He opened a small garage and service station in Memphis at 1656 Lamar Ave., where he began working to repair vehicles. Not long after, he started contemplating a better way of lifting cars in order to work underneath them. The archaic jack was just too difficult to make major repairs. He set out to use the pressure on cylinders from existing compressors to lift the cars.

Lunati was unsuccessful in his first attempt. He failed in his second and third attempts as well. In fact, he had many failures before he finally created a product that could lift the weight of a car and keep it off the heads of mechanics. In 1924, he perfected his lift, but engineers remained skeptical and said the new product would be difficult to sell. In 1925, Lunati obtained a patent, but he was challenged with manufacturing and selling his invention.

Lunati's patent attorney had another client with business acumen and finances to get the new product off the ground. Hence, the Automobile Rotary Lift Company was formed. The company's first office was on the eighth floor of the Exchange Building. Its manufacturing services were at 1055 Kentucky St. Like the inventor, the company had a rough start. It failed to make any money until its third year. By 1928 however, the young company watched its sales grow. In 1936, it dropped "Automotive" from the company name and expanded production to include elevators. In 1958 Rotary Lift Co. merged with the Dover Elevator Corporation, which had its headquarters in Memphis for many years. Dover elevators are distributed all over the world.

Peter Lunati loved his company, but his true desire in life was in ministry. Lunati faced deadly encounters in France, and he was determined to share his faith. He was content giving royalties to the church, and he built a church at the corner of Manassas Street and Looney Avenue. The nondenominational church was named the Christian Assembly, and Lunati began to preach there in 1930.

In 1935, Lunati purchased 1,200 acres of seemingly unsuitable land near Holly Springs, Mississippi. Friends told him the land was good for nothing, but Lunati turned it into a place with scientific farming, irrigation, and electric power. His goal was to build a religious school and tabernacle where students could work on the farm while completing their studies.

Peter Lunati could have pushed for more money, considering the influence he had in the rotary lift industry. Many people felt he did not get enough credit for his invention and he could have been a more successful businessman. However, Lunati was not a greedy man. He did protect his interests with a couple of victorious lawsuits, but he found joy in building his family a beautiful home and donating money to his church. Lunati was able to create what he wanted and do what he wanted with his life. He cared little about making money for money's sake. He was happy as long as he had enough to provide for his family and meet his goals. Few people ever attain that level of success.

As fate would have it, at the age of 56, Peter Lunati died on October 19, 1946. The rotary lift concept survived him, and his religious teachings were carried on by his son, Peter Lunati Jr.

R. Brad Martin
Saks Incorporated

"We think that work is a team process and that success is driven by a team."
-- R. Brad Martin

R. Brad Martin graduated from the University of Memphis in 1976. While he was a student, he ran for the Tennessee House of Representatives and became the youngest person, at the age of 21, to ever hold such a position. After he graduated from the University of Memphis, he continued in the state legislature while also working as a real estate developer. He then returned to school and received his EMBA degree in 1980 from the Owen Graduate School of Management, Vanderbilt University. In all, Martin served five terms as a state representative.

During the 1980s, Martin did a number of things, including launching a business in Nashville. The company became the largest corporate affiliated child care organization in the nation. He also became the principal investor in a group that purchased a department store chain named Proffitt's in October 1984. Proffitt's had five stores located in the Knoxville, Tennessee, metropolitan area. In 1989, Martin became more active in the company and simultaneously held roles of chairman, president, general merchandise manager, and chief executive officer. During his tenure, the company grew its annual revenue from $70 million to $7 billion.

In 1998, Proffitt's, Inc. purchased Saks Fifth Avenue. Saks Fifth Avenue was one of the premier department store chains in the country and had its beginnings in 1919. After the merger, the company began operating with a new name: Saks Incorporated. Under Martin's leadership as chairman and CEO, Saks expanded to 350 stores in 39 states. In addition to Saks Fifth Avenue and Saks Off 5th Avenue, these stores include Parisian, Younkers, Herberger's, Carson Pirie Scott, Bergner's, Boston Store, Club Libby Lu (for the pre-teen market, acquired in 2003), McRae's, and Proffitt's. In May 2005, Saks announced the sale of Proffitt's and McRae's for $622 million to Belk, a Charlotte-based department store company.

In addition to Saks, Martin has been a director with two public companies: First Tennessee National Corporation and Harrah's Entertainment. He has also had involvement in one private company: Pilot Corporation. In the fall of 1998, Martin participated in the Executive-in-Residence Program at Iowa State University's College of Business. He spoke at Vanderbilt University's Owen Graduate School of Management in 2002, as well as the 12th annual Fogelman College of Business and Economics Alumni Day luncheon at the University of Memphis in 2004. In 1983, Martin received the Distinguished Alumni Award from the University of Memphis.

In educational settings, Martin has shared with students his ideas for entrepreneurship and success in the corporate world. For him, the role of CEO is not simply to run operations behind a desk, but to visit stores in order to visualize the business from the customer's perspective. He has also met with vendors in order to solidify business relationships. In this way, Martin believes Saks can provide quality products and the best service to its customers. In fact, the manner in which he learned about the retail business was to ask himself a basic question, "Would this be something I would buy?"

R. Brad Martin believes in a company that is based on teamwork, service, and responsibility, where each person is counted on to deliver. Martin also believes that a measure of creativity, although risky, is necessary for any business to succeed. He must be doing something right, because *Forbes Magazine* listed him as one of America's most powerful people.

Bishop Charles Harrison Mason
Founder, Church of God in Christ

"Then I gave up for the Lord to have His way within me. So there came a wave of glory into me and all of my being was filled with the glory of the Lord.... When I opened my mouth to say 'glory,' a flame touched my tongue.... Oh! I was filled with the glory of the Lord. My soul was then satisfied."
-- Bishop C.H. Mason, commenting on speaking in tongues at the Azusa Street Revival, Los Angeles, 1907

In 1907, there were 12 large churches in the Beale Street area. One of these was a new denomination located three blocks from Beale Street at 392 S. Wellington (now named Danny Thomas Boulevard). Referred to as a sanctified church, it was founded by Charles Harrison Mason.

Mason was born on September 8, 1866, just outside of Memphis in Bartlett, Tennessee. He became a minister in the Baptist Church and entered Arkansas Baptist College in 1893. He withdrew soon after because he became dissatisfied with the manner of instruction and the approach used in teaching the Bible's message. In 1895, he met Charles P. Jones and other ministers who believed in the doctrine of salvation. In an 1896 revival in Jackson, Mississippi, Mason began to preach a doctrine of salvation through holiness. He preached with such fervor that he was excommunicated from the Baptist faith.

Because of hostility from the Baptist Association, when the group met the following year to hold another revival, they transferred their location to an abandoned gin house in Lexington, Mississippi. This revival brought together the basis of a Pentecostal church they named "Church of God." The name did not stay long, however. While walking down a street in Little Rock, Arkansas in 1897, Mason envisioned a change in the name to "The Church of God in Christ."

In 1907, at a convocation in a converted livery stable on Azusa Street in Los Angeles, Elder Mason and several members began to speak in unknown tongues. Mason believed he was being baptized by the Holy Ghost. After his experience at Azusa, Mason experienced all aspects of divine grace: regeneration, sanctification, and spiritual baptism. He believed he was completely prepared to assume the leadership of a church and its people. Upon returning to Memphis, he proclaimed speaking in tongues as a New Testament doctrine. Not every member of his church believed in it, however. During a meeting in Jackson, Mississippi, a church split occurred. From this, Charles Jones formed the Church of God (Holiness).

Those siding with Bishop Mason organized a church later that year in Memphis. Mason was appointed the general overseer and chief apostle of the church. He was given complete authority over doctrine, church appointments, and satellite congregations. He chose a 20 day annual convention based on the work schedule of their rural members from November 25th to December 14th, a timetable still followed today. The first national meetings were held in Memphis at Church's Park and Auditorium until an appropriate tabernacle was built. Finally, in 1925, a hospital at 958 South Fifth St. was converted into a tabernacle, but it was destroyed by fire in 1936. By the end of World War II, Mason Temple was dedicated. It had a seating capacity of 7,500 and was the largest tabernacle owned by an African-American religious group in the United States.

Mason Temple was the culmination of a dream by Bishop Mason. It coincided with the growth of the church under his guidance. In 1907 the Church of God in Christ had only 10 congregations. It grew because Mason and his ministers carried the holiness doctrine to others in various U.S. cities. As a result, others formed their own congregations. At the time of Bishop Mason's death in 1961, at the age of 95, membership was up to 400,000. As of 1997, it was the second largest Pentecostal group in America with more than eight million members. Church of God in Christ now has 5,000 churches throughout the world.

Tim McCarver
Athlete, Sports Announcer, Author

"I prepared for life after baseball (as a sports announcer) even while I played. To go through a 162-game season after 35 exhibition games, you have to be in condition, and I mean mentally as well as physically. It's a great education. It's great for learning to get along with people, to make adjustments."
-- Tim McCarver

The city of Memphis knew what it had in Tim McCarver. As a 15-year-old high school kid, he was being watched. Bill Dickey used to sit in the bleachers and think to himself, "I've got to sign this kid quickly." Two years later, he did. Dickey was a Hall of Fame catcher for the New York Yankees and worked as a scout for the St. Louis Cardinals when he first came across McCarver.

McCarver grew up a sports prodigy, if there ever was one. He excelled at both football and baseball at Christian Brothers High School. Universities tried to grab him as a football player, but he stuck with baseball. Upon graduation, he signed with the St. Louis Cardinals in 1959 at age 17. It was the jump-start of a major league career that lasted 21 years over the span of four decades. McCarver bounced back and forth between several minor league teams before becoming St. Louis' permanent choice for catcher in 1963.

The next year, McCarver won World Series Most Valuable Player honors after batting .478 and leading his team to victory over the Yankees. It was the first of three Cardinals teams he helped reach the World Series. Memphis papers described their hometown prized catcher as the "Boss of the Game." After the Cardinals beat the Yankees, McCarver flew to Memphis for McCarver Day. Memphis remained his home until 1978 when he moved to Philadelphia. Memphis then changed the name of its baseball stadium to Tim McCarver Stadium.

In 1969, McCarver was traded to the Philadelphia Phillies. The Phillies traded him in 1972, but then reacquired him in 1975 because of pitcher Steve Carlton's influence. The two were good friends and former teammates. McCarver contributed to three straight National League Championship Series appearances, and became Carlton's personal catcher. McCarver retired as a player in 1980.

Almost as soon as he announced his retirement, McCarver was asked to begin a broadcast career with the Phillies. Since that time, he has broadcast for the New York Mets, New York Yankees, and, most recently, the San Francisco Giants. In 1984, he began his stint as an analyst for ABC before switching to CBS Sports. He currently works for FOX. His national broadcasts have included championship, All-Star, and World Series games. In 2003, he set a sports analyst record by broadcasting his 13th World Series.

Today, McCarver is regarded by many as baseball's premier television analyst. His play by play announcements with Joe Buck for the FOX network have earned him three consecutive Best Sportscaster/Analyst Emmys. For several years, Tim had his own national radio show, *McCarver One-on-One*. In 1999, he began a weekly television show called *The Tim McCarver Show*, shown regionally. The show went national in late 2003 and captured the 2004 Telly Award for Best Sports Program. McCarver also authored five books including three best-sellers: *Oh Baby, I Love It*; *Baseball for Brain Surgeons*; and *The Perfect Season*.

In the 1960s, McCarver lived in Memphis during the off-seasons, while he played for the Cardinals. He pursued a college degree and participated in several local charities such as Muscular Dystrophy and Boys Town. It was tough for him to leave Memphis in 1978, where he grew up and still had many friends. He was pleased to hear the Memphis Chicks drew 300,000 in attendance in 1980, the year the stadium was named after him. McCarver is proud of his hometown and honored to have his name be associated with a Memphis tradition.

Allen B. Morgan Jr.
Morgan Keegan & Company, Inc.

"...the most important thing (in starting a business) is to have enough capital to start.... Second thing, surround yourself with top quality, talented people. And the third, I think you have got to be very serious and think long-term about your business as opposed to very short-term and being an opportunist."
-- Allen B. Morgan Jr.

Thirty-six years after founding the first investment firm based in Memphis, Tennessee, Allen Morgan Jr. remains at the helm of Morgan Keegan & Company, a firm now ranked among the nation's 25 largest broker/dealers. Morgan's dynamic leadership and entrepreneurial spirit created an environment that continues to thrive today.

Three years after graduating from the University of North Carolina, Morgan, along with Jim Keegan and two other young Memphians, founded Morgan Keegan in 1969 with $500,000 in start-up capital. Initially, Morgan's vision was to serve the investors of Memphis and to introduce regional investment ideas outside of the South. In 1970, Morgan Keegan became the first New York Stock Exchange member in the city. Morgan added fixed income securities to the product mix in 1972 – a decision that paid off handsomely in subsequent years. The Fixed Income division quickly grew to represent a significant portion of revenues. Bond underwriting remains important to the firm and the communities it serves, providing funds for the construction of schools and other key public projects.

Morgan's focus on the South remained steady and his goal became that of dominating the region as the premier provider of investment services. In 1983, the company went public, raising stockholder equity to expand its presence in the region. In the 1990's, the firm expanded through several acquisitions, including T.J. Raney & Sons, Arkansas' oldest investment banking firm, and Athletic Resource Management, a Memphis-based sports management agency. In 1994, Morgan Keegan was named the 3rd-fastest growing NYSE company by *Equities* magazine.

Throughout his career, Morgan garnered the respect of his peers and took on key industry leadership roles. In 1995, *Financial World* magazine named Morgan as one of three outstanding CEOs in the securities industry. He served on the NYSE Regional Firms Advisory Committee and held various positions with the Securities Industry Association, culminating with a term as the 2002 SIA Chairman of the Board. Morgan also shared his leadership skills with the greater Memphis community. In 1994, he was honored by The Memphis Society of Entrepreneurs. The following year, he was awarded the Memphis Carnival Business and Industry Cooke Halle Award for important contributions to the financial services industry. Morgan currently serves as a board member of Dixon Gallery and Gardens, Opera Memphis Foundation and University of North Carolina at Chapel Hill Foundation.

In 2001, Morgan brought Morgan Keegan into a partnership with Regions Financial Corporation based in Birmingham. By 2004, Regions had merged with another Memphis institution, Union Planters Corporation, to form one of the nation's 15 largest financial services providers. Today, Allen Morgan is both chairman of Morgan Keegan & Co. and vice chairman of Regions Financial.

Morgan Keegan has grown to 260 offices in 18 states with 3,200 employees and $550 million in equity capital in mid-2005. Allen Morgan's influence and contributions can be seen throughout Memphis and the South. From the landmark Morgan Keegan Tower on the Mississippi River, Morgan has made his mark on his hometown by employing many talented professionals, by supporting cultural and civic development, and by fostering the rise of entrepreneurial efforts in our community.

Joseph Orgill III
Orgill, Inc.

"All businesses are changing so rapidly that entrepreneurship is required - not optional - for today's manager. Traditionally, entrepreneurs were people who got new ideas, which often spawned new businesses. However, today even the best established business faces new challenges and opportunities. The creativity, capacity for risk, and vision traditionally associated with the entrepreneurs are becoming the characteristics of all successful businesses."
--Joseph Orgill III

Joseph Orgill III retired as chairman of Orgill, Inc. in 2004 after serving in that capacity since 1980. He graduated from Yale University with a Bachelor of Arts degree in economics, and then joined Orgill, Inc. in 1959 as a salesman. In January, 1968, he became president of the firm. In 1997, the company reached the milestone of 150 years in business. It is the oldest Memphis company to remain under the control of the family that founded it. In order to allow professional management to handle all operations, Orgill, Inc. implemented a rule that no family member can hold a job with the company.

Orgill, Inc. started as R.T. Lamb and Co. in 1847 with offices in Memphis. At the time, William Orgill was a silent partner. His older brother, Joseph Orgill, arrived first in New York from England to open a hardware business. William joined him a few years later as a salesman.

On a trip to Memphis, William Orgill saw great business potential in the city's location high on a bluff safe from floods. He was impressed with the use of the Mississippi River as a natural transportation system and the proximity of huge cotton plantations. William realized the necessary supplies for those traveling westward. After he bought a hardware business in Petersburg, Virginia, he and his new partner, R.T. Lamb, moved it to Memphis. Lamb ran the business, while William continued to work for his brother in New York.

William and Joseph Orgill never lived in Memphis, however. Following the death of their partner, Henry Lownes, in 1857, their youngest brother, Edmund, came to Memphis to take over the business. The company sold agricultural implements and supplies for blacksmiths, carpenters, coopers, and tinners. In 1850, it moved near Cotton Row to the corner of Front and Monroe, where the Shrine Building is now located. In 1922, Orgill Brothers moved to larger quarters at Tennessee and Calhoun. Currently they have a 650,000-square-foot warehouse at 2100 Latham. In the early 1900s, the company dropped retail sales and became a distributor. Now, it distributes goods to independent retailers, home improvement centers, and lumberyards.

During the 1970s, under the leadership of Joseph Orgill III, the company began to expand. It developed a version of the hub-and-spoke system with Memphis as its distribution center. Goods were sent to warehouses in other cities, and then smaller shipments were forwarded to retailers. This system was later dismantled to establish a series of national distribution centers. Orgill, Inc. now has five distribution centers and serves more than 60 countries.

Other innovative approaches involve E-Commerce and customer service. Through websites, the company allows its retailers to offer online shoppers access to the complete Orgill catalogue, consisting of more than 60,000 products. Orgill, Inc. also provides its clients with market research and international sales development. *The Home Channel News* trade publication recognized the company for these innovations.

Joseph Orgill III's civic interests include the United Way, the United Negro Fund, the 100 Club, and the Shelby County Hospital Authority, among others. He is also a member of several boards and has received numerous awards. He believes, to survive in the world market, one must work hard, hold costs down, alter tactics, and adapt to changing demands. Under his direction, Orgill, Inc. has become the world's largest independent hardware distributor.

Sam Phillips
Sun Records

"When you're talking about music, now that's my soul."
-- Sam Phillips

Most refer to Elvis Presley as "The King," an appropriate title for the man who many feel was responsible for the popularity of rock 'n' roll. However, even the most influential people rarely accomplish their feats on their own. If Elvis were alive today, he would undoubtedly agree. So who was the man behind Elvis' music? It was someone from a poor background who has been called a visionary and the inventor of rock 'n' roll - Sam Phillips.

The story of Phillips' life has its twists and turns. He was born in Florence, Alabama, in 1923. By the time he was in high school, he was already accomplished enough as a musician that he could play practically every instrument. He even conducted the school band. His youth was cut short when his father died, however, because he had to help support the family. To make ends meet, Phillips dropped out of high school and worked at a grocery store and a funeral parlor.

Phillips had dreams of becoming an attorney, but fate had another plan. He enrolled at Alabama Polytechnical Institute to major in audio engineering. He had worked at WLAY radio station in Muscle Shoals, Alabama, and at a radio station in Nashville before moving to Memphis in 1945. Phillips went to work for WREC, broadcasting big bands from the skyway of the exclusive Peabody Hotel. He hosted *Songs of the West* everyday at 4 p.m., as well as *Saturday Afternoon Tea Dance*, a show that aired nationally from The Peabody Hotel.

Phillips first came to Memphis, at the age of 16 with his older brother and three other friends. They drove down Beale Street and saw the Mississippi River and other areas. Phillips thought Memphis was the most attractive town he had ever seen. But what hit him the most was Beale Street, the place that W.C. Handy made famous in his songs. Handy was also from Florence. Phillips was always fascinated by Beale and its variety of music. He said, "It was like a land of milk and honey for people that wanted to have a good time."

In October, 1949, wanting to do something on his own, Phillips signed a lease on a small storefront located at 706 Union Ave. near downtown Memphis. The studio, named Memphis Recording Service, opened in January, 1950, with the slogan "We record anything, anywhere, anytime." Phillips recorded personal records, demos, and even weddings and funerals. He began to record blues musicians and he sold the masters to established companies like Chess and RPM. Phillips recorded such notable artists as B.B. King, Joe Hill Louis, Rufus Thomas, Howlin' Wolf, Junior Parker, Little Milton, James Cotton, Roscoe Gordon, and the record considered by many to be the first rock 'n' roll record, *Rocket 88*, recorded by Jackie Brenston and Ike Turner in 1951.

Eventually, Phillips quit his job with WREC and concentrated on his recording service and his own record label, Sun Records. His first release was by an R&B saxophonist named Johnny London on March 27, 1952. Phillips believed in taking chances and in trying to accomplish the seemingly impossible. His vision was to find a white artist who could perform in the style of a black performer.

In the summer of 1953, a young man came into Phillips' studio to record *My Happiness* and *This is Where Your Heartache Begins* for his mother. Phillips noted that this kid had a real grasp on ballads and put everything he had into a song. Phillips was impressed by what he heard.

A year later, Phillips asked the young man to come back and audition. The audition did not go so well at first. Phillips kept trying to pigeon hole the young crooner with the music of Bing Crosby and other ballad singers. It sounded okay, but it was not the sound he was looking for. After everyone took a break, the young

Cash recorded his first record for Sun in mid 1955, *Cry, Cry, Cry,* backed by *Hey! Porter. Folsom Prison Blues* was released a few months later (photo from Arcadia Archives).

Over the next several months, Elvis' popularity began to rise. Phillips sold his contract to RCA in the latter part of 1955 in a business deal that benefited both of parties. Elvis needed a national distributor and Phillips needed capital to work on his new crop of stars: Carl Perkins, Johnny Cash, Jerry Lee Lewis, Roy Orbison, and Charlie Rich, among others. Even with the sale of Sun Records in 1959, Phillips still maintained a record company and studio named Phillips International.

Sam Phillips believed people would not be satisfied if they did not follow through on their dreams. His dream was music, and his discovery of artists and entertainers from Howlin' Wolf to Elvis Presley changed the world of music forever.

singer picked up a guitar and started messing around, singing *That's Alright Mama.* He picked up the tempo as band members began to join in. Phillips stuck his head out of the control booth, convinced he had heard the sound he was listening for. He asked, "What are you doing?" The boys answered, "We don't know." As he turned on the tape, Phillips said, "Well, back it up, try to find a place to start, and do it again." Rock 'n' roll and the legend of Elvis Presley had begun.

Great Balls of Fire, Jerry Lee Lewis' follow-up to *Whole Lotta Shakin' Going On,* became another huge hit for him. It was recorded in October 1957 (photo from Arcadia Archives).

Sun Studio, the birthplace of rock 'n' roll (photo by Robert W. Dye).

Dewey Phillips (left) and Sam Phillips (right) were not related, but they were collaborators in the early history of Memphis rock 'n' roll. Dewey, a DJ on WHBQ, had his own radio show, "Red Hot & Blue." He introduced Elvis' first record, "That's All Right Mama" backed by "Blue Moon of Kentucky," on radio. It put Elvis in the spotlight and initiated his rise to stardom (photo courtesy of Sam Phillips Estate).

Abe Plough
Plough, Inc.

"Success in itself, no matter how modest, becomes an inspiration and makes people want to work out their own destinies. And then add to that inspiration, some ingenuity, and resourcefulness and you've got another set of building blocks to achievement."
-- Abe Plough

Harry S. Truman once said, "I studied the lives of great men and famous women, and I found that the men and women who got to the top were those who did the jobs they had in hand, with everything they had of energy and enthusiasm and hard work." This accurately describes the pattern of Abe Plough, a Memphis native who started his company when he was only 16 years old.

Abe Plough was born in Tupelo, Mississippi, in December, 1891, but within a year of his birth, Moses and Julia Plough moved their family to Memphis. The family settled in the "pinch" area of north Memphis, where Abe set up a clothing and furniture business. The area was multicultural, and had a significant Jewish population. Eventually, the Plough family included eight children.

Abe Plough attended Market Street School in Memphis until 1905. Lorena Banks, his first grade teacher, made her students do mathematical exercises. Young Plough was usually the sharpest. Much later, he sought her out to thank her because he had found the exercises very useful in his business. Although she had died, Plough ended up donating enough money for her adopted home (Decatur, Alabama) to build a library. It was a typical gesture from him.

When Plough reached the age of 16, he was ready to leave the clothing business and begin his own career. He was attracted to the pharmaceutical industry. In order to learn the trade, he worked for free at the George V. Francis drug store as an errand boy. He convinced his father to financially support his dream of entrepreneurship, so his father gave him $125 dollars in capital. In 1908, Plough Chemical Company was born in a single room above his father's store. Plough's first product, called Plough's Antiseptic Healing Oil, was a combination of camphor, cottonseed oil, and carbolic acid. It was mixed together in dishpans and then placed in a large copper dispensing kettle. His first delivery vehicle was a horse and wagon that carried his homemade remedies to country stores and farmers. Because his product was unknown, he had trouble selling it, so he traded it for other pharmaceuticals. It was also an effective way to expand his knowledge of the field.

Around 1914, Plough became the proprietor of Battier's Pharmacy on Beale Street, later to become the Pantaze Drug Store. Here he nationally marketed Black and White Ointment in 1916. It became his largest selling product. During the 1910s, Plough also added a cosmetics line.

Abe Plough hit it big in 1920. He purchased the St. Joseph's Company in Chattanooga, which had been in the public eye since 1878. The entire reason for the purchase was to market a brand of aspirin. Plough and his associates believed it would be best to market it under a nationally recognized name instead of a new one. With a clever advertising campaign – one of Plough's strong suits – sales were crisp, and the line became one of his best. Plough became a pioneer in the field of child medication, and he was the first to sell flavored, quarter strength aspirin. He made it a life ambition to research and develop products that would ensure child safety. For his efforts, he was given the first individual award from the U.S. Consumer Product Safety Commission.

Plough was quick to realize the potential in the foreign market. He hired Ramon R. Diaz in 1926 to build this market, mainly in Central and South America and in the Caribbean. By the end of the 1930s, they were selling products in 44 countries, and the company has since experienced an expansion on a worldwide level.

Part of Abe Plough's success resulted from his willingness to listen to and work with his customers. He made sure they were satisfied. In Central America, he lowered the price of products to fit the purchasing power of his customers. In a 1977 speech before prospective small business owners, Plough commented about the importance of personalizing a business. He pointed to several reasons for loss of business: discourtesy to the customer; grievances that were not adjusted; product prices not being low enough; and the influence outside sources have on customers. He commented, "Business goes where it is invited, stays where it is well treated, and grows where it is cultivated."

Beginning in 1957, sun worshipers around the world were not only treated to adorable ads of a dog tugging on the swimsuit bottom of a tan child, but to a product that would evolve into one of their best lines of defense against harmful sun rays. Coppertone suntan lotion has become one of the company's flagship product lines.

In 1971, Plough merged with another of the world's greatest pharmaceutical companies: Schering - the brainchild of German doctor Ernest Schering. Schering had created some of the world's leading antihistamines such as chlor-trimeton and the cold medicine Coricidin.

Following the merger, the company began production of Lotriman and Vanceril. In 1979, it acquired Scholl, Inc., which was a leader in the foot-care industry. Schering-Plough is also home to Maybelline cosmetics and DAP, a caulking compound. The company even expanded into the business of radio stations. Over its lifetime, Plough, Inc. has purchased or merged with 30 companies.

Abe Plough was nicknamed "Mr. Anonymous." He truly believed success came from helping others. He is responsible for millions of dollars in charitable contributions, most of which were given anonymously. "Integrity is what you do when no one is looking," as the saying goes. Plough's philosophy was "to help the greatest number of people in order to do the most good." Plough set up the Plough Foundation before his death in 1984 so that long after his death, others could continue to benefit from his generosity. His foundation supports educational causes throughout Memphis and Shelby County.

Abe Plough's legacy lives on throughout the world. Today, Schering-Plough is one of the leaders in its industry. His products and his contributions to the children of Shelby County make him one of Memphis' greatest innovators and human beings.

Plough surveys the front of his company in 1960, which had increased its net sales in that year to $45.9 million (photo from Special Collections Department, University of Memphis Libraries).

Elvis Aaron Presley
The King of Rock 'n' Roll

"I ain't no saint, but I've tried never to do anything that would hurt my family or offend God.... I figure all any kid needs is hope and the feeling he or she belongs. If I could do or say anything that would give some kid that feeling, I would believe I had contributed something to the world."
-- Elvis Presley

If a city's only claim to fame was Elvis Presley, it would be enough. His story has been told innumerable times, just as his recordings have been issued and reissued to meet the demand. School children may not know about pop stars from 10 years ago, but they know about Elvis. Some teachers even have their students do special projects about Elvis in their music history classes. One cannot bring up American music without talking about Elvis. Not bad for a poor kid from the small town of Tupelo, Mississippi.

Sam Phillips found in Elvis the type of performer he dreamt of - a white man who performed in the style of a black artist. Phillips soon learned how significant his musical discovery was. Elvis was not merely a good performer, but the "King of Rock 'n' Roll" icon who redefined American popular music and touched millions of listeners.

When commenting on his encounter with the young 19-year-old in Sun Studios, Phillips remarked that Elvis "tried not to show it, but he felt so inferior." Phillips then said, "Elvis Presley was probably innately the most introverted person that ever came into that studio." Others made similar observations. But when Elvis recorded two ballads for his mother at Sun Studios during the summer of 1953, Phillips took notice of his rising star. He said Elvis poured everything he had into his songs. This mild-mannered person became transformed.

Two composers and record producers named Jerry Leiber and Mike Stoller recorded Elvis on three occasions, one being the soundtrack for *Jailhouse Rock*. They were impressed by Elvis' variety of musical interests. He knew a lot about musicians and their songs. Similar to Sam Phillips, Leiber recognized Elvis' incredible talents when Elvis recorded the tune "Don't" with genuine emotion. As

he matured both as a man and a singer, Elvis developed into an unequaled balladeer.

Elvis had a quality to his voice that was unrivaled. It was smooth and seductive, and it reached into the souls of listeners. This quality came from the most significant music in his life – gospel music from church, and the music he heard in the African-American community. With a natural voice that was virtually flawless, he possessed the unique capability to capture nearly any style that he was asked to perform.

Throughout his career, Elvis racked up quite an impressive array of statistics. He signed with Sun Records at the age of 19, and by the time he turned 21, he was an international recording star. Elvis made 31 feature motion pictures, plus two theatrically-released concert documentaries. In the United States, 150 of his albums, singles, and extended plays have reached gold and platinum sales. Elvis has received gold and platinum records from more than a dozen countries. Internationally, sales figures have exceeded one billion units, making him the all-time leader in the industry. Of the 149 songs that made Billboard pop charts, 18 of them hit No. 1. Elvis' records also ranked highly on Billboard's country and R&B charts, which demonstrates the broad base of his appeal. In the gospel field, Elvis won three Grammys from the National Academy of Recording Arts and Sciences. He was nominated a total of 14 times.

The combination of musical talent with impeccable good looks, southern charm, youth, and a natural ability at showmanship marked Elvis' ingredients for success. But Elvis' star shined beyond the stage.

Elvis was a performer of the people. Everyone in Memphis seems to have an Elvis story, but their stories

portray Elvis as if he were just an ordinary person. There are stories of him buying cars for elderly strangers, renting out a local theater late at night so he could take Lisa Marie to a movie, and of eating lunch with an older woman who babysat him as a child. It seems as though he never forgot his friends, and he was generous with the spoils of his success. After all, at one time Elvis was just a kid in Memphis' Humes High School, from which he graduated in 1953. At the time, no one could have predicted the profound impact he would have on Memphis and the world.

On August 16, 1977, Elvis Presley died at his antebellum-style mansion, Graceland. His death sent ripples of shock around the world and triggered a period of public mourning. Now, the anniversary of the man's death has become a celebration of his life and music. Elvis named three people in his will, one of whom was his daughter, Lisa Marie. She became sole heir to the estate, but her inheritance was held in trust until she turned 25 in 1993. Priscilla Presley, who was married to Elvis from 1967 to 1973, was Lisa Marie's legal guardian. In 1981, Priscilla and her co-executors decided to open Graceland to the public. They hired Jack Soden, an investment counselor from Kansas City, to take over operations. He became CEO of Elvis Presley Enterprises, the corporate division of the Presley trust that was

formed to manage its assets and business affairs. When Lisa Marie reached her 25th birthday, she continued the successful management of the estate by forming a new trust. In 1998, she became more involved in managing Graceland, while Priscilla turned to other activities. In February, 2005, Lisa Marie sold off a major interest in Elvis Presley Enterprises.

Graceland remains a top attraction in Memphis, with more than 600,000 visitors per year. It is one of the top five home tours in America. As CEO, Jack Soden has witnessed the development of Graceland and its significance on the economy of Memphis. But he also has expanded Elvis Presley Enterprises to include control of the shopping mall across the street, an airplane exhibit, and the Elvis Presley Automobile Museum. In addition, he continues to supervise the worldwide licensing of Elvis products, music, videos, and publishing assets, among other things.

After Elvis died in 1977, people from all over the world made a pilgrimage to Graceland. Before the house was opened to the public, many wrote their names on the brick wall surrounding the house. Others attached remembrances and messages to the gate and wall, like votive offerings. Folk artists created sculptures and paintings, including one depicting Elvis walking up the path to a heavenly Graceland to be welcomed by his mother. Now, the pilgrimage extends from his birthday on January 8 to the date of his death. The house – along with the modest memorial garden where Elvis, his mother, his father, and his grandmother are buried – is the main attraction. All one needs is a little imagination to see Elvis playing the piano, cooking in the kitchen, kidding around with friends, or riding one of his horses.

And then there is the music. The effect of his death on people matches the power of his message in song. The stars who hit the stage with something to offer and leave the world with something to savor burn long after their time on earth has ended.

*While Elvis was still in the Army in Germany, a group of Shriners were invited to
Graceland in 1959 when this photo was taken (photo by Robert W. Dye, Sr.)*

*Elvis met 14-year-old Priscilla while in Germany in September 1959. They were eventually married
on May 1, 1967, in Las Vegas (photo from Memphis Room, Memphis Library and Information Center).*

Rev. Adrian Rogers
Bellevue Baptist Church; The Love Network

"Now our young people today, many of them, could not recite the Ten Commandments. Many of them are members of churches.... And these kids have those blue-faced computers and televisions in their room, but they're becoming road kill on the information highway. They do not understand the Word of God and the Truth of God. Put this down, big and plain and straight. There is no goodness without God."
-- Adrian Rogers, "Love Worth Finding" radio broadcast, April 23, 1998

As one approaches the junction of Appling Road and Interstate 40 proceeding east, three giant crosses mark the rise of a huge sanctuary just to the south of the exit. This is Bellevue Baptist Church, built in 1989 on 377 acres of land in Cordova. The pastor, Dr. Adrian Rogers, retired from his post in March, 2005.

The story of Adrian Rogers is inseparable from that of the Bellevue Baptist Church. He began his ministry in 1972, and he was only the sixth senior pastor at Bellevue. The first chapel, built in 1903, had one room and stood on the corner of Bellevue and Erskine Avenue. A new church, which could accommodate 3,000 members, was built in 1952 at 70 N. Bellevue. The new sanctuary in Cordova seats 7,000.

Dr. Rogers was born in West Palm Beach, Florida, where he was ordained by Northwood Baptist Church. When he agreed to be the pastor of Bellevue, he was serving as the pastor of the First Baptist Church in Merritt Island, Florida. He inherited a vibrant church in Memphis that, under the past leadership of Robert G. Lee and Ramsey Pollard, grew to 9,000 members in 1972.

Bellevue members were immediately taken by the style of Dr. Rogers' preaching and the pragmatic way he interpreted the Bible. The first time he preached at Bellevue, it was described as "electrifying." He not only impressed the Bellevue congregation, but outsiders as well. The current membership stands at more than 29,000. He used other techniques to draw attention to his message. Special events such as "Miracle Day," "The Feeding of the 5,000," and "Body of Christ Day" were quite effective.

Dr. Rogers was president of the Southern Baptist Convention three times. With 16 million members, it is the world's biggest Protestant denomination. He conducted crusades in Russia, Taiwan, South America, and other places. One of his important outreach undertakings, *Love Worth Finding Ministries*, is a syndicated television and radio program that he founded. The National Religious Broadcasters awarded the program the 1998 Program of the Year Award and the 2001 Radio Program of the Year Award. Rogers was inducted into the National Religious Broadcasters Hall of Fame in 2003. He wrote more than 30 books and pamphlets, and prepared 31 cassettes on various religious subjects.

The only thing different about Dr. Adrian Rogers' retirement is that he no longer was pastor of Bellevue Baptist Church. His commitment and passion for delivering his message of the Gospel continued with "Love Worth Finding Ministries" and at Memphis' Mid-America Theological Seminary, where he taught.

THY LIGHT AND THY TRUTH   Psalm 43:3

Michael D. Rose
Gaylord Entertainment Corporation, Promus Hotel Corporation

"Encouraging entrepreneurship has been a hallmark of our country's status as the world business leader. As we enter a true global economy, it is vitally important that American business leaders recognize and understand the role entrepreneurship has played in our success."
-- Michael D. Rose

From Holiday Inn to Promus Companies to Gaylord Entertainment, Michael D. Rose has reached a high mark at the corporate level. Rose graduated from the University of Cincinnati with a degree in business and from Harvard University with a law degree. He was convinced that a law degree would be helpful in the business world. But instead of pursuing business, Rose returned to Cincinnati to join a law firm named Strauss, Troy & Ruehlman. He also taught at the University of Cincinnati. At the firm, one of his clients would change the direction of his life.

Roy Winegardner, one of the most successful Holiday Inn franchise developers, was a self-made millionaire. He formed a new company in 1972 named Winegardner International, and Rose was asked to be executive vice president. Their company had developed seven Holiday Inns in the United States, Brazil, and Australia when Kemmons Wilson asked Winegardner to become vice president of Holiday Inn in 1974. Rose came to Memphis with Winegardner. In 1979, when Wilson retired from Holiday Inns, Rose became its president and Winegardner became the chairman of its board. Two years later, Rose also became CEO. After Winegardner retired as chairman in 1984, his position was filled by Rose.

While with Holiday Inn, Rose succeeded in bringing together three of its development divisions into a central hospitality group. It became Holiday Inn's largest income producer. One of his major contributions to the company's stability was in the area of strategic planning. The company sold off 30 businesses having little to do with the hotel business, and expanded into casinos and restaurants relating to its primary interests. This expansion included Harrah's, Embassy Suites, Crowne Plaza, Homewood Suites, and Hampton Inns. Because of this growth, the company's name was changed to "Holiday Corporation" in 1985.

Under Rose's continued leadership, Holiday Corporation expanded into China. In 1987, it became the first hotel to guarantee meeting facilities and services. The corporation also paid its stockholders a $65 per share dividend, and it gave head management executives 13.1 percent in company equity.

When Holiday Corporation was broken up in 1990, Promus Companies, Inc. was formed. Promus continued to control Embassy Suites, Hampton Inns, Homewood Suites, and Harrah's. Rose became its CEO and chairman. Five years later, Promus Hotel Corporation split from Harrah's Entertainment. Rose retired as chairman of Harrah's in 1996, and he left his position at Promus the following year.

In 2001, Rose became the chairman of Gaylord Entertainment, Inc., a company based in Nashville. Some of Gaylord's current holdings include Gaylord Hotels, ResortQuest International (the biggest vacation rental property management company in the United States), the Grand Ole Opry, Springhouse Golf Club, and WSM-AM. In May, 2005, Rose became chairman of the board's executive committee, a post he will hold until 2009.

Michael Rose has also served on the boards of Darden Restaurants, FelCor Lodging Trust, First Horizon National Corporation, Stein Mart, and General Mills. Mainly due to his 15-year service with General Mills, he was named by *Director's Alert* as one of corporate America's 10 outstanding directors in 2000. Rose is also a member of the Beta Gamma Sigma Director's Table, which seeks to promote the role of education in the training of effective business and managerial leaders. In addition, Rose sits on the University of Memphis board, and the university named a facility in his honor: Michael D. Rose Theatre and Lecture Hall.

Clarence Saunders
Piggly Wiggly

"Then it came to me that a fellow shouldn't depend on others for his ideas but should have them himself. I decided I ought to get up a new idea in the grocery business. I thought first of a name. In two hours I guess I had thought up 1,000, and decided I liked Piggly Wiggly best."
-- Clarence Saunders, 1938

If anyone should be given an award for persistence and determination, it is Clarence Saunders. Spending his entire life in the grocery business, Saunders lost two fortunes, yet he never ceased to develop new concepts. Shortly before he died on October 14, 1953, he was planning another technical wonder that he hoped would amass his third fortune.

Saunders was born in Virginia in 1881. His mother died when he was 4. His family moved near Clarksville, Tennessee, to a town called Palmyra, where his father worked on a tobacco plantation. By the time Saunders was 14, he had dropped out of school to clerk in a general store. He then moved to Clarksville to work for Hurst and Boillin wholesale grocers, first as a traveling rep, then as a salesman in the city. He bounced between jobs but decided to stick with the grocery business. Around 1904, Saunders took a job with Shanks, Phillips & Company, a wholesale grocer in Memphis. He worked as a salesman for the company until 1914.

Saunders was a very astute businessman, as well as salesman. He noticed there were major problems in retail grocery stores. Grocers frequently went under because of extending too much credit to their customers. The standard system was for grocery clerks to put together orders from lists provided by customers. Products were contained in huge barrels or bins, or on shelves behind the counter. In Saunders' opinion, this was not only a waste of time, but it also increased labor costs, contributing to high overhead and low profits.

Saunders envisioned a self-serve store with high volume and low profit margin. In addition, by having shoppers do all of the work, labor costs would decrease and, in turn, prices of groceries would drop. In 1915, the wholesaler Saunders-Blackburn Company was born. It stayed in business for about three years, and it supplied much of Piggly Wiggly's produce. On September 6, 1916, Saunders' first retail operation opened at 79 Jefferson St. – a self-serve Piggly Wiggly store. Many were skeptical about its success, however.

Saunders did not originate the concept of a self-serve store, but he contributed to its evolution. He took the basic concept and added to it a well thought out, highly organized system. Then, with clever advertising and salesmanship, he convinced the public of its utility.

Piggly Wiggly displayed a never-before-seen floor plan. Every one of Saunders' stores had a turnstile through which customers entered. Customers used wooden baskets and followed a specific route through the store. Every product was priced and easily viewed. Customers were offered a choice of national brands. Sections of the store were separated by wooden railings. Refrigeration reduced the amount of spoilage. Much of the equipment was patented, including the floor plan. When customers finished shopping, they moved toward the front to the checkout counter and paid by cash. All of these concepts, now routine, were revolutionary in 1916, and the brainchild of Clarence Saunders.

It is one thing to conceive a totally innovative system, but quite another to make it successful. Saunders was a marketing whiz and a superb salesman. He had a knack for the dramatic. He used gimmicks for his grand opening in 1916. For the opening, he advertised a beauty contest, gave $5 and $10 gold coins to every woman, handed out balloons and flowers, and entertained with a brass band. Even the name he chose for his store, "Piggly Wiggly," was an advertising gimmick. Some say he may have thought of it when he saw some pigs trying to scurry under a fence. In any case, Saunders' knack for catchy names was evident in his other stores as well: "Clarence Saunders Sole Owner of My Name Stores,"

"Keedoozle" (Key does all), "Zizz-Buzz" (You zizz right in and you buzz right out), and "Foodelectric." Each of these names was unique and reflected Saunders' personality and his sense of flair.

By 1923, one Piggly Wiggly store had grown into 2,660 national outlets. The company was doing business to the tune of $180 million annually, and Saunders was worth about $10 million. But then came the slide. Wall Street traders drove down the value of Piggly Wiggly stock. To counter this move, Saunders supposedly arrived in New York with a suitcase of $1 million to buy up every available share. If he had succeeded, he would have made $40 million. He was not so fortunate, however. Saunders claimed the rules were changed on him, and he lost everything, including control of his vaunted stores. Today, the Piggly Wiggly Company is a wholly owned subsidiary of Fleming Companies, which boasts the proud title as the largest grocery wholesaler in the United States. Saunders bounced back with Clarence Saunders Owner of My Name Stores, only to be wiped out in the depression.

Despite a string of bad luck, Saunders remained persistent. In 1937 he began to promote Keedoozle, a line of automated grocery stores with vending machines. When World War II interrupted his development, he

started to manufacture small wagons and pushcarts, and even ammunition boxes. Keedoozle finally made its appearance in 1948. Customers were given keys to move merchandise along a conveyor belt and dispense it down a chute. A year later, because the key concept was too complex, he revamped the store with push-button devices and renamed his business "Zizz-Buzz." At the time of his death in 1953, he had already built the prototype for his Foodelectric stores, another innovative vending concept.

Despite all of Saunders' problems in the grocery business, his attitude was certainly remarkable. He never stopped developing new concepts. He seemingly enjoyed his work. During the 1920s, he owned Memphis' only pro football team and named it "Sole Owner Tigers," or "Clarence Saunders Tigers." Though he lost money, he had fun and reaped the rewards of publicity. After the depression terminated his Sole Owner stores and the Tigers, he went to a store and began to hand out thousands of carnations. Police were called for crowd control. Think of the publicity.

In 1921, Saunders began construction of his home, which he named "Cla-Le-Clare" after his three children. The public referred to it as the "Pink Palace" because of its Italian pink marble. Saunders put $950,000 into his home before he went bankrupt in 1923. The property was donated to the city in 1926, and opened as a museum of natural arts and history in 1920. The home is a city landmark and a tribute to its original owner. A reproduction of the first Piggly Wiggly store can be found there.

Clarence Saunders contributed more revolutionary ideas to our nation's grocery business than anyone else. He was a man who totally outstripped everyone in developing novel grocery concepts and marketing them successfully. In the 1930s, Charlie McFadden implemented the name Piggly Wiggly in several versions of his blues with the lyric "My name's Piggly Wiggly, I've got groceries on my shelf." Although Saunders lost ownership of Piggly Wiggly stores, he is credited for its innovative concepts and well-known name.

Clarence Saunders' palatial home, which he never lived in, became the Pink Palace Museum in 1930. It is Memphis' history museum, containing exhibits on anything from African-American culture to technology (photo by Robert W. Dye).

Keedoozle No. 1, Poplar and Union Extended, opened in 1948 using a key and vending machine concept to dispense groceries. One year later, Saunders changed to a push-button concept and renamed his stores "Zizz-Buzz" (photo from Special Collections Department, University of Memphis Libraries).

Dr. John J. Shea Jr.
The Shea Ear Clinic

"A good life is a dream in youth, realized in maturity."
-- French poet Alfred de Vigny
(John Shea's life motto)

The Shea Ear Clinic is truly a family-operated medical clinic. The clinic dates back to 1926 when it was founded by Dr. John J. Shea Sr., who was an ear, nose, and throat specialist. The company not only continues to bear the Shea name, but also the family's belief in integrity, responsibility, and accountability toward its patients. As a result, the Shea Ear Clinic continues to maintain an enviable reputation for excellence in the field of otolaryngology. Dr. John J. Shea III, his grandson, currently heads his own clinic, Shea Center for Ears, Hearing and Balance. His son, Dr. John J. Shea Jr., is currently the head of the Shea Ear Clinic.

John Shea, Jr. served as a physician in the Korean War. In 1952, when he left military service, he became more interested in the treatment of ear disorders. He continued his medical studies in Los Angeles and at the University of Vienna, Austria. Dr. Shea developed several innovative procedures that are now standard treatments in the field. Dr. Shea believed innovation involved looking at a problem from a very different angle. It meant a return of hearing for thousands of people.

Dr. Shea perfected the stapedectomy in 1956. This procedure uses Teflon tubes and grafted veins from other parts of the patient's body to replace stapes in the ear. Once a highly risky endeavor, stapedectomies are now considered to be routine. Shea himself has performed some 40,000 of these operations with a success rate in excess of 90 percent.

Shea is credited with the procedure now used to correct perforations of the ear drum. This method utilizes the connective tissue underlay technique in tympanoplasty operations, as opposed to the previous and less successful overlay technique. Not only has he developed new ways of curing hearing disorders, Dr. Shea created most of the surgical equipment he uses to perform these procedures.

One of Shea's latest innovations is regarding the treatment of Ménière's disease. This disease is characterized by a group of symptoms including progressive deafness, ringing of the ears, dizziness, and a feeling of pressure in the ears. With the use of streptomycin perfusion, Dr. Shea is experiencing amazing results in the treatment of this disease.

In addition, Shea developed a procedure for those suffering from nerve deafness. He developed a cochlear implant, which can be discretely placed in the ear canal rather than being exposed. With Dr. Shea at its helm, the Shea Ear Clinic has garnered the highest international respect for its unique management of otologic diseases. Moreover, the Shea Ear Clinic handles all medical problems associated with the ear, nose, and throat, whether the issue is a minor ear infection, allergies, or cosmetic surgery.

Ever since Dr. Shea organized the Shea Ear Clinic Foundation in 1957, it has expanded to include otology research and physician education. The foundation's success is dependent on Dr. Shea and the Shea Ear Clinic's remarkable medical procedures. Shea spends his time serving as a clinical professor at the universities of Tennessee, Mississippi, North Carolina, and Tulane. Another facet of his foundation is to help indigent patients receive the same level of care that those with money and insurance receive.

Dr. John Shea Jr. believes that to be successful, "We must learn to live by our wits in this high-tech, computer-driven world." It seems he has done just that and more. He has lived out his life motto, which began as a youthful dream to help others. By following his dream, through hard work and determination, Dr. Shea has made a very noteworthy and significant contribution to world medicine and the well-being of mankind.

Cybill Shepherd
Singer, Actor, Author

""We have to keep trying things we're not sure we can pull off. If we just do the things we know we can do... you don't grow as much. You gotta take those chances on making those big mistakes."
-- Cybill Shepherd

When most people hear the name Cybill Shepherd, they are reminded of her television and movie roles. Even those who only watch a small amount of television recognize her name. People initially think about her beauty and her roles in shows like *Moonlighting* and *Cybill*. Acting was not her original love, however.

According to Cybill, her primary interest was singing. Cybill loved to sing from an early age, whether it was at the dinner table, around the camp fire, or in church. Cybill and her sister Terry had singing competitions as they sang along with Elvis' "Blue Suede Shoes." At age 16, Cybill began her formal training. When the Metropolitan Opera Chorus came to Memphis, she studied with its coach. During her years at Memphis' East High School, Cybill joined a band called Cybill and Friends. The group, inspired by Peter, Paul & Mary, made $50 a gig playing at parties. In 1966, Cybill won the Miss Teenage Memphis contest, as she sang Bob Dylan's "Don't Think Twice, It's All Right" while playing the ukulele for the talent segment.

Currently, Cybill has recorded more than 10 albums, including *At Long Last Love*, the 1975 musical of Cole Porter songs, and most recently, *At Home With Cybill*. Her repertoire includes pop standards and jazz. She made two albums of the latter in the 1970s, one with Phineas Newborn Jr. and the other with Stan Getz. She has also performed in front of sold-out crowds.

It was modeling, not her musical career, that jetted her into fame, however. She won the Model of the Year contest in New York in 1968. The next year, Peter Bogdanovich spotted one of her *Glamour Magazine* covers and cast her in his 1971 film, "The Last Picture Show." She continued to study opera, but Orson Welles advised her to pursue acting. Cybill began to face some very cruel reviews. One critic stated, "Cybill Shepherd cannot walk or talk, much less sing." Another wrote that "she had all the charm of a hamster."

Despite criticism, Cybill remained persistent. She continued her film career with such blockbusters as *The Heartbreak Kid* (1972) and *Taxi Driver* (1976). In 1977, she made her New York singing debut at The Cookery, where she had an opportunity to learn from the legendary Alberta Hunter. Cybill played other venues in New York, working with many prominent jazz musicians.

Cybill's role in the TV series *Moonlighting* made her a star. She won two Golden Globe awards as Bruce Willis' co-star. The show, which debuted in 1985, was cancelled in 1989. During the show's run, Cybill gave birth to twins. Her next TV hit was the 1995 series "Cybill," a show loosely based on her life. For her efforts, she won another Golden Globe.

Cybill recently published her memoirs titled *Cybill Disobedience: How I Survived Beauty Pageants, Elvis, Sex, Bruce Willis, Lies, Marriage, Motherhood, Hollywood, and the Irrepressible Urge to Say What I Think*. The title itself provides insight into the out-spoken, strong woman she has become.

Cybill Shepherd is a role model for women of all ages. She has accomplished tremendous success and learned to take life as it comes. She said aging "is not easy, but it is also another exciting stage. It can be explored. You can learn from it." By taking roles that portray the struggles and victories of women that society calls "past their prime," she has taught many how to poke fun at menopause, plastic surgery, grandparenthood and divorce.

Cybill Shepherd has referred to herself as a "brassy blonde," which underscores her strong-will, boldness, and passion. All of these character qualities have helped her survive in such a tough business. Instead of believing all the negative criticism written about her, she silenced her critics and believed in herself. Cybill is truly an inspiration for those who must overcome life's obstacles.

Fred W. Smith
FedEx

"The original idea for FedEx came when I wrote a term paper as an undergraduate...about a very simple observation: As society automated – as people began to put computers in banks to cancel checks rather than clerks, or people began to put sophisticated electronics in airplanes – society and the manufacturers of that automated society were going to need a completely different logistics (transportation and supply) system."
-- Fred W. Smith

Fred Smith envisioned that as technology advances, transportation must also evolve. Steamboats and trains were logistically suitable for American society during the 19th and much of the 20th century. Trucks then became a primary means of transportation, which is still the case today. But trucks are not alone. In this modern digital computer age, airplanes have become the most efficient means of moving goods over long distances. However, airplane delivery systems were not suited for express deliveries until Fred Smith conceived a special customized system. Despite many difficulties that would have overwhelmed most people, Smith stayed with his original concept and built a business that is now a household name around the world.

Smith was originally from Marks, Mississippi. His father, who died when Fred was only 4, founded and made millions off of the Dixie Greyhound Lines bus company. His grandfather rode the waters of the Mississippi as a riverboat captain. In 1965, while Fred Smith was attending Yale University, he wrote a term paper for an economics class in which he outlined the basis for FedEx. According to every source that tells this remarkable story, his professor gave him a "C," but Smith said he does not remember his actual grade. In his paper, he wrote about his experience as a pilot in New Haven. He noted that pilots spent too much time transporting spare computer parts to desperate companies. He also mentioned the inefficiency of the system.

The Vietnam War put Smith's career on hold. He served four years with distinction and received a Bronze Star, Silver Star, two Purple Hearts, plus several Air Medals. After he was discharged from the Marine Corps in 1970, Smith went to Little Rock, where his stepfather owned a company that worked on airplane engines. His idea about express shipping once again sprang to the forefront, since the company had trouble obtaining parts. Smith had inherited $4 million from his father. He combined this money with huge venture capital investments totaling $72 million, which took a year of gritty determination to get. In 1971, in Little Rock, FedEx was born with small aircrafts that were retrofitted as cargo planes. In 1972, Smith moved his headquarters to Memphis because weather rarely caused the city's airport to close. On April 17, 1973, FedEx began formal operations.

Smith's idea for packages was patterned after the bank's method of clearing checks overnight. From there he developed the hub and spoke concept, with Memphis serving as the hub for every single package that was shipped. Both surface and air transportation had grown up with a linear system of delivery. In contrast, by delivering everything to a central hub where packages were quickly sorted and shipped to various destinations, Smith's system saved time and money. Smith admitted that Delta airlines pioneered the hub concept, and he just capitalized on technology from pre-existing airplanes and trucks. But Smith's system was unique in the fact that everything was intertwined. Airplanes needed trucks to complete the delivery process.

More importantly, the entire system needed to function with complete punctuality, precision, and dependability. System claiming overnight delivery must adhere to a tight schedule. After packages were brought to the hub, they were flown out during the early morning hours so there was little competition from passenger lines. In addition, FedEx had to build an entire new industry to track its packages. The company printed sequential bar-code numbers that needed to be read by machines. For tracking purposes, a small handheld computer was designed named the "Supertracker." At

(photo courtesy of FedEx).

Security Task Force, and he is a member of the Business Council, the CATO Institute, and the Mayo (Clinic) Foundation. He was the chairman of the U.S.-China Business Council, and he is currently chairman of the French-American Business Council. In 1997, he received AMOD's Crystal Apple Award and the first Peter Drucker Strategic Leadership Award. In 2004, Smith was named *Chief Executive Magazine*'s CEO of the Year.

each stage on a package's delivery route, it was scanned so anyone could check on the item's location.

Beginning with a stable of 14 small aircrafts in 1973, FedEx now has 671 aircrafts worldwide. It currently serves 220 countries, uses 71,000 vehicles, and employs 250,000 people around the globe. FedEx handles more than six million shipments per day. Its annual revenue is $29 billion. The company offers integrated business solutions, expedited delivery of time-sensitive shipments, customs clearance, international freight forwarding, and trade facilitation. *Fortune Magazine* has consistently ranked FedEx high on many of its lists.

FedEx has made some strategic purchases over the years. To successfully compete against United Parcel Service, it bought RPS trucking. As part of its expansion into overseas markets, the company purchased Asian Flying Tigers Airlines. During the first quarter of 2004, FedEx acquired Kinkos. In this insightful move, Fred Smith realized the benefit of providing customers with a convenient place that combines mailing, printing, copying, and other business services.

Fred Smith has served on the boards of several companies, including that of St. Jude's. He is chairman of the Business Roundtable's

Fred Smith recalled two people who left a great impression on him. One was a friend and professor at the University of Yale, who impressed him with an individualistic lifestyle. The other was an uneducated Marine sergeant who had an incredible insight into the minds of working people, influencing Smith's managerial style. And just as Fred Smith learned something about life from the two of them, every aspiring entrepreneur can learn a great deal from Fred Smith. His drive and his dreams are an inspiration, as well as a virtual guidebook for success. One of Smith's bits of wisdom is to be eclectic in studies, because this type of background may help formulate ideas. Innovative insights may come sooner or later, but they will come, just as Fred Smith's did.

FedEx Forum, home of the Memphis Grizzlies
(photo by API Photographers, Inc.).

A fleet of FedEx planes are made ready at the Memphis International Airport for the world-wide distribution of packages during the wee-hours of the morning (photo by Robert W. Dye).

Maxine Smith
Civil Rights Leader, Educator

"Education will determine the food you eat, the job you hold."
-- Maxine Smith

Maxine Smith's goal was to become a teacher. She earned a bachelor's degree in biology from Spelman College in 1949, and a master's degree in French from Middlebury College, (Vermont) in 1950. Smith reached her goal, teaching French at the university level from 1950-56, including two years at Memphis' LeMoyne-Owen College. For her efforts, LeMoyne-Owen awarded her an honorary doctor of laws degree.

In 1957, Smith applied to the University of Memphis for graduate studies, but she was denied entrance because of her race. The incident brought her into the Civil Rights Movement. Smith chose to fight her rejection with education and non-violent activism. She became a board member of the NAACP, a position she holds to this day. In 1962, Smith became executive secretary of NAACP's Memphis chapter.

Smith's husband, Dr. Vasco A. Smith, received his dental training at Meharry Medical College. He was among several African-American dentists who took an active role in desegregation. Vasco Smith served as a Shelby County commissioner from 1972-95, where he advocated minority involvement in county decisions and county contracts. In 1980, the National Dental Association honored him with its Civil Rights Award. Vasco has been a board member of NAACP's Memphis branch since 1955.

The Smiths were at the forefront of the 1960s civil rights fight, traveling throughout the country. In Memphis, they attempted to desegregate hotels, public transportation facilities, department stores, drug stores, restaurants, and movie theaters through nonviolent methods such as sit-ins, demonstrations, and negotiations. As Vasco Smith said, "I don't know of anything that anybody did across the United States - other than carrying guns and threatening to shoot white folks - that we didn't do." Among other things, the Smiths' efforts helped lead to upgraded employment for blacks.

In 1961, Maxine Smith was part of the effort to desegregate four local schools. She also worked to have more black employees in the school system. In 1969, she presented school officials with 15 demands to fully integrate schools, but the response was negative. In support of the demands, 67,000 black students participated in school boycotts dubbed "Black Mondays." The protests led to a complete school board restructuring, which allowed African-American participation. Two years later, Smith was elected to the Memphis Board of Education, where she served for 24 years. While on the board, she was instrumental in hiring Dr. Willie Herenton as the city's first black superintendent.

As a result of her involvement in the Civil Rights Movement, Maxine Smith is passionate about reminding young people how fortunate they are. Smith appreciates the individuals who suffered for freedoms that so many now take for granted. Only by educating people about our country's tragic history can future generations appreciate each other and avoid evil acts of discrimination. Smith currently serves on the boards of the National Civil Rights Museum and Tennessee Board of Regents. A tribute to her accomplishments was presented at the Memphis Public Library. She received the annual Distinguished Friends Award, as well as the NAACP's Dr. Aaron E. Henry Lifetime Service Award. In 2003, she was honored with the Freedom Award.

After nearly half a century of marriage, the Smiths credit each other with their accomplishments – a tribute to solidarity, strength, and most importantly, love and respect. Their lives are reflected in the Martin Luther King statement, "The ultimate measure of a man is not where he stands in moments of comfort and convenience, but where he stands at times of challenge and controversy."

Dr. Willard R. Sparks
Sparks Companies, Inc.

"The single most important point in being a good entrepreneur is the willingness to give people responsibility and then hold them responsible for their decisions."
-- Willard R. Sparks

Dr. Willard Sparks became a very successful commodity trader, business consultant, and world leader in the agriculture and food industry. He has been at the forefront of researching and analyzing policies and regulations for various international governments, as well as the influences these policies have on agricultural enterprises.

Born in Dibble, Oklahoma, Sparks received his B.S. and M.S. degrees from Oklahoma State University, and a Ph.D. from Michigan State University, all in agricultural economics. Dr. Sparks came to Memphis in 1963 to work as director of economic research for Cook Industries, a major agricultural trading and exporting firm. He became senior executive vice president and director of Cook's International Agriproducts Group. While with Cook, Sparks orchestrated the first large sale of U.S. grain to the Soviet Union.

Fourteen years later, in 1977, Sparks founded Sparks Commodities, Inc., which was later changed to "Sparks Companies." As a world leader in agricultural market analysis, research, and consulting, the company had more than 750 clients, including major U.S. food companies. In 2003, Dr. Sparks sold his company to a British-based information provider that renamed the company "Informa Economics, Inc."

Dr. Sparks' main contribution was in the quantitative economics field, where mathematical models are employed in the commodities market to analyze and predict fluctuations. Such models are useful because the agricultural industry is constantly bombarded with situations, such as quickly changing market conditions, technological innovations, new markets, the weather, and varying consumer tastes. Currently, Sparks' approach is widely used by the U.S. Department of Agriculture. His advice on agribusiness and strategic planning helped many to achieve success.

Dr. Sparks was highly involved in a number of organizations and U.S. commodity exchanges. He was a co-founder of both Vining Sparks and Storage, USA, and a part-owner of both Cattlco and the Blues City Baseball, which is the management team that operates the community owned Memphis Redbirds baseball team. He also served on a number of boards, including those at Oklahoma State University and the University of Memphis. Dr. Sparks established the Sparks Family Chair of Excellence in International Business and the Sparks Family Marketing Center in the University of Memphis Fogelman College of Business and Economics. In 2003, in honor of his many contributions, the university renamed its Bureau of Business and Economic Research after him. For his community service, Dr. Sparks was honored with the Outstanding Philanthropist Award by the National Agricultural Alumni and Development Association.

In agribusiness, it is crucial to plan ahead and avert undesirable consequences, which is why Dr. Sparks' work has been so influential. His analytical models have kept the world aware of agricultural fluctuations. Sparks has helped agribusiness maintain maximum output and high productivity. His methods have assured us of an adequate food supply.

Mr. Sparks was named to the Hall of Fame by the alumni association of Oklahoma State University. He also received the Distinguished Alumni Award from the alumni association at Michigan State University. The Memphis Cancer Foundation presented its Spirit of Life Award to Dr. Sparks before he died of cancer on January 30, 2005, in Memphis.

(photo courtesy of the Sparks Family).

Jim Stewart and Estelle Axton
Stax Records

"When I think about...Estelle Axton being the co-founder with Jim Stewart, she was more than just a co-founder. She was...the reason why the Stax philosophy is as it is. She was a mother figure to most of us.... She and Jim created an environment where people could be themselves, where people could come to work and enjoy being in the environment. And they were not subjected to the racial slurs and the hostilities that were so prevalent outside in Memphis at that time, and in the United States."
-- Deanie Parker, Stax publicist, singer

Think for a moment on the names of Otis Redding, Isaac Hayes, Dave Porter, Sam and Dave, the Staple Singers, and Booker T & the MGs. Reflect, if you will, on the songs "Sittin' on the Dock of the Bay," "Soul Man," "Green Onions," and "Respect Yourself." Then realize that these legendary musicians and hit songs are just the tip of the iceberg when it comes to the history of Stax Records.

Stax Records is responsible for many landmarks in the music industry. Within 15 years of its inception, Stax placed 167 hits in the top 100 on the charts and launched the careers of a multitude of young stars. Perhaps one of the most notable facts about Stax is that it came together during the worst civil unrest in the nation. Despite this, it managed to become one of the most integrated businesses in the country. The company's history is quite remarkable.

Estelle and Jim Stewart were born in Middleton, Tennessee. They grew up on a farm operated by their parents. Both enjoyed music, but Jim had plans to become a fiddler with a country band. He played fiddle on the side while he worked for First National Bank. Jim attended the University of Memphis and studied business management. He continued his fiddle playing in the Army. He had aspirations of becoming a banker, but it did not work out.

In 1957 Jim began to record country music in his wife's uncle's garage under the name Satellite Records. He also picked up a couple of business partners. None of their recordings sold well. Estelle, who by this time was married with two children, was working as a teller at Union Planters Bank in Memphis. Jim convinced Estelle and her husband to mortgage their home to help him

purchase badly needed recording equipment. He also needed money so he could buy out his partners. With Estelle as an equal partner, they relocated the studio in 1959 to a storehouse in Brunswick, Tennessee, where Jim recorded his first black group, the Veltones. The record was picked up by Mercury for distribution, but it did not sell well.

In 1960, Estelle and Jim moved their studio to Memphis, renting the old abandoned Capitol Theater at 926 McLemore Ave. The studio's first hit was a duet with local disc jockey and entertainer Rufus Thomas, and his daughter, Carla. The song was called *Cause I Love You*, and it gave Estelle and Jim hope. Although they did produce a few more country records, they felt their niche was in R&B. Their first national hit was Carla Thomas' *Gee Whiz*. It reached No. 5 on the R&B charts and No. 10 on the pop charts.

The record company had even more success with the Mar-Keys, a name coined by Estelle. The group was comprised of a white high school R&B band called the Royal Spades and a few black session musicians. Their song "Last Night" reached No. 2 on the R&B charts and No. 3 on the pop charts. But more importantly, it shaped the Stax sound of Memphis soul. Because the name "Satellite" was being used by another company, Jim Stewart decided it was time for a name change. He took the first two letters of his last name (ST) and the first two letters of his sister's last name (AX) to form the new name, Stax. The hits continued to pour out from the old theater for the next 15 years.

In 1962, the studio welcomed the young Otis Redding, whose career skyrocketed with the label. In 1965, Sam and Dave began releasing hits by Stax writers

Standing left to right, Steve Cropper, Jim Stewart, Estelle Axton; seated, Carla and Rufus Thomas, signing contract, 1965 (photo by API Photographers, Anxton, Estelle, Stewart, Jim, Inc.).

Soulsville USA, 1967 – home of the Stax Record Co., 926 McLemore Ave. It was in an old theater that Estelle Axton and Jim Stewart renovated to make Memphis music history (photo API Phographers, Inc.).

Isaac Hayes and David Porter. The hits kept on coming. Stax's success would be dampened by tragedy, however. In 1967, the plane carrying Otis Redding and the Bar-Kays crashed, killing Redding and most of the group. Redding's hit song, *Sittin' on the Dock of the Bay*, was released posthumously. It immediately topped both the pop and R&B charts.

With a huge number of stars and hits, Stax Records had experienced success. But there was another aspect to Estelle and Jim's accomplishments: the revitalization of a neighborhood. Many of their musicians came from the local area, and in this sense, Stax Records became part of the community. Estelle was a very important figure. She operated the Satellite record store in the theater, using it as a test kitchen for ascertaining the musical tastes of local black youth. As many have pointed out, she was the glue that bound together black and white artists, and she made others feel at home. Her personal touch is difficult to find in any business.

A huge hit for Sam & Dave, as well as for its composers, Isaac Hayes and Dave Porter. Recorded in 1966, it hit No. 1 on the R&B charts and No. 21 on the pop charts (photo from Arcadia Archives).

In the 1970s, Stax fell on hard times and faced many legal battles. The suits proved to be overbearing for the company, which had earned eight Grammy Awards and an Oscar. In 1977, Stax's master tapes were sold at a bankruptcy auction for $1.3 million – much less than their value. The studio itself was razed in 1989. In February 2004, Estelle Axton passed away at the age of 85.

The sun has yet to set on this Memphis multimedia company. In the year 2000, Soulsville announced plans for the Stax Museum of American Soul Music, Music Academy, and Performing Arts Center. The idea has now come to fruition with the construction of a theater that closely resembles the original, which houses the museum. Next to it is the Music Academy. This salute to the musicians, writers, performers, and creators of Memphis Soul is an amazing tribute to Stax and the music industry.

Jim Stewart and Estelle Axton sacrificed so much to fulfill their dream. Estelle took a great risk in mortgaging her house to pay for the studio. It was indeed an act of faith, and demonstrated her belief in her brother's ability. As a result of their efforts, another layer was added to Memphis' rich musical heritage.

Recording session at Stax, 1967. Isaac Hayes at the piano, with Dave Porter to his left, and singing sensations Sam & Dave (photo by API Photographers, Inc.).

A collage of Stax recording artists, with some notable exceptions, from around 1968 to 1969 (photo from Arcadia Archives).

Danny Thomas
St. Jude Children's Hospital

"Success has nothing to do with what you gain in life or accomplish for yourself. It's what you do for others."
-- Danny Thomas

The son of Lebanese immigrants, Danny Thomas started life in 1914 with the name of Muzyad Yahkoob. He struggled with his career at first, singing on the radio and performing stand-up comedy. In 1937, while taking a break during one of his emcee jobs in Detroit, a drunken person approached Thomas and told him how he prayed to St. Jude to cure his wife of cancer. The prayer was effective. Thomas recognized the power of prayer and, that evening, he prayed this to St. Jude: "Help me find my place in life, and I will build you a shrine."

A couple years later, Thomas hit it big in Chicago. His nightclub and radio acts became hot property. His career began to flourish. He moved his family to Hollywood and appeared in films such as *Call Me Mister* with Betty Grable, and the 1953 version of *The Jazz Singer*. But the one act that solidified his stardom was the 1953 TV comedy series *Make Room for Daddy*, which was later called *The Danny Thomas Show*. Thomas formed a production company with Sheldon Leonard. The company garnered one success after another with such comedy hits as *The Dick Van Dyke Show*, *The Andy Griffith Show*, *The Real McCoys*, *Gomer Pyle*, and *The Joey Bishop Show*.

Thomas' pledge was not uttered in haste to only be forgotten as he climbed the ladder of success. He intended to fulfill his promise. Originally, Thomas thought that a statue or small chapel would be appropriate. But after discussions with friends and associates, the path wound toward a full-fledged children's hospital. In the 1950s, Thomas' friend Abe Lastfogel, who was also head of the William Morris Agency, suggested that he visit Cardinal Stritch of Chicago. After hearing Thomas' wish to honor St. Jude and build a children's hospital, Cardinal Stritch suggested that he visit Edward Barry in Memphis. Barry was a lawyer and the owner of the Memphis Chicks baseball team. He arranged several meetings with prominent businessmen and city government officials. It was not long before the idea of a hospital dedicated to curing catastrophic illnesses in children began to take form. This hospital was not just meant for treating illnesses, however. It was meant to be a leading research facility as well.

To raise funds, Thomas rode across the country with his wife, Rose Marie, to talk with potential donors. On one trip, they stopped at 28 cities in 32 days. Thomas' friends were also active in supporting the idea. Abe Lastfogel and others in California established the St. Jude Foundation to raise funds. With all of their successful efforts, they grew a need to have an annual fund-raising organization. For this, Thomas turned to his roots as a Lebanese American. He and 100 others formed ALSAC – The American Lebanese Syrian Associated Charities - in 1957. The group, headquartered in Memphis, is responsible for all the hospital's funding. It has a network of more than a million volunteers nationwide.

On February 4, 1962, St. Jude Children's Hospital opened its doors. Today, its mission remains as strong as ever. Researchers are currently working on new methods in bone marrow transplantation, chemotherapy and radiation, and gene therapy. In addition, they are developing treatments for diseases of the blood, hereditary and infectious diseases, pediatric leukemia, and even the psychological issues involved in dealing with such experiences. St. Jude has been the leader in pediatric cancer research since the 1960s. The survival rate for leukemia therapy has risen from four to 80 percent under the hospital's leadership. Other forms of childhood cancers are experiencing similar leaps in recovery.

Perhaps the most amazing characteristic of St. Jude Children's Hospital is that it maintains the same philosophy Thomas so strongly believed in when he

started it. Children will never be turned away as a result of their parents' lack of finances. Families without insurance are never asked to pay. The hospital has treated children in about 70 countries since its inception.

Today, Danny Thomas and his beloved wife are buried on the grounds of the hospital. Their children – Terre, Tony, and actress Marlo Thomas – are carrying on his dream. Marlo views her father's work as a legacy that will forever remain in his children's lives. She has continued in her father's path of raising funds by hosting the annual St. Jude Hollywood Gala, and an hour long TV special, *Time to Live*. She also donates all the profits from her book, *The Right Words at the Right Time*, to St. Jude.

Even though Danny Thomas could easily have ridden his wave of fame, he will be best remembered for his drive and energy toward building a children's hospital. Seven years prior to his death in February 1991, President Reagan awarded Thomas the Congressional Medal of Honor for establishing St. Jude Children's Hospital and making a lifelong commitment to support it.

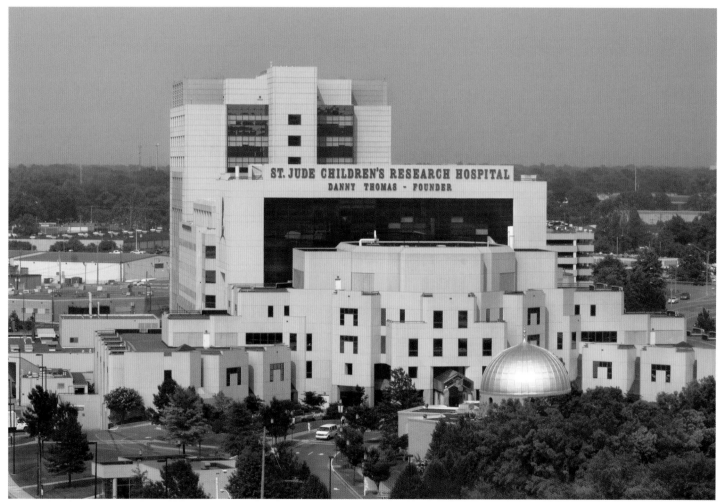

Main portion of St. Jude Children's Research Hospital with the gold-crested dome of the ALSAC (American Lebanese Syrian Associated Charities) Pavilion. Danny Thomas, founder, and his wife Rosie are buried in a crypt on the side of the pavilion (photo by Robert W. Dye).

During a dedication for a new seven-story addition to St. Jude in 1975, Danny Thomas receives a check from the parents and brother of a young patient who had died at the hospital of leukemia. The family pledged to raise $100,000 from Virginia residents (photo from Special Collections Department, University of Memphis Libraries).

Pat Kerr Tigrett
Pat Kerr, Inc.

*"Entrepreneurship embodies the spirit of the creative world of business and separates it from the mundane....
Strive to become what you were born to be. Many people travel life's journey not finding
this simple key to happiness."*
-- Pat Kerr Tigrett

As a farm girl growing up in Savannah, Tennessee, Pat Kerr Tigrett seemed to know what she wanted to do with her life. All the women in her family did some form of handiwork. After her mother opened a floral and gift shop in Savannah, Tigrett amused herself for hours in the back area by designing clothes from leftover pieces of lace. Her childhood experiences served as groundwork for what was to follow – a world-class reputation as a designer.

Tigrett attended the University of Memphis. While there, she was voted Miss Memphis in 1960. After graduating with a degree in fine arts in 1963, she spent three years at the Memphis Academy of Fine Arts and was honored as Miss Tennessee in 1964. During a modeling trip to the Orient in 1965, she bought antique lace in Hong Kong. Her purchase started a massive collection that now includes lace pieces ranging from the 16th century to modern times. Some of her items were previously owned by Queen Victoria, Edward VII, Marilyn Monroe, and Princess Diana. Many of her unique pieces were purchased in England, where she lived for 20 years. Neiman Marcus said her lace collection is one of the best and largest collections of Victorian and Edwardian lace in the world. The Metropolitan Museum of Art and the Tennessee State Museum in Nashville have each exhibited part of her collection.

Pat Kerr Tigrett married John Tigrett in 1973. John was friends with some of the world's most important movers and shakers, from Winston Churchill to J. Paul Getty. John started as a bus company executive. He then became a successful investment banker and made it big with his patents. The first of John's patents was "Glub-Glub," the drinking duck. He also marketed mesh playpens and retractable tape measures. In the mid-1960s he moved to London, where he worked with Armand Hammer to negotiate oil rights. John also worked with Sir James Goldsmith regarding corporate takeovers. After the Tigretts married, they spent the good part of 20 years between London and Memphis. John is perhaps best known for his negotiations in building the Pyramid, which defines and dominants the Memphis Skyline. Isaac Tigrett, John's son from a previous marriage, is the co-founder of Hard Rock Cafe.

Meanwhile, Pat Kerr Tigrett continued to pursue her love for clothing design. In 1978, Neiman Marcus of Dallas bought the bulk of her inventory and placed an additional $100,000 order. Shortly, Pat Kerr, Inc. was born. With Tigrett as CEO, the company designs fancy lace bridal gowns, cocktail dresses, suits, and debutante and christening gowns that have been purchased by royalty, socialites, and celebrities. Tigrett refers to her stylish clothes as "couture." Her lace dresses have been deemed fashionable and artistic, and future heirlooms.

Many magazines, newspapers, and books have featured her designs, such as *Town and Country, L'Officiel, Vogue, Tiffany's Wedding Book*, and The *New York Times*. She has also appeared on several TV shows including *Oprah* and *The Today Show*. Of her numerous awards, the first one she received was the 1983 Marketer of the Year Award. She has also received design, fashion, and civic awards.

Tigrett has devoted herself to numerous charitable events, including the Big Dig, the Bridge of Lights, the National Civil Rights Museum opening, and the Smithsonian Rock 'n' Soul Museum grand opening, among others. She helped found the Jingle Bell Ball and the Nutcracker Ball, as well as the Blues Ball. Tigrett is not only a world-renowned designer; she has greatly benefited the city of Memphis. Showcasing her talents as a world-renowned designer, Tigrett's 25th Anniversary Fashion Show was held in September, 2005. In keeping with her past efforts, it created a fashion scholarship at the University of Memphis and benefited other causes.

Henry M. Turley Jr.
Henry Turley Co.

"All my planning of downtown became easier once I realized what its value was. Its primary value is a place where everybody has a stake, where everybody can come together."
-- Henry M. Turley Jr.

Henry M. Turley Jr. was a key engineer of Memphis' downtown revitalization. For his efforts, he received numerous awards from such groups as the American Institute of Architecture, the Chickasaw Group of the Sierra Club, and the Downtown Memphis Association, among others. Turley was honored with the Mr. Downtown Award, and his name has become synonymous with making Memphis' downtown a great place to work and live.

Turley family members have lived in Shelby County as far back as the 1820s. Henry's father worked as a cotton merchant with Anderson Clayton Co. and FM Crump & Co. for a number of years, until he joined his son's real estate business. After graduating from the University of Tennessee in 1963, Henry Turley Jr. went to work for Percy, Galbreath & Son as a property manager. The company later promoted him to executive vice president. Turley Jr. started the Henry Turley Company in 1977 based on a belief that downtown housing would sell if it was properly developed. Initially, the business focused on property management.

In 1979, Henry Turley Jr. and a group of investors bought the Shrine Building. They finished renovating the building into apartments in 1981, the same year The Peabody Hotel reopened. The renovations marked the beginning of a downtown revival. Turley then had a string of projects: Paperworks; Union Commons; Parking can be Fun Garage; and several factory and warehouse renovations on South Main. Most of Turley's locations were transformed into apartments or condominiums. In 1986, he refurbished the beautiful Memphis Cotton Exchange into office space, where his company still maintains its headquarters on the 12th floor.

Turley and Jack Belz's 1989 partnership allowed Harbor Town to become one of the most desirable places to live in Memphis. Located on a narrow sliver of land separated by the Wolf River, Harbor Town is a planned community of national praise. The basic concept was to build homes and apartments, as well as other amenities common to any community. Harbor Town has a beautiful layout with its ponds, small parks, trails, playgrounds, and marina. It also has a Montessori school and a small grocery store. The neighborhood contains Victorian architecture and old-time lampposts, and purple martin birdhouses are everywhere.

Turley and Belz also worked together on Oak Court Mall and South Bluffs, another planned residential community. Their recent "Uptown" project will consist of homes and apartments for lower-income residents, and will be built on the Hurt Village project site. These undertakings follow Turley's belief that the downtown is for everyone, and all people should have access to a certain quality of life. In keeping with his interest to promote downtown, Turley teamed up with Pat Kerr Tigrett in 1986 to sponsor and stage the lighting of the Hernando-DeSoto Bridge. The duo also initiated the Pyramid's Big Dig groundbreaking in 1989.

There has been a vibrant renewal of Memphis' downtown with the hustle and bustle involving its tourist attractions. Henry Turley's contribution was in providing opportunities for local citizens to live, work, and enjoy downtown's amenities. He supplied citizens with a wide variety of apartments, condominiums, and homes. Turley's approach to development blends in with his view that a downtown's main function is to integrate all types of people into a common community.

Kemmons Wilson
Holiday Inn

"It is the entrepreneur who takes the risks necessary to turn new ideas into realities. A person has to take risks to achieve. These very risks inspire creativity and the desire to succeed – two of the most important elements in any business venture."
-- Kemmons Wilson

Kemmons Wilson was an interesting man from a multitude of aspects. He did not graduate from high school, though he wished he would have. He quit two months before graduation and got a job to help pay his mother's hospital expenses. Because of this, he came to realize the necessity of hard work. In fact, while addressing a graduating class of high school seniors, he said, "I really don't know why I'm here. I never got a degree, and I've only worked half days my entire life. I guess my advice to you is to do the same. Work half days every day. And it doesn't matter which half, the first twelve or the second twelve." He went on to say, "Too many people only want to put in a 40-hour week. I always told my managers that you can't be successful if you don't tell your wife not to expect you home for dinner." Such was the wisdom of Kemmons Wilson.

There is another reason for Wilson's hard work and long days. Nine months after he was born in Osceola, Arkansas, his father died. "I was so hungry when I was growing up that I was scared that I might be hungry again," he said. "I became a hard worker. I enjoy working."

Wilson's mother moved the family back to her hometown of Memphis. When he was 14, Wilson was struck by an automobile and ended up in a full body cast for a year. His mother worked extra hours, and she even went without food in order to pay his expenses. He returned the favor many times. No wonder they were so close. Wilson's mom became his biggest supporter, and she later helped him in his various enterprises. When he was 20, Wilson purchased a popcorn machine and operated it in a movie theater. He was so successful, the theater's owner bought him out. He then pursued a Wurlitzer jukebox franchise, a string of movie theaters, and the construction business.

In 1951, Wilson saw his biggest opportunity. With his five kids piled in the car, he and his wife left on vacation to Washington, D.C. While staying in a hotel, the family suffered from uncomfortable beds, overcrowded conditions, high prices, and unattractive facilities. But the one factor that bothered Wilson the most was the fact that he was charged extra for each of his children. On the trip, he even began to take measurements of the rooms. In a true entrepreneurial spirit, he resolved to do a better job, and that is exactly what he did. The man who started out by selling popcorn created the largest hotel chain in the world.

Kemmons Wilson was determined to give the American traveling public nice places to stay, complete with air conditioning, clean rooms, phone service, restaurants, comfortable beds, and free lodging for kids. He wanted his chain to be known for these things. He called it "standardization." His dream was for people to know that they could expect value and comfort from every Holiday Inn, regardless of where it was. In fact, that became one of its slogans: "The best surprise is no surprise."

Even the name lends itself for an interesting story. When the designer of the hotels, Eddie Bluestein, turned in his plans to Wilson, the words "Holiday Inn" were inscribed on the bottom. Bluestein must have seen the movie starring Bing Crosby, and the name stuck. Wilson also wanted a sign that was at least 50 feet tall and gave the impression of a movie theater marquee. He built his first hotel at 4941 Summer Ave. in Memphis. It opened on August 1, 1952. It was wildly successful and soon, three more just like it appeared. In 1953, Kemmons Wilson and home builder Wallace E. Johnson partnered in the construction of Holiday Inns. By 1972, *Time Magazine* featured Wilson, who boasted a franchise of 1,405 Holiday Inns. He was proud of his hands-on company approach, and his love of the "hunt."

The Man with 300,000 Beds

TIME

Innkeeper
Kemmons
Wilson

Holiday Inn

WEL

Environment Report: The Energy Crisis

The company's early location sites were ideal, perhaps because of Wilson's relentless searches for the perfect places. He said, "For that kind of man, no job in the world could offer more: a chance to chase daylight around the world, clambering over hills, slogging through rain forests, stalking through prairie grass in a never-ending hunt for the perfect motel site."

In 1976, Wilson retired as CEO of Holiday Inn. He always believed one should not be afraid to fail. "I've made more mistakes than anyone else," he said. "That's why I'm so successful." Through the years, Holiday Inn has tried many approaches to business, but the company always returns to Kemmons Wilson's methods of doing things. With many attempts at different slogans and campaigns throughout the years, one seems to best embody the spirit of its founder: "Relax. It's Holiday Inn." Following his retirement, he continued to work and constructed a huge resort in Orlando, Florida, then launched another hotel chain, Wilson World.

Kemmons Wilson relaxes in front of a popcorn machine, his first business venture, and Holiday Inn, his biggest (photo from Kemmons Wilson, Inc.).

Like others in this book, Kemmons Wilson continued to give back to his community and the business community as a whole. He regularly spoke to large groups about the importance of entrepreneurship, and he encouraged people to discover and follow their dreams. "The business world of today and the future will always have a place and need for entrepreneurs," he said. "I cannot imagine how we can achieve true progress without them." Kemmons Wilson's legacy continues, not only through his hotels and legendary reputation in the hotel industry, but in his children.

At the age of 90, shortly before his death in 2003, Kemmons Wilson donated $15 million to build the Kemmons Wilson School of Hospitality and Resort Management at the University of Memphis. It is not only a school, but an active hotel. In a sense, his gift is a delayed certificate of graduation that reminds others, "Opportunity comes often. It knocks as often as you have an ear trained to hear it, an eye trained to see it, a hand trained to grasp it, and a head trained to use it."

The first Holiday Inn opened in August, 1952, at 4941 Summer. This photo was taken in 1953 (photo by Robert W. Dye, Sr.).

In November, 1968, Holiday Inn changed its motto from "The Nation's Innkeeper" to "The World's Innkeeper," which showed its expansion to overseas markets. Kemmons Wilson proudly points to the new slogan, while George Conway looks on (photo from Special Collections Department, University of Memphis Libraries).

Frank Wright
Wright Medical Technology

"We are dedicated to continuously improving patients' lives by providing our customers with orthopedic products that address their greatest clinical challenges. We will provide uncompromising service to our customers, foster the development of our employees, and reward all those with a vested interest in our business. We will operate our business profitably, with a sense of urgency, and in a manner that is beyond reproach."
-- Wright Medical Technology Mission Statement

Often we hear stories of faithful employees who invent a product they believe in, only to discover their bosses do not. Such is the story of how Wright Medical Technology began. In 1944, Frank Wright became the Memphis sales representative for Richards Manufacturing Company, a manufacturer of orthopedics. He developed an all-rubber walking heel for leg casts, making it easier for these patients to move around. His employer did not see a use for it, though. Even so, Wright acquired a patent on the device, and he and his wife Carolyn founded Wright Manufacturing Company in 1950 on Jackson Avenue in Memphis.

The rubber heel was just the beginning. Bone plates, orthopedic implants for major joints, and necessary accessories soon followed. Before long, the Wrights were producing wheelchairs and a multitude of medical devices aimed at making life easier for patients facing orthopedic difficulties.

In 1975, at the time of Frank Wright's death, the company moved just east of Memphis to Arlington, Tennessee. Two years later, it was bought by Dow Corning, becoming Dow Corning Wright. There have been other mergers and name changes over the years. Today, the company is named Wright Medical Group, Inc., and it is comprised of four worldwide companies. Its headquarters in Arlington is called Wright Medical Technologies.

Despite many changes, the mission of the company has stayed the same. It has held to that pledge. Since its early years, Wright has gone on to develop and distribute a vast array of orthopedic implants and instrumentation for the hip, knee, and small joints. It also has developed a unique line of biologic products, including calcium sulfate-based bone graft substitutes. Wright has become a solid name in the industry by solving many problems that orthopedic professionals face.

Perhaps because of its early roots, Wright has continued to foster research and development innovations. It has crossed the threshold into spinal stabilization, trauma, and arthroscopic products. The company's employees are becoming pioneers in biotechnological research.

Wright Medical Technology's level of quality is uncontested. It has been an ISO 9001 certified designer, manufacturer, and distributor for more than 50 years. This world is indebted to Frank Wright and his refusal to give up on his rubber heel. Wright recognized the needs of certain patients, and firmly believed in the value of his invention. Instead of backing down when others failed to see its benefits, he seized the opportunity and began his own company. From a rejected product came a state-of-the-art company that is dedicated to healing and relieving pain around the world.

Partners in Progress is an in-depth look at those businesses, professional groups and community service organizations that have supported this book and its objectives. The company summaries offer further insight into the entrepreneurial spirit which flourishes in Memphis and the Mid-South.

API cine
A division of API photographers, Inc.

As a child, William Walton Carrier exercised his creativity at the Brooks Academy of Art. He earned his photography merit badge as a Boy Scout and served his time in the darkroom as a teenager. After developing award-winning photography, Carrier became active in Professional Photographers of America and Cameracraftsmen of America. He has received Master of Photography, Craftsman and Electronic Imagery degrees. His photographs have been exhibited, published, and awarded national recognition. Excellence in still photographic imagery served to inspire his career in cinematography.

Bill Carrier believes the future will be formatted in High-Definition video. He chooses HD as the originating medium for video production. Whether it's a production for the Discovery Channel or a music video for MTV, Carrier travels the HD highways and airways covering everything from accident/helicopter rescue reenactments to Peruvian artifacts and international art exhibitions.

The International Photography Hall of Fame recently recruited Carrier to develop and capture, on DVD, nearly two centuries of worldwide professional photographic history. He has completed projects for huge international companies including American Express, Burlington Northern Sante Fe Railroad, Wal-Mart, International Paper, and FedEx. He was also Director of Photography, 2nd unit, on many feature films including "Silence of the Lambs" and "The Firm." He remains the only local Director of Photography sanctioned by the International Cinematographers Guild. Carrier's honors include many Tellys and Addys, Silver and Gold Awards at the Chicago and Houston International Film Festivals, and several prestigious Cine Golden Eagle awards.

Honors aside, home is where the heart is. Bill Carrier believes that through teaching and sharing information, everyone wins. Giving back to the community through professional organizations has been a great way to accomplish this. He was instrumental in the planning of the Memphis and

Carrier with Arri 35 mm, lensing the show "Cybill" starring Cybill Shepherd.

Shelby County Film & TV Commission, and continues to serve in promoting Memphis as a location for national news, MTV, and independent and major motion pictures. Through his participation with NARAS (National Recording Arts and Sciences), he was given the honor of judging the Music Video Grammy Awards. Carrier pulls together multiple art forms to share moments, capture our emotions, and elicit a response. He attributes his success to his dad's lessons on empathy and his family's ability to share his vision of the light.

For over 25 years, Carrier has promoted the development and hiring of local crews, artist, musicians, and theatrical talent. He believes that students who achieve competency and excellence in life and career skills hold our very future in their hands. These students are the life blood of our future workforce in business, industry, and government within our city and our nation. Kudos to Junior Achievement for seeing the vision, and thanks for making Memphis a better place to grow in.

2nd Unit Panavision Super 35
Carrier with Robert Duvall on the set "A Family Thing."

Carrier directs High Definition for Signature Advertising.

Super 16 mm in Studio B with University of Memphis football team for Sossaman & Associates.

Staff still photographer Bill Kingdon, for Kiva Sound Studio, Ransom Group, Lawnboy, and aerial for Memphis Regional Chamber.

Director/DP Carrier uses High Definition with Tyler midmount gyros discussing helicopter flight plan with pilot Allen Burnett for the Hospital Wing reenactment.

Bob Richards' Jewelers, Inc.

Bob Richards' Jewelers, a third generation family business located on Wolf River Boulevard near Germantown Road, provides fine jewelry and related services to the Mid-South and beyond, with clients from Alaska to St. Thomas. The family-owned-and-operated business, known as a purveyor of heirloom-quality fine jewelry, is one of a very few jewelry stores in the area to provide in-house watch and jewelry repair, with two Rolex-certified technicians and two jewelers on staff.

In 2003, the store was selected as an independent "Official Rolex Jeweler," a distinction afforded very few retailers. The process required to become a Rolex dealership, according to Richards, is a slow one because Rolex scrutinizes potential dealers before entering into a relationship. Rolex is just one of the luxury watch lines offered by Bob Richards' Jewelers; other lines include Tag Heuer, Cyma, and Swiss Army. The store maintains a wide selection of fine jewelry from designers such as Tacori, Hidalgo, Martin-Flyer, Sequoiah, Simon G, Mastoloni Pearls, as well as giftware by Waterford and pens by Porsche Design and Cross."

Three Generations of Jewelers

Bob Richards has been in the jewelry business his entire life. "It never occurred to me to pursue any other profession," he admits, revealing that his formative years were spent in the family's retail operation in Selmer, Tennessee; his father established Richards' Jewelry there in 1927. Richards's father died when Richards was 15, and his brother took over the family business. Richards, after finishing high school, attended watch-making school at Gem City College in Quincy, Illinois, graduating in 1968. After returning to Selmer to work in the family store for a couple of years, he decided to move to Memphis, going to work for Sears until 1975 repairing watches.

Broadnax – which were the premier stores in Memphis at the time – offered him a job working in the Laurelwood store and doing the repairs for five of their other stores. During his tenure at Brodnax, Richards attended Rolex technical training in New York in 1977 and 1980 for his Rolex certification. In 1984, changes in ownership of the Broadnax chain gave Richards reason to leave. This was the beginning of Bob Richards' Jewelers, which was originally located in the Hickory Hill area of Memphis. In 1999, the need for a larger space and different location brought him to his present location in the 2,400 square-foot store on Wolf River Boulevard.

Bob Richards' Jewelers has remained a family business. Two brothers, Jerry and Ron, provide jewelry repair and custom design work. Richards comments, "Having Jerry and Ron here has been a real asset to our business. Their many years of experience show through in the quality workmanship of each piece they produce." With the addition of his son Anthony, the family business has now expanded to its third generation of family participation. Anthony, a Certified Public Accountant and finance major, handles the store's accounting and computer duties (he's that computer guy), and he is also one of the store's main buyers.

The operation has expanded dramatically since Richards opened his 750 square foot store in 1984 with the hiring of family members and the need for more employees, the "adopted family" has all developed long-term relationships with clients. Richards's wife Polly, who has worked by his side since opening the store, comments, "We cannot begin to describe how special the relationships with our clients have been. We have been there through all their occasions, the happy ones and the sad ones. We have watched their children grow up, and now they are coming in for their engagement rings. We have made some treasured friends and have some wonderful memories."

Bob Richards (l.), with wife Polly and son Anthony, provides fine jewelry and related services to the Mid-South and beyond from their store on Wolf River Boulevard.

Giving Back to the Community

Bob Richards Jewelers knows the importance of contributing to community organizations such as donating valuable merchandise to local charities and the WKNO and Orpheum auctions. According to Richards, his most rewarding work is with St. Jude's Children's Research Hospital Foundation, donating his time appraising the donated jewelry items and selling some of the estate pieces for the organization.

Looking Forward

Richards plans to continue growing his company as his father did more than 75 years ago, by, in his words, "giving good value for your dollar, personal attention, staying educated on the ever-changing world of jewelry, and having the ability to service the client's cherished items. We will always strive to live up to our slogan: 'The only jeweler you'll ever need.'"

Coleman-Etter, Fontaine Realtors

The traditional practices utilized in real estate are changing; adapting to those changes is what puts Fontaine Taylor, President of Memphis real estate firm Coleman-Etter, Fontaine at the top of her field.

Innovation seems to be second nature to Taylor who, in 1985, joined Marjorie Coleman and Fran Etter, the founding partners of Memphis's only (then and still) wholly female-owned and female-managed real estate company. After two years with Coleman and Etter, Taylor bought out her partners and has never looked back.

Serving Clients' Needs

Under her leadership, Coleman-Etter, Fontaine is immensely successful, growing to a company with forty full-time agents, of which some eighty-five percent are female. Taylor doesn't release sales data, but those in the know acknowledge that her company is consistently among the top producers in this market, maintaining a reputation for selling high-end homes, primarily within the confines of Memphis.

However, Taylor is careful to note that her agents possess first-hand knowledge of area properties, and maintain market share by consistently selling homes throughout the area, including midtown, Germantown, Collierville, and other suburban locales. "My goal is to make sure that we have agents who are highly aware of trends in real estate and keep on their toes with related technologies," she said, adding, "My job is to research the market and adapt to changes in the marketplace. My stick-to-it-tiveness assures that Coleman- Etter, Fontaine's agents possess all the tools they need to be successful."

Tools of the Trade

Among those tools have been a number of innovations, including the use of the internet as a real estate sales tool. Veteran real estate maven Taylor was the first in Memphis to offer what has come to be known as "virtual tours" – 360° mini movies that depict residences, inside and out, in living color. Although Coleman-Etter, Fontaine is now one of many Memphis-area realtors offering virtual tours and other internet-related services on their company website, Taylor maintains her policy of seeking out innovations that will enable her agents to render top-notch service. "We have the largest support staff of any Memphis-area realty company in terms of support staff members per agent," contends Taylor.

There are other innovations Taylor has used to further shape her future, including several innovative personnel policies. Taylor says that hers is the only company in town with a policy prohibiting its realtors from serving as both the buying and selling agent for their clients. "With separate agents you make sure that the best interests of both parties are served," Taylor notes. She adds, "The bottom line is not as important as treating clients fairly," explaining that it is very difficult for a real estate agent to represent both a buyer and a seller simultaneously and oversee the best interests of both.

Coleman-Etter, Fontaine employs only full-time agents, another rather innovative approach in this market. Most Coleman-Etter, Fontaine realtors are long-time, experienced agents. "That is not to say I never hire new agents," Taylor carefully explains. "I like growing my company. It's just that a typical new agent at this office brings a history of previous sales and/or experience to our table. We want informed agents so they can provide a great service," Taylor adds.

A Permanent Change in the Industry

Coleman-Etter, Fontaine co-founder Marjorie Coleman was once characterized as having "long been known as a trailblazer in the real estate world [who] forged a path for other women who would come along, ensuring a permanent change in the industry." Taylor has followed in the footsteps of that innovator, and has paved the path blazed by Coleman with success after success, garnering both personal honors and acclaim for her company.

In 2003, Taylor was chosen as the 2002 REALTOR® of the Year by the Memphis Area Association of REALTORS® and was honored for this accomplishment by the Tennessee General Assembly in 2003. A past president of the Memphis Area Association of REALTORS®, the Mid-South's largest real estate trade association, Taylor has also served as president of the Tennessee Real Estate Education Foundation (TREEF) and as a director of a plethora of local and national realty associations. Coleman-Etter, Fontaine was among honorees of the Business and Industry Salute by Carnival Memphis as it celebrated the accomplishments and contributions of an industry vital to the economy of the Mid-South. Taylor has also been a multi-year recipient of the Top 25 Female-owned Businesses Award, and in 2005 was a recipient of the Top 10 Women in Business Award.

"I believe our success has come from our mission -- to provide unrivaled service by informed agents in a pleasant, pleasing atmosphere," commented Taylor. "We look forward to the future and to our continued success."

Fontaine Taylor, President

Boyle Investment Company

In the early 1900's, Memphian Edward Boyle had a vision for his hometown. A descendant of Memphis co-founder John Overton, Boyle, believing the city would continue its eastward expansion, developed a new subdivision. Stately Belvedere Boulevard, still today one of Memphis' most prestigious addresses, was the first of many Boyle developments founded on the principle that properties are long-term investments. Company President Henry Morgan notes, "We've built a strong company because the family, from the beginning, has been committed to developing for long-term value. We operate on the belief that properties are long-term investments that should be carefully planned, built, and maintained."

In 1933, Boyle's sons - Snowden, Charles and Bayard Boyle, Sr. - founded a company based on this principle and dedicated to the continuance of their father's vision: development of land in the city's key growth corridors. Bayard Boyle, Sr.'s strategic acquisition of acreage developed with an eye for longevity has resulted in a company recognized as a key player in the development and management of property in Memphis.

Boyle Investment Company got its start in the property management business but in the late 1930's, when the need in the city for new housing grew, Bayard Boyle, Sr. shifted its main focus to buying land and developing it into subdivisions and shopping centers and to relationships with several prominent insurance companies to offer residential and commercial loans for property acquisition and development. The company created a real estate sales organization that, in the 1950's, grew to a full-service real estate investment operation. In 1970 Boyle began development of the former Ridgeway Country Club at Poplar and 1-240, then well to the east of the city's population center. The innovative move paid off as the population center continued to shift. Boyle's 204-acre Ridgeway Center, recognized as one of the area's first and finest office parks, is home to many national and international companies including Morgan Keegan, ServiceMaster, Marsh USA and Sedgwick CMS.

Boyle's real estate developments, when viewed on a map, are clustered just east of the Poplar and I-240 and Walnut Grove and I-240 Interchanges and then dot the landscape farther east. On the eastern perimeter of Ridgeway Center sit the Morgan Keegan Building and Marsh Center. Nearby are the stylish Humphreys Center and Regalia, retail and office developments featuring upscale restaurants and shopping.

Boyle's business has evolved into the development, leasing, sales and management of major developments including River Oaks and Farmington (at Germantown). The offices, retail establishments and private homes at these sites continue to be some of the city's most desirable properties. The Village Shops of Forrest Hill, developed in the mid-nineties, sits on the east side of Germantown between these developments and fast-growing Collierville. Most recently, Boyle has put its energies into the master-planned Schilling Farms community in Collierville. Schilling Farms is a 443-acre, $350 million innovative multi-use development offering residential, retail and office properties within a people-friendly, self-contained community.

The Schilling Farms Project is one of a series of successful joint ventures with landowners that have resulted in the development of some of Memphis' premier properties. In each case, Boyle has worked closely with the landowners to develop a strategic vision for their property.

Morgan Keegan Building in Ridgeway Center

Memphis and Beyond

In the last few years, Boyle has developed a number of office buildings for major companies including the Southeast Regional Headquarters for the United States Postal Service, the corporate headquarters for Thomas and Betts at Southwind, the headquarters facility for Baptist Memorial Healthcare Corporation at Humphreys Center, and headquarters for Helena Chemical Corporation at Schilling Farms. These developments – totaling more than 5 million square feet of space developed and owned or managed by Boyle – are just the ones located in Shelby County, Tennessee.

Boyle has developed or currently manages a growing list of properties outside of Tennessee, including sites in Mississippi, Arkansas, Texas and Florida. Boyle's first venture in the Texas Metroplex was the highly successful Preston Shepard Place. The partnership, of which Boyle was managing partner, sold the property in July 1996 for $47 million. Boyle also developed and still owns the Southwest Crossing power center in Ft. Worth.

In 2001, Boyle entered the Nashville market and opened an office led by a team of seasoned real estate professionals. Boyle Vice President Paul Boyle says, "We will continue to be an active player in the Memphis market, but we are also focusing our attention on Nashville. We're excited about the company's future, and we remain dedicated to maintaining a long-term vision that delivers enduring value for our partners and tenants."

Following one of the successful models used in Memphis, the Nashville office has formed a joint venture with descendants of the Berry family to create a 600-acre community to realize the Berry's vision of a legacy compatible with Franklin's vibrant vision for its future. The Nashville office in partnership with Northwestern Life Insurance Company recently purchased two Class A office buildings at Cool Springs in Franklin, totaling slightly less than 300,000 square feet and has several properties under contract.

Regalia Shopping Center

Long-Term Family Ownership

Boyle, which began as a family company, today remains a family company. Headed by Chairman Bayard Boyle, Jr. (son of co-founder Bayard Boyle, Sr.) and his brother-in-law, President Henry Morgan, Boyle Investment Company is located at 5900 Poplar Avenue in Ridgeway Center. Boyle's commitment to visionary projects and long-term ownership has resulted in a strong portfolio of commercial and residential developments that have become landmarks in the heart of the Mid-South. The Boyle family – including the fourth generation represented by Paul Boyle, Henry Morgan, Jr. and Bayard Morgan – has remained in direct control and ownership for more than seventy years, spanning a period of three wars, recessions, a quadrupling of interest rates and double digit inflation, and through the emergence and disappearance of numerous real estate fads.

Throughout this period, Boyle has maintained the same value-oriented principles of hiring people of high integrity and good judgment to create a cohesive team of internal experts, careful demographic and growth pattern analysis, and a commitment to excellence in projects developed. The consistency of results over many decades has confirmed this approach, which continues to deliver enduring value for Boyle's projects. Boyle's commitment to hiring and retaining the right key employees, according to Chairman Bayard Boyle, is its secret to success. "Our greatest asset is our team of seasoned professionals. We have a number of executives in key positions who have been with the company for more than 20 years and who we believe are tops in their field."

Henry W. Morgan, President; J. Bayard Boyle, Jr., Chairman; Paul Boyle, Vice President

Boyle is a privately held, family-owned and operated organization structured to provide clients and employees with the tools to achieve success in multi-use and single family land development, office, retail and industrial development, commercial property sales and acquisitions, and office, retail and industrial leasing and property management. Boyle also has a commercial construction company and a general insurance agency. With its corporate motto: "Excellence in Real Estate," Boyle continues to uphold its reputation for innovative developments that endure the test of time.

Innovators may not have much in common, but one thing they all seem to share is the ability to recognize opportunity. Innovator William B. Clark (who gave prominent Memphis landmark Clark Tower its name) always seemed to be ready when opportunity came knocking.

Although the late William B. ("Bill") Clark is no longer at the helm of the firm he founded in the early 1920's, his innovative approach to the development of residential and commercial property is still the guiding spirit of Clark & Clark, the family-owned and operated company that remains an industry leader today.

Clark & Clark was established when Bill Clark envisioned the development of family-owned land on Mitchell Road into residential subdivisions. His success in that venture led Clark to develop property throughout the city's then most noteworthy neighborhoods, including Vollentine-Evergreen.

After the Depression, Clark noticed that Memphians were becoming increasingly interested in property in the eastern portion of the city and, once again seizing opportunity, put his money into developing neighborhoods in the Poplar-Goodlett area. Known as Galloway Terrace, Belle Meade, and The Village, Clark's stately neighborhoods quickly ranked among Memphis' prime residential real estate.

Over the next twenty years, Clark continued to believe that opportunities for growth for his company were linked to the expansion of Memphis eastward. In the 1940's he began to purchase acreage on the

fringes of the city, securing a portion of the 9,000-acre White Station Plantation. He augmented his holdings in 1958 when he bought, at a price of upwards of $11,000 per acre, adjoining land for what would become the site of White Station Tower. His plan was to construct the first office tower to be located outside of downtown Memphis.

The Clark family says that although their ancestor was criticized and even ridiculed for his vision, he persisted. In 1965, Clark broke ground at 5050 Poplar for the 24-story building that would contain 278,000 square feet of office space. Clark anticipated that it might take as long as five years to lease all the space, but he surpassed all expectations by fully occupying White Station Tower shortly after it opened. The building remained in the family until it was sold in 1998 for $18.4 million.

The success of the White Station Tower project led Clark and his son Buck (William B. Jr.) to begin construction on an adjacent building that, at 34 stories, was to be even grander than the 5050 building. It was a project that proved to be unpopular with many of the city's civic leaders because they feared it would have a draining effect on business in downtown Memphis. However, Clark persevered, and the 670,000-square-foot Clark Tower opened in 1971 at a cost of $21.3 million; it sold in 1984 for $44.7 million.

"My grandfather had amazing vision, and he never hesitated to pursue it," says Partner Nick Clark. "I think it is really difficult for most people to comprehend the widespread opposition and ridicule he faced as he planned and executed these projects. But they became Memphis' defining landmarks."

Clark, Sr. credited his son Buck with the success for the Clark Tower project as it was Buck who secured the financing for the project, a joint venture with the Metropolitan Life Insurance Company. "The project might not be there if it weren't for him," Clark said in an interview conducted several years before the Clark family patriarch died.

The Clark family's vision didn't stop at White Station Road. As early as the 1960's, the Clarks foresaw that Memphis would continue expanding eastward, predicting it would "build all the way up to

Nick, Ben, and Diana Clark break ground for Clark Tower as Bill Clark (second from l.) watches.

Clark & Clark has remained committed to building the city's future for more than 80 years.

Collierville, and East Memphis will be in the center of what is now metropolitan Memphis." They have been proved correct, as the opening of the Bill Morris Parkway/ Highway 385 to Collierville in 2000 has fueled growth along the 385 Corridor.

The Clarks' role in the emergence of Bill Morris Parkway/ Highway 385 has been spearheaded by Clark brothers Ben and Nick. At thirteen, the twin sons of Buck and the grandsons of Bill Clark, Sr., made a bargain with their 70-plus-year-old grandfather to join the business when they came of age, with the understanding that Bill would keep Clark & Clark in the family.

The Clarks acted on their vision for development around the Nonconnah corridor when, in 1995, Clark & Clark began construction of Lenox Park, the first speculative Class A office complex to be located in this area. Consisting of seven 97,000-square-foot buildings, Lenox Park forms the largest integrated-technology office park in Memphis. The $84 million complex, which houses Clark & Clark's corporate headquarters, is located near Kirby Parkway and Bill Morris Parkway/ Highway 385 and is home to high-profile tenants including FedEx, Pfizer, and International Paper.

The buildings that comprise Lenox Park, designed by award-winning architectural firm Looney Ricks Kiss, incorporate what at the time was considered to be the first use in Memphis of a composite bar joist system made with three-foot-deep steel bar joists. This system incorporates the joists and the concrete floor together as a system allowing for reduced structural steel costs without compromising

strength. Additionally, the buildings offer extra electrical circuitry for computers and other office equipment. The buildings were designed with both horizontal and vertical conduits to make installation of future systems easier as technology advances.

In a book currently being written about Clark patriarch Bill Clark and the Clark real estate dynasty, Memphis writer David Yawn notes that Lenox Park "evokes several common threads in the Clark family tradition, such as a commitment to quality, an ability to project future demand, and the kind of pioneering spirit that turns vision into reality in spite of risk. Success is also on that list."

Nick Clark thinks the company's success along the Bill Morris Parkway/ Highway 385 is tied to the success of what has come to be known as the Technology Corridor. To that end, Clark organized the 385 Technology Corridor Association, whose mission is to provide a venue for interested parties to work together to develop the corridor to its fullest potential. Clark says that marketing the area as the Technology Corridor is a key element in the economic and community development of this region and is "influencing the quality of the growth for the betterment of all."

He and his brother Ben know something about growth and development, having learned from their father and their grandfather that visionaries always look to the future with expansion as a primary goal. For more than eighty years, Clark & Clark has been committed to the growth and development of Memphis and the surrounding area, and the Clarks intend to continue this commitment well into the future.

Lenox Park, which houses Clark & Clark's corporate headquarters, is the largest integrated-technology office park in Memphis.

Duncan-Williams, Inc.

Like many business success stories, the history of investment-banking firm Duncan-Williams, Inc., began with a vision. According to company president Duncan F. Williams, that vision of treating customers and employees like family began in 1969 when his father, the late A. Duncan Williams, established the securities firm.

Led by the elder Williams' tireless dedication to the achievement of success, Duncan-Williams, Inc., became a major force in municipal underwriting in the Southeastern United States during the 1970's and 80's. While tax free bonds are still an important part of the firm, it also now excels in US Government and Agency Securities, CMO's, corporate debt, SBA's, mutual funds, CD's, IRA's, DUS Bonds, portfolio management and stock transactions.

A Family Affair

After the untimely death of her husband in 1989, Carolyn Williams decided to retain the investment banking firm in order to provide her children, Duncan F. and Emily, the opportunity to operate the company after they graduated from college. During this time, Carolyn spent many hours at the firm letting everyone know that the company was strong and moving forward. She assured all of the employees that their jobs were safe and that no radical changes were going to be made. Carolyn also relied upon a select group of trusted associates to help her with the continued success at Duncan-Williams. Serving as

Duncan F. Williams

Company President was its former corporate attorney, Donald Malmo, who, along with Frank Reid as Chief Financial Officer, and Sharon Dunn and Leonard Richman, were engaged in the day-to-day operations of the firm.

After graduation from the University of Alabama, Duncan worked three years for another regional broker before joining Duncan-Williams. Duncan joined the firm with hopes of continuing what his father had started over two decades before. Once Duncan began his employment with the firm, he knew he needed to work in several different capacities to earn the respect and loyalty of the employees. He wanted everyone to know that he believed, like his father did, that if you treat someone with respect and honesty, that their loyalty will not be far behind. After seven years of working with the firm, Duncan became President in May of 2000. With Trey Fyfe, Don Clanton, and Jim Pauline added to the management team, Duncan has continued the expansion of the business which now includes branches in four states and customers in all fifty states, as well as Israel, South America, Europe and the Caribbean.

Carolyn Williams Bennett is shown here with the third generation leaders of Duncan-Williams, Inc.: Mary Franklin Williams (standing), Duncan Ware Williams (in her lap) and William Stovall Dunn (sitting on steps).

Customer Service as the Key to Success

The success of Duncan-Williams, Inc., rests both on the wide array of products and services it provides as well as its philosophy of providing unequalled customer service through personal relationships with its clients. "We are a Memphis-based company with over 6,000 customers all over the world. This may mean we have to go the extra mile to make sure the customers know this company and their brokers and are comfortable with them – but that's what we do," explains Duncan.

The philosophy must be working. In the past five years, revenues have averaged an increase of approximately 20% per year. In the past ten years, Duncan-Williams' revenues have more than tripled. "Our customers include a cross-section of the investing world," Williams says. "They include banks, money managers, pension funds, insurance companies, mutual funds, corporations, trust departments, churches and credit unions along with municipalities and individuals."

In January 2003, Duncan-Williams moved into its new corporate headquarters that was designed expressly for the financial industry. It is serving Duncan-Williams' 110-plus professionals and gives them all the advantages of any Wall Street firm. The site includes custom-built workstations which provide multiple flat-screen computer terminals and a phone system linked to the computers and the internet. This gives management and the sales staff an opportunity to listen and learn from their own phone calls. The company invested between $4 million and $5 million to streamline its services, a huge benefit to the customers. Longtime employee Sharon Dunn says the young President's willingness to employ innovative techniques was no surprise. "Duncan is an innovator, which means he is open to trying new things."

The company solely manages financings in excess of $145 million, safe keeps security assets for its customers in excess of $1.3 billion

and also maintains more than $150 million in lines of credit to support daily trading and underwriting activities. In addition to the Memphis headquarters, the firm maintains offices in Baton Rouge, Louisiana; Charlotte, North Carolina; Houston, Texas; and Jackson, Mississippi.

Maintaining a capital base well in excess of regulatory requirements, Duncan-Williams, Inc., operates under provisions of the Securities and Exchange Act of 1934 and is a member of the National Association of Securities Dealers, Inc. (NASD), the Municipal Securities Rulemaking Board (MSRB) and the Securities Investor Protection Corporation (SIPC).

Duncan-Williams, Inc., was also rated in the "Top 100" of the Weiss Guide to Brokerage Firms in 2003-2004. This is quite an accomplishment of which the Company is very proud.

After 35 years, the focus of Duncan-Williams will remain on its vision of growth and the principles that were started by its founder and followed by everyone who is working at Duncan-Williams. Mr. Williams' mission statement was to:

'WORK HARD, REMAIN LOYAL TO YOUR EXTENDED FAMILY OF COWORKERS AND EMPLOYEES, AND GIVE YOUR CUSTOMERS BETTER SERVICE AND PRODUCT THAN YOUR COMPETITORS."

This belief remains the cornerstone of the Duncan-Williams company today. At this time, 20% of the total employees with the company have been there for 20 years or more. This says volumes about company loyalty to its employees and the loyalty of employees to Duncan-Williams, Inc.

Duncan proudly points out, "This company is over 35 years old. Over those three-and-a-half decades, it has grown and extended itself across not only this country, but also to other places in the world. Now we are on the threshold of an exciting future – one that requires satisfying every customer. That is what counts; that's all that counts."

The Williams family is also involved in the ownership and management of several apartment communities in Memphis and Jackson, Tennessee, as well as a farming operation in the Mississippi Delta.

EnSafe

Innovation is not happenstance at EnSafe Inc. The Memphis-based firm views innovation as the normal course of business in providing engineering, environment, health & safety, and technology services to clients worldwide.

EnSafe prides itself on using creative thinking to develop custom solutions, whether it's developing ground-breaking technologies for environmental remediation, interpreting regulatory requirements for our clients' benefit, or communicating with clients creatively. "What really sets us apart from other professional services companies is our 'outside the box' thinking that leads to innovation and cost-effective solutions," says EnSafe President Phillip G. Coop, CHMM, who founded the company in 1980.

EnSafe's staff of 250+ develops innovative approaches that can be either low-tech or high-tech, depending on the client's unique situation. "We hire people with expertise and talent, putting them together with other professionals from diverse areas, and we then encourage them to cross their traditional boundaries so that their solutions have a broader perspective than might otherwise occur," Coop says. This broad perspective has benefited EnSafe's clients in many ways.

Innovation in Remediation— Creative thinking came into play when EnSafe was biologically treating soil to clean up contaminants. The process required providing nutrients to microorganisms that would consume the soil contamination. Because the commercial nutrients were rather costly, EnSafe used creative thinking to find another plentiful and inexpensive source — chicken manure from nearby poultry farms.

"When it comes to environmental and advanced monitoring problems, there are no cookie-cutter solutions," Coop says. EnSafe's custom solutions have won awards recognizing innovation in environmental remediation. In three out of four years, EnSafe earned the American Council of Engineering Companies of Tennessee's Engineering Excellence competition Grand Award. It also has earned three top category awards — environmental, engineering studies, and surveying/mapping — since 1999. In all cases, EnSafe has developed innovative solutions that have saved clients significant dollars.

EnSafe scientist collects samples in Baku.

On the national stage, EnSafe's innovation in perchlorate remediation earned the Secretary of the Navy 2000 award for environmental restoration, as well as the precursor Chief of Naval Operations award.

Regulatory Innovation— EnSafe's commanding knowledge of evolving environmental regulations allows it to make regulatory interpretations that benefit clients. EnSafe was asked to develop a petition to have a chemical reclassified as nonhazardous so it could be burned in a facility's boiler. After reviewing the waste data, EnSafe concluded that a little-used section of the federal hazardous waste rules could make the petition unnecessary. With regulators' concurrence, the client saved more than $200,000 in fees it would have paid EnSafe for preparing the petition as well as more than $500,000 annually in future disposal costs.

Innovation in Client Service— Innovation is not limited to EnSafe's environmental and engineering work. When projects require collaboration and critical decision-making in real-time, EnSafe leverages secure websites to share information using web-based databases and Geographic Information System technology. Extranet websites are

developed by EnSafe's Technology division, which has grown from an internal support operation to a client-service division. EnSafe's technology services cover envisioning, planning, design, implementation, and management. Its expertise includes software engineering like e-governmental portals (www.dpdgov.com) to outsourced networking infrastructure management.

EnSafe continues to diversify both in practice and geographic reach through the growth of its safety engineering services and remedial construction arm, Ops Contracting Services, LLC, which manages clients' environmental liability on a turnkey basis. Geographically, EnSafe's ability to respond worldwide — the company has worked in more than 35 countries so far — is enhanced by offices in Central Europe and Central Asia and projects in Russia's Sakhalin Islands, Kazakhstan, Serbia, and Azerbaijan.

EnSafe's vision is to continue to grow and innovate in the course of serving clients' needs, even the most challenging ones. In EnSafe's view, where there is challenge, there is opportunity. And innovation is not happenstance; it's business as usual.

Fleming/Associates/Architects

As one of the region's premier architectural firms, Fleming/Associates/Architects (F/A/A) offers an array of services including: master planning, feasibility studies, architectural design, and interior design. Projects of local interest include the Collierville Town Hall, Crew Training International's World Headquarters, and Hope Presbyterian Church.

F/A/A serves governmental entities, major corporations, developers, private companies, and individuals. Although the firm services a multitude of industries, its arenas of concentrated expertise are: institutional, educational, religious, recreational, medical, housing, and commercial (including restaurants and office facilities).

Memphis Roots for Over Fifty Years

Robert Fleming began practicing architecture in the early 1950's in Memphis, Tennessee. After establishing his own firm, he built the business that his son Scott joined in 1981. Scott served in the family business until 1994, when he bought the company from his father and formed Fleming/Associates/Architects, P.C. In the ensuing years, F/A/A president and owner Scott Fleming has grown the professional corporation from a staff of six to more than thirty.

In 1998, architects Lisa Namie, Ben Witt, and Gary Gibson joined F/A/A as Principals/Owners. A year later, F/A/A added Interior Design to its portfolio of services. The Interior Design department, led by Director Debbie Ross, offers services to clients on either a stand-alone basis or as an adjunct to a F/A/A architectural project. Offerings available through the Interior Design group at F/A/A include: interior architecture, programming and space planning, architectural finish selection and coordination, and furniture and accessory selection.

A Cornerstone of Quality

According to Scott Fleming, the firm's success is built on quality. "We are an architectural firm committed first to meeting our client's needs while maintaining a quality of life and practicing our profession in a responsible and satisfying way," he explains. The firm's commitment to quality is evident both in their work product as well as in their community service efforts. Fleming notes, "Many firms say they focus on quality work, but to us, it's much more than a credo. At F/A/A, we consistently devote the preponderance of our practice to work which satisfies our personal need to produce aesthetically pleasing and highly functional architecture within the confines of our client's budgets. It's at the core of our business model and principles. The delivery of quality services and personal attention are considered the key ingredients we provide our clients. Our list of repeat and long-standing clientele is evidence that the design approach we implement is successful."

Quality of Community

Noting that the best plan constructed of the best quality products is not quality work if erected in a less than desirable area, Fleming and his coworkers dedicate part of their professional and personal time to fostering a better community in the Memphis area.

To this end, Fleming sits on the Crichton College Board of Directors, the Land Use Control Board and the Streets Ministries Board of Directors. Other principal/owners are active in the Brooks Museum League, Phoenix Club of Memphis, National Eagle Scout Association, Bartlett and Germantown Chambers of Commerce, and the Tennessee Health Care Association.

The focus Fleming/Associates/Architects P.C. has on quality is not limited to the work they produce, but rather it extends to the communities they serve – a fact the firm continuously demonstrates. "The measure of our success is how we enrich the lives of our clients and the communities in which they, and we, live," says Fleming. Pausing, the architect adds, "In short, we try to make the world a better place."

Fogelman Properties

Fogelman Properties is a privately held, third-generation company specializing exclusively in multi-family apartment housing. The firm operates as the holding company for its two subsidiaries, Fogelman Management Group (FMG) and Fogelman Real Estate Services (FRES). Headquartered in Memphis, and with regional property management offices in Atlanta and Louisville, FMG manages more than 15,000 apartment homes throughout the Southeast and Midwest. FRES handles all asset management activities relating to the properties in the Fogelman portfolio, including property acquisitions, placement of debt/equity financing, and investment services.

The roots of Fogelman Properties can be traced back to 1941 when Morris S. Fogelman opened Fogelman and Company in a one-room office at 127 Madison in downtown Memphis. The company at that time specialized in the sales of single family homes and insurance. In 1963, his son Avron joined him and formed a local property management firm servicing the Memphis metropolitan area. Under Avron Fogelman's leadership, the company expanded rapidly in the 1970's and 80's throughout the Southeast and Midwest. Today, Fogelman Properties is one of the country's largest privately held operators of multi-family apartment communities. Avron's son Richard (Rick) serves as President/CEO of Fogelman Properties and another son, Mark, is President/COO of Fogelman Management Group, managing properties in Memphis, Nashville, Atlanta, Orlando, Kansas City, Raleigh/Durham, Savannah, Ft. Wayne, Indianapolis, Lexington, Louisville, and St. Louis. A third son, Hal, owns and operates a local market research firm.

Rick Fogelman uses the terms "family" and "home" to describe the Fogelman companies' culture and focus. "We're extremely proud to be a third generation family business that views our Fogelman associates as extended family. My father and grandfather built the foundation for this company, one based upon hard work, integrity, professionalism, and the never ending quest to be the best. We take great pride in perpetuating this legacy today. With an outstanding group of over 400 dedicated Fogelman associates, we strive every day to provide the highest level of service to our property owners that we represent and to the residents who call our Fogelman communities their home," he stated.

FMG's organizational structure is flat by design. Mark Fogelman, President of FMG, explained, "We are structured to provide maximum service to our property owners and residents. We strive to maintain our flat organizational structure because we feel it enables us to provide rapid responses to changing markets and property-level trends. Not having to work through unnecessary layers of middle management allows us to react fast. Indeed, it's our lack of red-tape bureaucracy that has

In 2003, FMG received two top industry honors from the National Apartment Association: 1) National Property of the Year for its Fountains of Andover Apartments, (Lexington, KY, shown above) and 2) Property Manager of the Year to FMG Regional VP Sheila Pennington.

proven to be one of FMG's major advantages when competing against other property management organizations."

All three generations of Fogelmans have been active in community efforts, believing that true success is measured by what is given back to the community. The family's charitable efforts center on public education. In 1987, Avron Fogelman established the Fogelman Scholars Program to provide scholarships to low-income graduates of Memphis public schools. With generous donations by Avron and his brother Robert Fogelman, the University of Memphis business college established the Fogelman College of Business and Economics with its Fogelman Executive Center and conference facilities. The family also endowed the Morris S. Fogelman Chair of Excellence in Real Estate, to honor the family patriarch. Additionally, the company has been a corporate sponsor of Richland Elementary since 1981. Fogelman's corporate sponsorship of Richland Elementary includes the funding of activities such as Arts in the Schools, honor ribbons, and pizza parties for students designated as "Most Improved" by their teachers.

Avron Fogelman (2nd from l.) with sons (from l.) Hal, Rick, and Mark.

Fred L. Davis Insurance

Fred L. Davis Insurance is a full service agency providing an entire array of financial services to individuals as well as small and large businesses, both locally and regionally. Through partnerships with global providers, the agency serves the deferred compensation plans of sizeable clients such as the Memphis Convention Center, Tri-State Bank, FedEx Forum, Memphis Airport Authority, and Memphis Light Gas and Water, as well as a multitude of smaller businesses in need of bonding and liability services.

Being First is a Way of Life and Business

Davis has a history of "firsts" in both his personal and professional lives. In 1955, when he was inducted into the Society of Entrepreneurs, Davis explained his feelings about entrepreneurship, saying, "The risk takers of the world are the people who are most responsible for the innovative progress from which we all benefit."

This was not lip service from Davis, as evidenced by the following list of just some of his many "firsts":

1967 – Opened the first African American-owned, independent insurance agency in the South that represented a multi-line company

1968 – Elected to the first Memphis City Council representing District 4, a predominantly white district

1970 – Helped establish the city's first non-profit healthcare clinic to offer evening hours – The Orange Mound Health Clinic (now Christ Community Heath Services)

1972 – First African American to chair the Memphis City Council

1972 – As City Council Chairman, created the first Memphis Music Commission to promote the heritage of Memphis Music.

Mentoring Opens Doors for Others

If you ask Davis about his proudest moments, he'll tell you stories about men and women he has mentored over the years and how they have made a difference in our community. A self-effacing man, Davis is reticent to talk about himself. For insight into the watershed events in Davis' life, one needs to visit his protégés.

Howard Eddings, President of the Memphis Leadership Foundation, Inc., and Crichton College President Larry Lloyd have much to relate about Davis. Eddings was 16 when Davis, with Orange Mound dentist Dr. Charles Pinkston, sponsored the Melrose High School baseball team in the American Legion League. The sponsorship represented two additional "firsts" for Davis – the first black team in the American Legion and the first team sponsored by an African American-owned business. "I was 16 when I met Mr. Davis and he has mentored me throughout my adolescence and adult life," Eddings said.

Though Eddings no longer lives in Orange Mound, the neighborhood where Davis continues to live and conduct business, the Memphis Leadership Foundation President continues to support the neighborhood of his youth. Through alliances such as the Orange Mound Collaborative and the Orange Mound Development Foundation (OMDC) – both organizations initiated by Davis – Eddings has collected funds to build a homes for under-resourced families, which, in turn, begin its helped OMDC housing initiatives. Eddings went on to become one of the next generation of leaders in Memphis. "I don't think you can find anyone that has contributed more to our community than Mr. Davis. His mentoring and ability to connect different business leaders to one

A Rich History of Community Involvement

The accomplishments of Fred Davis went far beyond his success as a businessman and mentor, and his stints as a Memphis City Councilman. Davis was chairman of the Public Works Committee in 1968 when the sanitation workers went on strike. Urging the City of Memphis to recognize the sanitation worker's union, Davis was joined by leaders from the NAACP and the Southern Leadership Conference to help contend with the volatile situation that ensued when the police threatened violence against the striking sanitation workers.

"Dr. King never lived to see it, but, as I understand it, a deal was finally worked out with the city and the workers - thanks to the work of Davis and a whole host of others working behind the scenes. He was one of a handful of people that kept this city from blowing up," Lloyd said. He considers Davis a "quiet and gentle leader; he's not loud but when a crisis hits, he's there."

> *"I have always strived to open doors for people that either didn't know the door was there or didn't know they could go through it. I feel very lucky to have had opportunities to do that."*

another has truly made a difference in our community," Eddings related.

Larry Lloyd also shares the Orange Mound Connection. In the mid-seventies, Lloyd graduated from Rhodes College and took a job in his first non-profit position. He wanted to bring the Young Life program to an inner city Memphis neighborhood. "I met Mr. Davis while in the process of selecting a target neighborhood in which to nurture a Young Life program. It was 1975 and he introduced me to Orange Mound and Melrose High School. We (Young Life) choose Melrose for two reasons: first and foremost, because of Fred Davis and second, because we thought it was the best place to create a new generation of leaders," he explained.

Davis' efforts have undoubtedly made Memphis a better place to live and do business.

Fred Remmers Rug Cleaners and Oriental Rug Gallery

For more than a century, Fred Remmers Rug Cleaners and Oriental Rug Gallery has responded to customer's requirements and desires. This emphasis on service has allowed the oriental and antique rug cleaning, repair and sales business to survive economic downturns to become a rarity in business – a fourth-generation family-owned enterprise.

A Memphis Institution

In 1881, Carl Hilstrom, Fred Remmers Jr.'s great uncle, started the business with a bucket and a hand brush. Since that time, the company has employed the latest technology for rug cleaning and investment rug restoration, beginning in the early 1900's with Hilstrom's first automated cleaning appliance for rugs. Called the Star Duster, the machine was designed to replace the then-standard practice of hanging and manually beating rugs to remove dust. In the early 70's, Remmers purchased the first fully automatic rug-cleaning machine in Memphis, demonstrating the family's commitment to innovation in their industry.

Interestingly enough, says Fred Remmers Jr., the latest technologies have actually taken their business back to the basics of hand tools. In their plant located behind the Remmers' office and store on Central Avenue, workers utilize hand tools, with compressed air and compressed air under water, to clean and restore investment quality rugs. Regardless of the quality of the individual rug, all fringe work is painstakingly done by hand.

Pamela Remmers Oates is the family member responsible for overseeing the rug-cleaning business today. Fred Remmers and Pamela Remmers Oates both agree that Remmers has always done whatever it takes to get the rug back to the best it can be. To illustrate the point, Oates related that her father once cleaned a rug intertwined with gold thread using a hand brush and a solution made especially for that rug. She added, "It's like he says, 'Sometimes you've got to go back to the time the rug was made.'"

Creativity Equals Success

The success of the business has required that the Remmers family be creative. In the late 1940's and early 1950's, wall-to-wall carpeting surpassed the popularity of rugs with consumers. At that time, Fred Remmers, Sr. got into the business of both cleaning carpets as well as selling and installing carpeting. After a resurgence of popularity of decorative rugs in the 1980's, Remmers eliminated their carpeting businesses and focuses entirely on oriental rugs.

This focus included the 1989 opening of the Fred Remmers Oriental Rug Gallery boasting an inventory of over 500 antique and semi-antique rugs that are almost exclusively Persian. The gallery's business continues to grow but still runs a distant second to the company's main business, which is rug cleaning and restoration. The approach to rug restoration, like rug cleaning, is undertaken at Remmers with painstaking care, stitch-by-stitch, by workers in the repair department located above the store.

Withstanding the Test of Time

The business of rug cleaning and restoration, according to Remmers, is a good barometer of the economy. "Rugs are a luxury item," he said, adding that "people aren't as quick to write checks for them in slow economic times as when business is booming." He noted that the cleaning business also suffers with the economy because rugs often don't appear to be dirty, even when they are, prompting people to postpone their cleaning.

Despite the ups and downs of the economy, Remmers has withstood the test of time. The fourth-generation firm has been a Memphis institution for over one hundred years, and there are no plans for this to change any time soon. Rug aficionados in the area will most certainly be happy to hear this.

Glassical

Memphis company Glassical, Inc. offers the services of skilled craftsmen who are changing the look of glass in businesses and fine homes nationwide. Glass-lovers who venture to the company's unassuming Summer Avenue location can't help but notice a sign by the door that beckons them with the words, "Imagination Welcome."

Once inside, the reasons for the sign's statement about imagination become clear: imagination is often turned into reality at Glassical. In addition to its sweeping array of contemporary furniture, shoppers discover other glass items that embody style and design: desktop accessories, etched glass awards, decorative glass vanity tops and even national memorials showcase their craftsmen's handiwork.

An Unlikely Beginning

When discussing Glassical's origins, owner Bryan Carter refers to his former career as a mechanical engineer for Western Electric, noting "I was fortunate to be involved in the early days of electronic circuit manufacturing, now commonly called 'computer chips'." He adds that, "This work led into the engineering of the photographic masking process and chemical etching of the very small and very accurate circuits; at that time I never anticipated how these technical skills would later come into play."

When Carter relocated to Memphis to work for Binswanger Glass, he quickly found that his interest in engineering emerged as a passion for solving the design challenges presented in the company's Glasscraft division. Already the leading fabricator of thick glass tabletops, Binswanger management asked Carter to develop new applications for their thick glass product. The young engineer then began to design "all glass" tables, focusing on solid glass table bases made possible by the application of the emerging science of structural adhesives.

In 1980, company president Milton "Mickey" Binswanger asked Carter to meet long-time family friend Eleanor Hawkins, working at that time on the restoration of the Peabody Hotel. A talented artist, Hawkins was in charge of restoring or recreating much of the art for which the hotel had been known in its heyday. Bringing Carter the only few scraps of glass that remained of the hotel's original lobby skylight, she enlisted Carter's aid in rendering a new skylight to serve as the lobby's centerpiece. "That combination of artistic talent with an engineering approach," Carter explains, "was the beginning of 24 successful years of glass etching.

A Monumental Job

It was Carter's experience with etching that made him a candidate to do the etching of the names of the fallen and missing soldiers featured on the Vietnam War Memorial erected in the nation's capital. The candidates competed in two categories: quality of etching and price. The Memorial Committee selected Carter to do the job which balanced both engineering wizardry with artistic sense. Carter is justifiably proud of this work that he says, "forever linked engineering and art as my life's work."

After etching the monument in Washington, Carter felt the time had come to own and direct a glass business in Memphis that could respond to both the artistic and custom needs of consumers. With the blessings of his former employers at Binswanger, Carter opened Glassical, Inc. at its Summer Avenue location, taking with him several members of the team of craftsmen he had put together.

Glassical owner Bryan Carter (l) and Theresa Batty stand next to the "practice panel" used to hone their etching skills for the Vietnam Veterans Memorial.

A Giant Leap

Today, Glassical offers a wide range of products from simple glass tabletops to projects Carter describes as "funky", all made possible by craftsmen such as veteran glass grinder and polisher David McLaurin. With 30 years experience, McLaurin performs a bevy of glass grinding tasks each day, from working on a single-piece, ¾ inch by 15 foot curved glass countertop to a simple medicine cabinet shelf.

Other Glassical craftsmen perform exacting tasks necessary to produce the pieces offered by the company. For example, glass cutter Danny Sisco relies upon his experience of 24 years to accurately cut

pieces of glass typically measuring 96 inches by 130 inches when they arrive at Glassical. Doug Dubose, a skilled glass decorator and sandblast etcher, provides glass carvings to meet the strong demand for creative designs set out in the sketches and concepts of artist Theresa Batty.

Given their craftsmen and the amazing products they create, it is no wonder that Carter expresses excitement about Glassical's future. "While our sales are nationwide," he explains, "the opportunity for those special glass lovers to come in and work directly with us on challenging projects keeps us on our toes and excited about doing what we love."

Kemmons Wilson Companies

He has been called "the personification of entrepreneurial spirit." In other words, Kemmons Wilson, the man who dreamed up the Holiday Inn concept, was an exemplar of the notion of "supreme innovator".

After all, the late Kemmons Wilson not only began the world's first motel chain; he also redefined the time-share industry with Orange Lake Resort & Country Club (OLCC) and grew a business, Kemmons Wilson Companies (KWC), that has owned and operated over 400 different businesses in a variety of industries since 1948. Although many of the companies initially supported home building activities and, later, the growing Holiday Inn chain, KWC became more diverse over time. KWC's previous industry experience includes automobile distribution, TV & radio broadcasting, healthcare, food and product manufacturing and banking.

At present, KWC is still made up of a diverse group of businesses including resort time-sharing, hotel management, insurance, aviation, real estate development and private investments. Although there are numerous successful family companies in business today, few take the idea more to heart than KWC. Years ago, Kemmons Wilson passed the leadership role on to his three sons, Spence, Bob and Kem and their children, who run the company alongside a group of experienced executives and thousands of committed employees. By words and deeds, KWC believes in investing in people and in enriching the lives of others.

Spence L. Wilson is the eldest of Kemmons' three sons and serves as President of KWC and Chairman of OLCC. He attended Vanderbilt University (1964) where he earned a B.A. with a major in economics and minor in Business Administration, then went on to earn his Masters degree at Harvard Business School (1968). He maintains board positions for Regions Financial, Bulab Holdings, Inc., Memphis Tomorrow, Rhodes College and Thomas W. Briggs Foundation.

Robert (Bob) A. Wilson is the second oldest of Kemmons' three sons and serves as Executive Vice President of KWC and President of Wilson Air Center (WAC). He attended Southern Methodist University (1967) earning a B.B.A. with a major in marketing and general business and Harvard Business School where he attended the Small Company Management Program (1979). He serves on the Southern Methodist University Business School Executive Board and is a current member of the National Business Aviation Association Security Council.

C. Kemmons (Kem) Wilson, Jr. is the youngest of Kemmons' three sons and serves as Executive Vice President of KWC and President of

Spence L. Wilson, Robert (Bob) A. Wilson and C. Kemmons (Kem) Wilson

Wilson Hotel Management Company (WHMC). He attended the University of Alabama (1968) where he earned his Bachelor of Science and also attended the Small Company Management Program at Harvard Graduate School of Business (1979). He maintains board positions for Region's Financial Corporation, Furman University, University of Alabama, Hope Christian Community Foundation, Baddour Center, Memphis Literacy Council, Baptist Memorial Healthcare Foundation, and Country Place Ministries.

Starting with a grove of orange trees near Disneyworld in Orlando, FL, Kemmons redefined the time-sharing business through his creation of Orange Lake Country Club. OLCC has grown to become the largest, single-site time-share resort in the world. Encompassing 1,500 acres, OLCC is the premier vacation spot for over 95,000 owners. At 2000 units and still growing, the resort boasts award-winning championship golf, tennis facilities, an 80-acre recreational lake as well as an abundance of activities and amenities one expects from a full-featured resort.

Wilson Hotel Management Company (WHMC) is active in both the development and management of hotels across the country but primarily focuses on the southeast region. With brands such as Holiday Inn and Hampton Inn, WHMC has also broadened the scope of traditional hospitality offerings with projects developed for the US Army, St. Jude Children's Research Hospital and The University of Memphis to provide lodging and other services.

KWC corporate headquarters is located in the company's latest office park development, Tournament Trails

In 1952, Kemmons Wilson Insurance (KWI) was created as an independent broker to provide insurance for the growing Holiday Inn franchise interests, handling all types of insurance products marketed through various national carriers. Today, still marketing through nationally recognized insurance carriers, Kemmons Wilson Insurance has become a leading insurer of hospitality risks throughout the country and delivers all types of property, casualty, life and health products to each of their clients. In addition to the hospitality niche, KWI provides coverage to over 1,100 businesses.

It was son Bob's idea to open a new corporate air center at Memphis International Airport. An avid pilot himself, Bob knew what was needed to bring hospitality to the fixed-base operation. Wilson Air Center opened in 1996. The one-of-a-kind facility features the world's largest canopy (to protect passengers from the elements) and offers comprehensive executive services, military and freight handling, aircraft for sale or charter, maintenance facilities and services and special customer events. In 2005, WAC expanded to Charlotte, N.C. The company has been a regular recipient of top industry honors since inception.

Orange Lake Resort & Country CLub is the world's largest single-site time-share resort.

In the Memphis area, the company has long been and today remains a key player in real estate development. With the relocation of the KWC corporate headquarters to their latest office park development, Tournament Trails, KWC initiated step one of its plans to develop commercial office and retail space in the park-like setting located just off Nonconnah Boulevard (385 Corridor) in what has come to be known as the "High Tech Corridor." The development comprises 38 acres and will feature, when complete, four class-A, multi-story office buildings totaling more than 400,000 square feet of office space.

Other KWC developments in the Memphis area are the Legends, The Oaks at Schilling Farms in Collierville and The Oaks at Appling

> Mission Statement: "To perpetuate and enhance the philosophy and entrepreneurial spirit of its founder, Kemmons Wilson."

Road developments. Legends features 26 two and three acre estate home sites, and is located on Houston Levee Road, minutes from public schools, recreational facilities and high-end retail establishments. The Oaks' communities offer the area's first ranch-style, empty-nester condominiums. With four different floor plans, The Oaks provides a village-like atmosphere complete with community clubhouse and pool.

Through the Private Investment arm of the business, the company continues to seek out and invest in highly select, non-publicly traded companies that possess the potential for significant appreciation at an appropriate level of risk. These are companies that KWC will identify with, in some cases, for generations to come. KWC's objective through its Private Investments' initiative is to significantly outperform, over long periods of time, the potential return of a prudently invested portfolio of marketable securities.

Kemmons Wilson was known, not only for his entrepreneurial acumen, but also for his generous spirit. That tradition continues through the Kemmons Wilson Family Foundation (KWFF). The Kemmons Wilson Family Foundation is a family-run foundation which honors the legacy of giving established by Dorothy and Kemmons Wilson. The goal of KWFF is to offer financial assistance to organizations that focus on community outreach and development, advancement of youth, enrichment of education, faith-based ministries, health and research-related organizations and to other initiatives that benefit the Greater Memphis community and reflect the family's passions. Some of the organizations currently receiving funding from the Foundation include Junior Achievement, Bridges Inc., University of Memphis, Dixon Gallery and Garden, Neighborhood Christian Center, Memphis Union Mission, The Memphis Zoo and St. Jude Children's Hospital.

Wilson Air Center, Memphis International Airport

Harding Academy

Harding Academy, a Christian college-preparatory day school serving the Memphis area since 1952, has a history of providing innovative approaches to education. In 1962, the Academy's leadership began expanding the school by opening elementary locations in church educational buildings, allowing young children to attend school near their homes. This innovative, multi-campus elementary structure helped establish the school as a leader in private education, not only in the Memphis area, but throughout the entire country.

Multi-Campus Structure Promotes Growth

In the ensuing forty-plus years, this multi-campus tenant structure has worked well for the Academy, allowing the school to steadily increase enrollment. Since the first satellite location was opened at Holmes Road, Harding Academy has held classes on 14 different tenant campuses. The multi-campus structure is cost effective, allowing Harding to follow its students as populations shift in the Memphis community. Churches have found this system also helps attract young families to their congregations. Other private schools in Memphis, and across the nation, have studied and implemented Harding's multi-campus pattern.

The first class of Memphis Christian School, now Harding Academy, 1952-1953

Today, Harding continues the multi-campus system on four tenant elementary campuses. The Academy also has Early Childhood programs at two locations: a free-standing, 700-student capacity elementary school in Cordova, and a junior-senior high school in the heart of east Memphis at Park Avenue and Cherry Road. Harding President Tom Dickson notes, "The Academy is large enough to provide a variety of experiences and yet small enough to provide individualized attention for all students."

As Harding plans for future generations of students, the Academy's Board has announced its intent to relocate the junior-senior high operations of the Cherry Road campus to eastern Shelby County. The Academy leadership is currently seeking 100-plus acres on which to build the new middle and upper school.

Mission Statement: Harding Academy is dedicated to fostering each student's academic excellence and faith in God through a Christ-centered education, which emphasizes intellectual, spiritual, social, and physical development.

From Books to Head to Heart

At Harding Academy, the educational process of a student is described as moving "from books, to head, to heart." The Harding experience is designed to instill in each student the knowledge and skills necessary to succeed academically and a love of learning that will benefit each young person throughout life.

Academic quality is only part of the Harding story. To appreciate what makes Harding special, one must also examine the Christian character of the Harding community. Every class is taught from a Christian perspective. The core values of integrity, service, and excellence are woven into the fabric of all that occurs at Harding Academy, not only in Bible class and in chapel, but also in math class, during Student Council activities, or on the athletic fields. This focus is what sets Harding Academy apart from other schools.

A quality Christian education. That is what awaits students at Harding Academy.

Memphis Business Interiors

"The office of tomorrow is our business today," says Scott Messmore, President of Memphis Business Interiors (MBI), the Midsouth's largest office furnishings enterprise. "We're more than furniture. We aim to help our customers do business better. Beyond furniture, our clients are concerned with organizational productivity including: technology, value, image, comfort, efficiency and so much more. Through our experience and expertise, we can actually help a business address these issues through professional office design."

Building the Office of Tomorrow...Today— MBI focuses on helping clients utilize the full potential of their office spaces. "When clients come to MBI, they can expect so much more than a great selection of desks and chairs," Messmore explains, "They can expect guidance, expertise and a complete understanding of what makes an organizational environment work."

Memphis Business Interiors differentiates itself from the competition by offering a complete range of services, from design, planning, and application, to financing, installation, and move management. MBI was founded in 1995 to represent Steelcase Office Furniture in the Memphis area.

The office of today takes into account ergonomics, productivity, image and technology.

Cutting-edge Offices— Among technological innovations currently in use in the Memphis area are the Polyvision® presentation board and the Room Wizard®, both in use in the recently-opened FedEx Institute of Technology at the University of Memphis. The Polyvision® presentation board features a powerful combination of projection screen and erase board that includes touch-screen capabilities and internet access. The Room Wizard®, a wall-mounted touch-screen, electronically schedules meetings via either touch-pad or the Internet. Also housed at the FedEx Institute of Technology is "BlueSpace," a collaborative effort between Steelcase and IBM touted as "the tech office of the future." IBM describes "BlueSpace" as "a new office environment that integrates the physical workplace with advanced computer, sensor, display and wireless technologies." MBI was

instrumental to the set-up of this cutting-edge office environment that offers employees the ability to be comfortable and productive, from rotating computer arms and mobile furniture to lighting options and in-office presentation tools.

MBI Anticipates Modern Office Needs— "Just a few decades ago, offices consisted of rows of desks with telephones and typewriters on them," Messmore says, noting that the effects of noise level, proximity to others, and the amount of paperwork adversely affected efficiency and morale. "'Business has changed, and so the office conducting business must change along with it," Messmore explains, adding, "We stay ahead of these changes, anticipating services and products that will heighten image and employee satisfaction while decreasing cost and inefficiency."

Technological Innovation— In an ever-changing work environment, MBI offers clients the technology required for such options as scheduling meeting rooms online from remote locations, printing or downloading erase board notes to a computer, or the simultaneous delivery of PowerPoint presentations to multiple locations. "We look at technology as a major innovation in helping businesses connect faster, perform better, and produce more," Messmore explains.

The offices of Memphis Business Interiors, including its 20,000 square foot showroom, are located at 4539 West Distriplex Road in the Distriplex Park at the corner of Shelby Drive and Getwell Road in Memphis. The client list of MBI includes Federal Express, Memphis Grizzlies, First Tennessee Bank, Hilton Hotels Corporation, and Medtronic Sofamor Danek, to name a few. For more information on MBI, call (901) 360-8899, or visit www.GoMbi.com.

Typical office environment a few decades ago.

Memphis Convention & Visitors Bureau

The Memphis Convention & Visitors Bureau (MCVB) is a private, not-for-profit subscriber corporation responsible for marketing Memphis and the Shelby County area as a destination for visitors and a meeting and convention site for businesses and organizations. Rather than adopt a convoluted mission statement, the MCVB states their mission simply: "To let people all over the world know about the one-of-a-kind trip that awaits them in Memphis."

Promoting Memphis is big business. It is estimated that visitors to Memphis have an economic impact of $2.4 billion annually, generating 50,700 jobs with an estimated payroll of $1.8 billion and providing more than $174 million in local taxes.

Regena Bearden, MCVB's Vice President of Marketing, emphasizes that the reasons to visit – and revisit – Memphis are constantly increasing. She says, "Not only have almost all of the city's attractions improved over the last 15 years, but we have added many new ones including four museums – the Fire Museum, The Children's Museum, Rock 'n Soul, and Stax," adding, "and then there is the Pyramid, Autozone Park, the FedExForum, the zoo expansion, the trolley – I could go on and on."

Bearden believes that the improvements, expansions and new venues exemplify the cooperation among the city's local government, its hospitality industry and private developers who, she says, "have joined forces to create a one-of-a-kind destination without destroying the city's heritage of music and cotton and that rural-meets-urban appeal that Memphis has always had for visitors."

Recently, the FedExForum, new home to the Rock 'n Soul Museum, opened; the Wonders International Cultural Series began "The Art of the Motorcycle"; the Stax Museum of American Soul Music opened and the city welcomed Ride the Ducks of Memphis to its ever growing list of attractions. Looking ahead, the Grizzlies will begin their fourth season in 2005 and in 2006 the pandas at the Memphis Zoo will be getting new neighbors as construction is completed on the new Northwest Passage exhibit which will house polar bears, seals and sea lions.

2005 promises to be another banner year for Memphis. In honor of B.B. King's 80th birthday September 16th, the city will tell the world that We Have the Blues and Many Ways to Cure it as it launches its Blues campaign. "Our promotions offer us the opportunity to secure in the minds of the consumer that Memphis is a must-see music city that can deliver what no other city in the world can," Bearden comments, adding, "We continue our branding strategies of Memphis as the music-lovers' destination to get the word out that this city, as the undisputed home of the blues, the birthplace of rock 'n' roll, and the cradle of soul is not to be missed."

The city's location as the only metropolis between the Mississippi River and the Mississippi Delta had much to do with the convergence of several musical genres: rhythm and blues, country, rock 'n' roll, gospel and soul music derived from the blending of music from the then-segregated black and white populations. For decades, musicians and music aficionados came to Memphis from nearby towns and states to play and listen to music. Nearly one in five of the earliest inductees to the Rock 'n' Roll Hall of Fame grew up within a 100-mile radius of Memphis. No other city can make that claim. And everybody knows that it was Memphis where Elvis Presley was discovered, and Memphis where he lived and died.

Beale Street – Home of the Blues

Just as important as the musical heritage is the availability of live music today. Kevin Kane, the Bureau's President & CEO agrees. "In terms of a 20th century music experience, Memphis is a destination that every music lover wants to see. The recent opening of the Stax Museum, Rock 'n Soul's move to the FedExForum, and the dozens of live music venues available on any given night makes Memphis on the top of any music lovers list of places to go."

The Magic of Memphis

One of the fastest growing markets for Memphis tourism is the European Market, Bearden explains, noting that most of these visitors are either from the United Kingdom or Germany. "Europeans love to travel and they spend more money on travel than Americans. We were hearing from travel agents that their clients had been to the US several times and wanted a different type of travel package. By partnering with New Orleans and cities in Mississippi and Tennessee, we are able to package a musical tour of 'Real America' that European travelers truly crave. The average international traveler on a musical heritage tour spends 13-17 days visiting three or four states. They stay 3-4 nights in Memphis and spend an average of $155 per day." last year, their expenditures translated to more than $23 million.

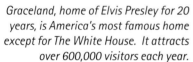

Graceland, home of Elvis Presley for 20 years, is America's most famous home except for The White House. It attracts over 600,000 visitors each year.
© EPE

Memphis Sets the Beat for Meetings and Conventions

The assets that make Memphis a desirable destination for tourists also make the city an ideal venue for meetings and conventions. As meeting planners know, adequate meeting space and lodging for convention-goers is essential. Memphis is home to a diverse array of facilities that can host meetings of almost any size: downtown, the Cook Convention Center boasts 190,000 square feet of exhibit space in a facility with 350,000 total square feet.

Memphis offers more than 20,000 hotel rooms citywide, including almost 4,000 downtown rooms. And our centralized location makes getting here easy and affordable by planes, trains, boats, or automobiles. Memphis International airport, only 12 miles from downtown, is easily accessible from any other part of the city. Once in Memphis, convention attendees enjoy our downtown's $5 billion expansion, area attractions, and incredibly affordable food and lodging. Memphis is a superb place to host an event – a fact proven by the large number of groups that meet in Memphis year after year.

The Future of Memphis Tourism

According to Kane, the Memphis tourism industry looks bright and believes the FedExForum will be key in enhancing the image of the city internationally. "I feel the FedExForum will provide a spotlight for our city like we've never seen. Aside from hosting an NBA team, the signature events the forum can host are monumental," he notes.

The MCVB CEO also believes that both the convention and visitor's markets for Memphis will benefit from the FedExForum's events, explaining, "Our convention trade will continue to grow at its good pace and we expect to become a new vacation destination in the minds of many new audiences in the near future. The growth will come from a combination of our marketing efforts and word-of-mouth from satisfied visitors. As our mission statement says, we offer a one-of-a-kind experience; once people come to Memphis, they'll come again and they'll tell their friends to come."

The mighty Mississippi

Memphis Light, Gas and Water

Since 1939, Memphis Light, Gas and Water has served as a .stone of the Memphis community, delivering vital utility services to local business and residential customers alike. During this time, Memphis has experienced exponential growth and with it, MLGW has remained one step ahead of municipal progress, expanding its utility infrastructure and adding a variety of services to support the populace now exceeding 1 million residents and making MLGW the largest three-service municipal utility in the nation.

At first glance, such utility service provision may appear to be a rather routine undertaking. But contrary to this notion, the tasks involved in MLGW's operations are as myriad and diverse as the customers it serves. Fulfilling these duties while investigating new ways to ensure affordable rates and reliable service often requires resourceful insights and innovative approaches, especially in a global climate of rising energy costs.

In recent years, MLGW pursued new ways to insulate local utility customers from such price volatility. As a result, a groundbreaking concept was born in 2000 that came to be known as the "MLGW Electric Wholesale Power Stabilization Plan." Under the plan, MLGW would issue $1.5 billion worth of tax-exempt bonds from its water division to pre-purchase electricity at a discounted rate from the Tennessee Valley Authority. The discounted rate would save MLGW and its customers $15 million per year over the 15-year term of the arrangement for a total savings of $225 million.

While a grand idea in theory, it posed some major obstacles in reality including the fact that federal policies opposed the use of tax-exempt bonds for electric prepayments. Rising to the challenge, MLGW worked for nearly two years on local, state and federal levels to gain approvals needed to proceed with this novel transaction. After

countless hours of congressional testimony and meetings with state and local officials, MLGW succeeded and the transaction was completed in 2003 marking the largest bond issuance in Tennessee history. This was truly an innovative undertaking mutually benefiting all parties involved by generating funds for TVA to use in completing some of its pending projects and by offering MLGW and its customers a long-term plan for the containment of electric costs. The transaction stands as one of MLGW's most pioneering initiatives and exemplifies MLGW's desire and ability to look beyond the short-term to find long-range, innovative solutions to meet the growing needs of its customers.

Eager to optimize the quality of customer service in the Customer Care Center (CCC), MLGW has pursued another innovative initiative by upgrading its Customer Information System (CIS). Unlike its outdated predecessor, the new CIS system consists of more than 2,500 computer system programs and affects some 650 business processes within the utility. The system interfaces many company functions, thereby reducing wait times for most inquiries and offering real-time account updates for utility customers by centralizing numerous operations. The new system also allows customers to request service changes online at their convenience and enables the CCC employees to view the same bill onscreen that their customers see, making communication much easier. The efficiency of this technologically advanced CIS system, combined with the added phone line capacity of the Netters Business Center where the CCC is now located, has dramatically reduced call waiting times to just a few seconds on average.

Through the years, MLGW has applied progressive thinking and actively sought innovative ways to improve the quality and affordability of its processes and services. Such commitment has enabled MLGW to offer its customers some of the lowest utility rates in the nation. Due to its forward-thinking and unparalleled success at serving more than 421,000 customers, the utility is highly revered among industry professionals nationwide and has even been examined by international dignitaries who view it as a good role model for their own utility organizations.

Under the leadership of MLGW President and CEO, Joseph Lee III, MLGW will continue to be an innovative leader in the energy industry in its endeavor to be the "Best Utility for Our Customers."

Residence Inn by Marriott

Walking into the downtown Memphis Residence Inn by Marriott is like stepping back in time. The historic art deco-styled structure, built as the William Len hotel in 1927 at Main and Monroe, opened last year following its conversion to a 90-suite, extended-stay hotel. A great deal of effort went into keeping the building true to its history while adding all the modern comforts.

General Manager Tricia Weatherford enjoys giving tours, and she is quick to note that the art deco feel of the property, preserved throughout the building, is especially noticeable in the hotel's lobby, the building's most architecturally significant space. There, the ironwork around the staircases and mezzanine reflects the art deco design of the hotel's original logo, a theme carried throughout the lobby and common areas of the hotel in the intricate inlaid woodwork. The vertical marble columns, the ornate elevator doors, and the light fixtures are all original to the building, and gilded mirrors and modernist furnishings are used to heighten the period look throughout the hotel.

A Quick Conversion

Memphis-based Wright Investment Properties spent 10 months converting the 12-story property to its present extended-stay status. Company president Larry Wright explains that a quick conversion of the property was possible because the historic building had been completely renovated in the 1980's when the landmark hotel was adapted for use as an apartment building. In an interview with The Commercial Appeal when the property opened, Wright noted that the conversion left a perfect footprint for his hotel venture, commenting, :The footprint and the size of the rooms fit the Residence Inn room size, so it was an easy transition to make from an apartment building to an extended-stay hotel."

The extended-stay concept, Manager Weatherford points out, allows guests to enjoy all the amenities of a fine hotel without sacrificing the conveniences of home such as a full kitchen including stove and oven, microwave and refrigerator. All rooms have high-speed Internet access and the lobby and common areas provide wireless Internet access. However, says Weatherford, her property was designed as an alternative to the traditional Residence Inn property: "The idea was to achieve a more up-scale, boutique concept Inn."

It is the attention to detail that makes this National Historic Register property special. From its original art deco details and its period look to its amenities, the downtown Residence Inn offers the special touches that sets it apart. For instance, all the beds in the hotel are feather beds and are triple sheeted. "In terms of bed comfort, this hotel always ranks in the top 95 percentile when compared to other hotels," Weatherford says with obvious pride.

Photo by The Commercial Appeal

A Rich Memphis Heritage

The building, which was placed on the National Historic Register in 1984, was begun in 1927 and completed in 1930. Its name was chosen by Grady Manning, who at that time was president of Southwest Hotels, Inc., the company operating the hostelry. Grady Manning's named the hotel in honor of his father-in-law, wealthy Arkansan William Len Seaman. Formerly of Savannah, Tennessee, Seaman became one of the wealthiest and best known citizens of Arkansas in the early part of the 20th century. At its opening, the William Len was heralded in the Memphis Press Scimitar as a grand hotel with 250 rooms, 250 baths, and "an artificially-cooled lobby and barbershop." Longtime Memphis mayor "Boss Crump" had his hair cut in the mezzanine barbershop of the William Len on a regular basis.

The hotel closed in 1970, reopening in the early 1980's when an investment firm converted the building's 250 rooms into 89 apartments. The Hertz Investment Group purchased the property in 1994, holding it until 2000 when it was donated by the Hertz family to Neve Yerushalayim, a college for women based in Israel. Larry Wright and his partners bought the building from the non-profit organization with the intention of turning it into an extended-stay property, the only property of its type downtown. Although the latest renovation kept the same configuration of rooms, the division of a large rooftop apartment allowed an additional unit.

Memphis Center City Commission president Jeff Sanford has called the restoration of the William Len "a great example of a sensitive renovation of an older building." In its new incarnation, it brings to downtown Memphis the style of a bygone era and the comfort and convenience of the 21st century.

Morgan Keegan & Company

Morgan Keegan & Company, Memphis's first homegrown investment firm, has been recognizing innovative ideas and sharing them with investors throughout the country for 35 years. Allen Morgan Jr., with three other young Memphians, launched Morgan Keegan as a specialty research boutique in 1969. Their mission was to spread the word to the investment community outside the region about up-and-coming companies based in the South.

During Morgan Keegan's history, there have been many "firsts" recorded by the firm and its associates – "firsts" that have resulted in national recognition. Today, Morgan Keegan is the region's largest full-service investment firm. Through more than 240 offices in 18 states, Morgan Keegan's 3,275 associates serve the investment needs of a broad range of individual and institutional clients. In 2004, Morgan Keegan reported record revenues of $727,000,000 and equity capital of over $500 million.

Under the leadership of Morgan Keegan Chairman Allen Morgan and Regions Chairman Carl Jones, the union of the two firms is regarded as one of the most successful bank-brokerage mergers on record.

From Memphis Beginnings to National Prominence

In those early days, Morgan Keegan watched many entrepreneurial concepts materialize and grow to become successful companies and even industry leaders. For example, Morgan Keegan executed the initial trade in Federal Express Corporation stock on the New York Stock Exchange in 1978, and provided research coverage on then relatively unknown companies like Wal-Mart and AutoZone. Today, Morgan Keegan continues to uncover the opportunities developing in its own backyard, while leading the industry in developing innovative financial services for its clients.

From the beginning, the firm grew at a rapid pace; and its founders soon expanded their mission to reflect their belief that Morgan Keegan could become the region's premier securities firm. A seat on the New York Stock Exchange was purchased in 1970 and, as the first Memphis firm to do so, Morgan Keegan quickly gained credibility among investors throughout the South. By 2002, Morgan Keegan owned five NYSE seats and a significant presence on the prestigious exchange floor.

In the early 1970's, Morgan Keegan broke new ground among industry peers by becoming one of the first firms to open branch offices, initially expanding in Jackson, Mississippi, and Memphis. Today the firm's 220 Private Client Group offices are found in numerous metropolitan areas across the South, Midwest and Texas — from Richmond, Virginia to Ft. Lauderdale, Florida, from Houston, Texas to St. Louis, Missouri.

Innovative Services for Investors

Morgan Keegan's Fixed Income Capital Markets division is recognized as one of the most extensive bond sales, trading and underwriting operations outside of Wall Street. Since the mid-1970's, the firm has provided bond underwriting for municipal governments, raising funds to build infrastructure such as schools, highways, hospitals and utilities throughout the South. From 1993 to 2004, Morgan Keegan led the nation in underwriting municipal bond issues in the South Central Region which includes Alabama, Arkansas, Kentucky, Louisiana, Mississippi and Tennessee. In 2003, the firm ranked 5th in the world for government agency underwriting, and was among the top 10 underwriters nationally for long-term municipal issues for the first quarter of 2005. (Source: Securities Data Company)

Among the innovations attributable to Morgan Keegan is a state-of-the-art proprietary analytical tool called eFolio®. Introduced in 1999, eFolio represents the first interactive, online portfolio management system for institutions. Today, more than 1,800 financial institutions have adopted the eFolio system to manage their bond portfolios.

Morgan Keegan's corporate finance effort has raised over $20 billion of growth capital since 1991, helping bring a number of dynamic Southern companies into the public eye. Through the firm's Mezzanine Fund and Opportunity Fund, Morgan Keegan provides capital to emerging small and mid-sized companies with promising futures.

From Morgan Keegan's equity trading floor, traders Hedi Reynolds and Bill Kitchens are in constant contact with the major exchanges.

New Opportunities on the Horizon

In 2001, Morgan Keegan forged a partnership with Regions Financial. Three years later, Regions merged with another Memphis-based institution, Union Planters Corporation, forming one of the nation's top 15 financial services providers. Becoming a part of Regions has created opportunities for growth and expansion within Morgan Keegan. With five million customers, 1400 branches and a similar corporate culture, Regions provides an unlimited opportunity for Morgan Keegan to expand its investment services to the bank's clients. Today, several Morgan Keegan financial advisors work from offices in Regions Bank branches, while Morgan Keegan oversees nearly 1000 bankers who offer insurance products to banking customers through the firm's Financial Sales Associate program. Additionally, the three

organization's trust divisions have been combined under the Regions Morgan Keegan Trust banner which operates as an affiliate of Morgan Keegan.

In its 35-year history, Morgan Keegan has become an established leader in the financial services industry, without forgetting its roots in the Memphis community. Guiding the firm's direction in the future will be its mission to advance the financial interests of individual and institutional investors, corporations, and public issuers through sound financial advice, comprehensive and timely research, and responsive and accurate service.

Morgan Keegan Tower corporate headquarters on the banks of the Mississippi River is a standout on the Memphis skyline.

National Bank of Commerce

Memphis' National Bank of Commerce (NBC) has offered innovative programs and products to meet customers' needs since its inception on the banks of the Mississippi River in 1873. NBC, long known as "The Cotton Bank", was once the world's largest processor of cotton collateral documents. In fact, in the early 1990's, the bank was instrumental in creating an electronic clearinghouse for tens of thousands of cotton documents that for decades had been manually processed in their original paper form.

This innovation is only one of many developed by NBC and its sister banks in the multi-billion dollar National Commerce Financial Corporation (NCF), a top-performing banking company for more than twenty-five years. Perhaps the best-known and most-emulated innovation pioneered by NBC has been its extended-hours bank branches in grocery stores. Although not the first to launch in-store banking centers, NBC was the first bank to focus its distribution network within stores.

NBC as Innovator

This innovation is only one of many developed by NBC and its sister banks in the multi-billion dollar National Commerce Financial Corporation (NCF), a top-performing banking company for more than twenty-five years. Perhaps the best-known and most-emulated innovation pioneered by NBC has been its extended-hours bank branches in grocery stores. Although not the first to launch in-store banking centers, NBC was the first bank to focus its distribution network within stores.

NBC opened more extended-hours bank branches than any bank in the world under the leadership of then Chairman and Chief Executive Officer Thomas M. Garrott. Garrott came to National Commerce Financial from the supermarket industry where convenience for customers is vital for success, and he implemented a focus on convenience at NCF that garnered national prominence for the organization.

The first of the new banking centers, then called Money Market branches but later renamed Super Money Market® branches, opened in a suburban grocery store in September of 1985. Within seven years, NCF (then known as National Commerce Bancorporation, or NCBC) operated 39 Super Money Market® branches and was recognized across the country as an innovator in the retail banking arena.

The Ins and Outs of Banking

In the meantime, NCBC had created a supermarket affiliate called National Commerce Bank Service, Inc., to license the concept on a nationwide basis to other banks. Since then, NCF has operated a successful consulting subsidiary that teaches its competitors the ins and outs of supermarket banking.

The bank's focus on maximizing the convenience of their in-store branches has not been limited to supermarket banking centers. In an article published in 2001, former Chairman Garrott noted that maximizing convenience for the bank's customers was the bank's primary focus during his tenure, commenting, "It's the same way we looked at account structures, branch locations, credit programs, Internet banking, and every other aspect of our business." Garrott added, "We knew that service and convenience make the difference for busy customers."

Garrott, who has served as Chairman of the Executive Committee of NCF since his tenure ended as Chairman of the Board of NCF, joined the Board of Directors of SunTrust Banks when it completed its $7 billion acquisition of NCF late last year. (For more information about Thomas M. Garrott and his role as a Memphis innovator, see his profile on pages 74 and 75 of this book.)

NBC Merges with SunTrust

National Commerce Financial Corporation, the parent company of National Bank of Commerce, was acquired in May, 2004, by SunTrust Banks, Inc. in a merger that creates the 7th-largest bank in the United States, with $148 billion in total assets in 11 states and the District of Columbia. The combined company, to be based in Atlanta, will operate as SunTrust, which means that by the end of 2005, the National Bank of Commerce name will be a thing of the past.

However, according to NCF president and CEO William R. Reed, Jr., the community and NCF customers will be gaining much more than is being lost. Says Reed, "This merger means great things for NCF employees, for our shareholders and especially for our customers,"

adding, "From a cultural perspective, SunTrust operates a similar banking model of regional banks, with local decision-making that keeps the bankers in tune with and responsive to customers' needs. Customers will have access to a deeper and broader array of products and services in a larger geographic footprint. We believe they will continue to see the benefits of our merger as we couple the strengths of SunTrust with the high entrepreneurial energy of NCF, with a sustained focus on retail growth, community banking, operating efficiency, asset quality and continued investment in de novo opportunities. And because there is little overlap between our footprints, our customers will continue to do business with the people they know and trust."

"The banking industry has changed a great deal. But the one thing that has not changed, throughout our history, and will not change in the future, is the quality of our people. They are our greatest asset." – Bruce Campbell, former Board Chairman

Orgill, Inc.

Innovation is clearly one of the essential components of success. When innovation is combined with creativity, foresight and good business sense, the sky is the limit. Just ask the folks at Orgill, Inc., the nation's largest independent hardware distributor which, in 2005, will rack up nearly a billion dollars in sales – an increase of some 400 percent over the last ten years.

Founded in 1847, the Memphis-based company has successfully adapted to the ever-changing hardware industry: in the last several years, Orgill has emerged as a major player in the field by adding prestigious accounts (Sears Hardware and 84 Lumber, as well as hundreds of independent stores, home centers and lumberyards) while increasing its distribution centers and expanding its geographical territory and its international business.

Head-On Competition

Orgill's dealer division, which supplies independent hardware stores, home centers and lumberyards, competes directly with three major hardware cooperatives – True Value Corp., Ace Hardware and Do it Best Corp. But the Orgill name isn't visible on any store fronts, and that is the way Orgill wants it. "We play to the uniqueness of each operation and try to establish the individual dealer as the brand. There are no Orgill stores out there unless we have a customer whose store name happens to be Orgill," explains Ron Beal, president and CEO.

An Industry Powerhouse

The Orgill name may not be displayed, but it is certainly a force in the industry -- with customers, with competitors and with industry analysts and the media. Home Channel News (HCN), the home improvement industry's premier trade publication, has showcased the privately owned hardlines distributor in three special issues in as many years. At a special awards dinner held in conjunction with this year's National Hardware Show in Las Vegas, Orgill was named Retail-Partner of the Year. At the same event, Joseph Orgill, III (Chairman of Orgill, 1980- 2004) was selected as one of four charter members of the newly established Home Channel Hall of Fame.

Such accolades are nothing new. In 1999, HCN recognized Orgill as E-tailer of the Year in its annual Year in Review segment. This award was based on the success of Orgill's QuikShip program, an electronic

commerce program that allows retailers to offer internet shoppers the ability to order any of Orgill's 60,000 plus products through the dealer's corporate website. The program, which began with some 200 sites, has enjoyed continued success since its inception.

Orgill was named one of the five most innovative companies within its industry that same year, a distinction explained in a write-up entitled "Why It Is Innovative" in the National Home Center News. Noting that the hardlines distributor provides more than just product to retail clients, the publication revealed that not only does the company successfully handle the basics; Orgill also "offers a complete menu, including market-based research, international sales development, and online order fulfillment over the internet."

While Orgill has been recognized for its E-Commerce and customer service programs, it has not neglected investing in computer and logistical systems. Orgill was the first company in the hardware distribution industry to install a computer in the 1950's, and has maintained its leadership in the use of computers since that time.

In the distribution centers, Orgill makes use of the latest bar code systems and scanners, as well as modern conveyor sorting systems to stage orders for accurate loading for delivery. In addition, Orgill maintains and operates a modern truck fleet of almost 200 tractors and 600 trailers to deliver products to their customers.

Numerous other services are available to Orgill's clientele including its Pro Source program, designed to help its pro dealers more successfully merchandise products for their customers who are plumbers, electricians, carpenters and others in the building trades. Pro Source incorporates a number of elements including product assortments, store planning and layout, and pricing.

A "Best Practices" Operation

Orgill's success as both a retail partner and with E-tailing are just two of the many reasons that Orgill is, according to Home Channel News's Jeff Arien, "a best practices kind of operation." Known for decades as a regional wholesaler, the hardware supplier has been quietly expanding. Since the 1970's, Orgill has been acquiring distributors both in the Memphis area and beyond; the purchase of its 13 acquisitions to date were a component of its plan for expansion calling for the company's emergence as a nationwide distributor.

Distribution centers have also expanded as the customer base has grown. For years, Orgill's dealers have been concentrated in the South, Midwest, and along the Eastern seaboard. These customers – independent lumberyards as well as corporate accounts like 84 Lumber – have primarily been serviced through the company's four distribution centers in Memphis; Inwood, West Virginia; Vandalia, Illinois; and Tifton, Georgia.

In the Family for Four Generations

Orgill, Inc., founded some twenty years before the Civil War began, is one of the oldest businesses in Memphis. The company began when Englishman William Orgill joined his brother Joseph's New York-based importing company. During his travels, William purchased the inventory of a hardware business being sold in Virginia and shipped it to Memphis where he opened the first Orgill's hardware store on April 1, 1847. Brother Edmund moved his family to Memphis where he actively managed the business, known then [and for most of its history] as Orgill Brothers & Company, Inc.

In the succeeding years, the company has continued to be controlled by Orgill family members who, in the early 1900's switched the focus of the company from retail to distribution and shortly thereafter expanded operations outside of Memphis. Today, Orgill, Inc. is one of the few American companies that has operated throughout its history as a family-owned, privately-held enterprise.

Former Chairman Joe Orgill, III, announced late last year that Fondren would take over the job as Chairman as part of the company's succession plan. In the 1970's the board decided to rely on professional management to guide the company. Orgill and his partner (and cousin) Michael McDonnell will remain on the board and will continue to play an active role in the company's business.

After 158 years, Orgill continues its pursuit of excellence. With a history marked by Tradition, Innovation, and Service, and its mission for success for its customers, it is safe to say that the best is yet to come!

Westward Ho!

Orgill decided to expand the company's territory and, in 2002, hired industry hardware veterans to carry out its westward expansion. Since then, many customers have been added in western states like Nevada, Colorado and California, which led to the opening of Orgill's third freight-handling facility, an export consolidation warehouse in Los Angeles.

Building on this momentum, Orgill opened a new distribution center in Hurricane, Utah, in the Spring of 2005 as part of its ongoing plan to develop a national network of distribution facilities and services. "We needed a physical presence in the West," explains Orgill's newly named Chairman Bill Fondren, who adds: "We can now compete and service customers in a way nobody ever thought possible."

Fondren, who led the company as president and CEO for almost twenty-five years, is quick to explain that expansion is consistent with Orgill's corporate objectives. He says, "Our mission remains in place: helping our customers be successful. We will now be able to offer our products and services nationwide."

Renasant Bank

Within three years of its start-up in 1999, Renasant Bank of Germantown grew to become a $225 million dollar bank with a commitment to operating like the community banks of the past – banks that put customers and employees first. This has not changed since Renasant's merger late last year with Peoples Bank & Trust based in Tupelo, Mississippi.

Renasant is retaining its name and charter and its President and CEO, Frank Cianciola, who explains that "the merger is really more a blending of two like banks. The only change for our customers will be an expanded number of choices of products and services and additional locations." Cianciola, a Memphis native who has made a career of banking, notes that Renasant and Peoples Bank share commonly-held operating philosophies, financial strengths, products and services, and cutting edge technology. "We also share the community bank perspective, that the people we serve and the people we employ come first."

This philosophy is the reason that Cianciola, with friend and business partner Jack Johnson, initially formed the new bank (known then as Community Commercial Bank). Opening in 1999 with Cianciola as President and Johnson as Chairman of the bank's holding company, Renasant quickly established itself as one of the area's premier community banking operations. Renasant's unique name was coined to embody the spirit of the Renaissance – a time of renewal, the rebirth of learning and the beginning of banking. Renasant currently has two banking offices in Germantown and Cordova and is building a new headquarters in East Memphis and an office in Collierville to open later this year.

Merger Expands the Market

Cianciola, who will sit on parent company Peoples' board while overseeing the operations of all of the holding company's offices in Shelby and DeSoto counties, says that the merger has allowed People's Bank to operate from a position of strength in this market. "We are growing and the combination of what we're seeing here in our area and down in DeSoto County bodes well," he notes, adding, "At present, we are larger in Shelby County than in DeSoto, but DeSoto is gaining ground so rapidly as a market that we're really excited."

Renasant will operate as an indirect subsidiary of People's Holding Company. The management and board of Renasant Bank will remain in effect while Cianciola and Johnson will serve on the PHC board. The bank will continue to operate as it always has, as a full-service commercial banking institution offering services to both commercial and private customers, but with a community orientation.

The Community Philosophy

The Peoples Bank name exemplifies the attitude that both Renasant Bank and its new merger partner share. As Peoples President and CEO E. Robinson McGraw puts it, "Over the years, we have consciously chosen to grow, progress, and offer leading edge technology, but never at the expense of the people we serve, or the people we employ."

Cianciola agrees with this philosophy, admitting that it was his desire to remain close contact with his employees and his customers that led him to form Renasant Bank with associate Jack Johnson. Cianciola, who worked his way through undergraduate school at the University of Memphis by working at First Tennessee bank, moved to Union Planters upon graduation, and later earned a Master of Science Degree in Finance from the University of Memphis, eventually moving to Commerce Union Bank in 1984 to become its Executive Vice President. With his help, the bank grew to become a $500 million dollar bank in eight years.

When Commerce Union was acquired by NationsBank, Cianciola was discomfited by the size of the operation. "The bigger we became, the less I liked it; I knew I didn't want to be a part of a bank the size of NationsBank," he explains. This led to the decision to accept Victory Bank's offer to become CEO of their small bank in 1995. Cianciola and his management team grew Victory to more than double its size; in 1998, when it was acquired, Cianciola began to seriously consider the possibility of forming a new, small bank.

Although Renasant (like Cianciola's other banking success stories) has grown to become a $225 million dollar bank, it has maintained its commitment to operating like the community banks of the past – a bank that puts its customers and employees first. And because Peoples Bank shares that philosophy, the merger means that the only change that Renasant customers will experience is a greater number of financial choices available through the association with the larger Peoples Bank & Trust Company.

The Crump Firm, Inc.

Long recognized for design excellence, The Crump Firm, Inc. continues its role as one of the leading architectural firms in Memphis with its reputation for producing innovative, high-quality designs for a distinguished group of corporate, healthcare, institutional, educational, religious and governmental clients, locally and nationally. An architectural practice established in 1970 and incorporated in 1985, The Crump Firm is a client-oriented, full-service, architectural, planning, and interior design firm. Its thirty-one staff member staff has completed diverse projects in twenty-nine states. With its ten architects and seven interior designers, the firm is well known for working closely with its clients to produce award winning designs within clients' budget and schedule.

The Crump Firm, Inc. specializes in designing the following project types: corporate headquarters, tenant office buildings, healthcare clinics and facilities, schools, college and university buildings of all types, performing arts centers, worship facilities and church additions, distribution centers and a broad range of governmental projects.

Recently completed office buildings include the International Place Tower III and two-three story office buildings in the Shadow Creek Office Park at Southwind for Highwoods Properties. The Crump Firm's corporate headquarters designs include buildings for Allenberg Cotton Company, Hohenberg Cotton Company, Orion Packaging Systems and Physiotherapy Associates.

The firm's healthcare clients include Baptist Memorial Health Care, Campbell Clinic, Semmes-Murphy Clinic and the Stern Cardiovascular Center for which The Crump Firm recently completed a new two story clinic in Germantown. Recently completed school projects include: a complete new upper school, campus center and lower school expansion for Memphis University School; a new upper school for St. Mary's School; Millington Elementary School for Shelby County Schools; Craigmont Middle School for Memphis City Schools; the new Federal Express Institute of Technology Building at the University of Memphis with LRK. The Crump Firm's designs of college buildings include seven new buildings and twelve renovations for Rhodes College.

The Crump Firm, Inc. is also known for its designs of new and innovative churches, fellowship halls, auditoriums and performing arts centers. Some of these projects include the Bartlett Performing

Arts Center, the Rose Theater in the Buckman Hall Performing and Fine Arts Center at St. Mary's School, the Performing Arts Center in the recently completed St. Benedict at Auburndale High School. The firm's design of religious facilities include numerous and varied projects for the Catholic Diocese of Memphis, the Episcopal Diocese of West Tennessee, Presbyterian churches including Second Presbyterian Church and Independent Presbyterian Church, Bellevue Baptist Church, Trinity Baptist Church and most recently, major additions and renovations to Temple Israel.

The firm's governmental projects include numerous designs for the

City of Memphis, Shelby County Government, the State of Tennessee and Memphis / Shelby County Airport Authority. The firm's services also include site analysis, master planning, feasibility studies, interior space planning and a full range of interior design services with licensed interior designers. The firm is also well known for assisting its clients with contractor selection and with attentive project administration during construction.

The Crump Firm, Inc. has completed numerous renovations and additions at the Memphis International Airport. This work began in 1988 and includes expansions throughout all three concourses including the Federal Inspection Station for international arrivals completed in 1995. The firm is now designing an expansion to double the current capacity for arriving international passengers. Currently, the firm also is completing its design of the new Tennessee Air National Guard Base at Memphis International Airport. The Crump Firm, Inc. will participate in the program management team on behalf of Memphis / Shelby County Airport Authority to assure that the new base is built in accordance with the approved design.

Additional current projects include new Early Childhood buildings for St. Mary's School and Presbyterian Day School, the proposed Memphis Belle Museum and a broad range of other new buildings, renovations and additions. The Crump Firm is led by its two principals, Metcalf Crump, FAIA, President, and David Hoback, Vice President. All principals, associates and staff members are dedicated to fulfilling the mission statement of The Crump Firm: to create inspired architecture which will endure. More complete information may be found on the firm's website: www.crumpfirm.com.

Saint Francis Hospital

Saint Francis Hospital has a history of providing innovative, critical medical services to Memphis and the Mid-South market. It was the first full-service hospital located in the Memphis suburbs, the first in the city to operate a Chest Pain Emergency Center, and it has now opened the first full-service hospital in Bartlett.

Saint Francis Hospital-Bartlett and Saint Francis Hospital in Memphis are part of Tenet Healthcare Corporation, the nation's second largest health care network with affiliations with many acute-care hospitals around the United States. Saint Francis has continued the trend of tremendous growth, beginning with its Chest Pain and Stroke Emergency Centers designed to provide the resources needed to both save lives as well as limit residual damage from those victimized by catastrophic strokes and heart attacks. In August 2004, Saint Francis was designated a UnitedHealth Premium cardiac specialty center, reflecting national recognition of the cardiac care it provides.

Yet, Saint Francis' efforts have not been limited to just one area. Besides founding one of the area's first heart centers, the hospital was also one of the leaders in establishing admission-to-discharge outpatient departments as well as a Women's Center. And its original 15-story hospital building is an early example of incorporating seismic specifications in Memphis construction.

A Personal Approach to Healthcare

Saint Francis, according to hospital spokesperson and professional basketball player Shane Battier, "takes a personal approach to healthcare, providing services for the entire family from birth to senior care." Saint Francis has established a number of specialty centers to meet this objective. The recently opened outpatient Surgery Center at Saint Francis, conveniently located in front of the hospitals' Park Avenue entrance, was designed to accommodate patients requiring specialized treatment without a hospital stay. At more than 16,000 square feet, the one-story facility contains four operating rooms and two procedure rooms.

Also offering personalized healthcare are the Cardiac Care and TotalCare Diagnostic Centers, combining dedicated customer service with some of the latest in diagnostic technology. The Family Birthing Center, the Diabetes Care Center, Cancer Care Services, and the Center for Health and Wellness (including its Center for Surgical Weight Loss) all provide specialized services designed to enhance the delivery of healthcare options to Saint Francis Hospital patients.

Additional hospital programs

include the Joint Replacement & Orthopedic Center at the Park Avenue facility and the Sports Medicine and Rehabilitation Centers located in Memphis, Bartlett, Collierville and Millington. The Behavioral Health Center offers inpatient and outpatient programs for adults and adolescents dealing with substance abuse and other behavioral problems, while the Sleep Center helps those who suffer from sleep disorders such as sleep apnea, recurrent awakening and daytime fatigue.

The Saint Francis mission is "To heal, support, and comfort all whom we serve in the tradition of Catholic healthcare." This was the aim when the hospital took the name of the Saint known for his compassion, and that has not changed. Today, as Saint Francis prepares to mark the anniversary of its thirty year tradition of healing, its mission is being carried out in both Memphis-area hospitals through myriad programs by hundreds of healthcare professionals, all devoted to providing quality healthcare for its patients.

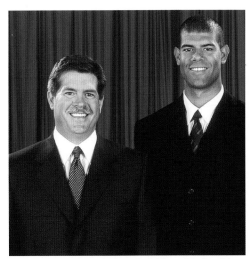

Current Saint Francis Hospital Memphis President and CEO David L. Archer with hospital spokesperson Shane Battier.

"First in Bartlett...Second to None" — In 2004, the new Saint Francis Hospital-Bartlett opened as a full-service 90-bed hospital, the first in the Bartlett community. Featuring birthing rooms, surgical suites, and an emergency room, the facility is located at Kate Bond road and Highway 64.

Staying True to its Roots

With its many programs, Saint Francis continues its leadership in delivering quality healthcare while remaining true to its Catholic roots. Initially positioned as a satellite facility for Saint Joseph Hospital in downtown Memphis, Saint Francis opened in 1974 under the name Saint Joseph Hospital East. The name was changed to Saint Francis Hospital in 1980. Operated as an independent Catholic hospital, the facility proudly boasts another first: the first woman president of an area hospital. Rita Schroeder, formerly Sister Rita, served Saint Francis tirelessly for twenty years. The force behind the founding of the hospital, Schroeder was also instrumental in the facility's extraordinary growth.

Current President and CEO David L. Archer was hired in 1997. Today, Saint Francis boasts over 500 beds in the original 15-story building on Park Avenue and the six-story Thompson Tower patient wing. The hospital shares its campus with a 197-bed nursing home, two medical office buildings and the University of Tennessee/Saint Francis Family Practice Residency complex.

The hospital has a long-standing association with the University of Tennessee Center for the Health Sciences' Family Practice Residency program, reflecting a strong commitment to both physicians and the quality of medical care they provide. The U.T. program utilizes the hospital's facilities for teaching and clinical experience for student physicians who often choose to stay in the community once their training is complete.

Saint Francis Hospital's Physician Referral Service directs patients to doctors who can address their healthcare needs. The Saint Francis medical staff includes over a thousand area physicians, representing many medical and surgical specialties. CEO David Archer explains: "Our doctors are integral members of the Saint Francis healthcare team and many of them serve in important administrative and board leadership roles. We are especially proud of these dedicated men and women of medicine.

Sedgwick CMS

Sedgwick Claims Management Services knows that bad things sometimes happen to good companies and to good people. Companies are sued over parking lot mishaps and employees are injured in workplace accidents. When bad things happen, Sedgwick CMS is ready to help by providing its clients with timely and accurate management of claims processing.

Sedgwick CMS is a leading provider of innovative claims and productivity management solutions to many of this country's largest employers. Clients include four of the top five firms in the Fortune 500 and 25 of the top 100. The company's specialty areas include workers' compensation; general, auto and professional liability; and short and long-term disability claims. Sedgwick CMS employs approximately 4000 colleagues in more than 80 offices across the United States and Canada. More than 400 colleagues work in the firm's North American headquarters in Memphis.

Memphis-Based by Choice

Sedgwick CMS has deep Memphis roots through the organizational lineage of the E. H. Crump & Company insurance agency, founded in the early 20's by late Mayor E.H. Crump. The business that evolved directly into today's Sedgwick CMS, however, opened its doors in 1969 in Los Angeles and San Francisco and later moved to Chicago. The decision to maintain and expand a national headquarters operation in Memphis was made by the current leadership – President and CEO David A. North and James B. Wiertelak, Executive Vice President and COO – both Memphians by choice.

Both North and Wiertelak were transplanted to Memphis during transition years that brought ownership changes and personnel shifting among cities all over the country. Wiertelak moved to Memphis from New York in 1993; North relocated from Chicago in 1995 upon being named president. Following changes in its parent company's ownership in 1998, Sedgwick CMS in 1999 became an independent company with a self-governing board representing its investors.

Elaborating on the decision to retain the Memphis headquarters, Dave North says, "In 1998, we knew we had the choice of several cities to call home. We were all very pleased with what Memphis had to offer. Of course, the central location is an obvious plus for a national company. Other things that we and our colleagues had come to appreciate about Memphis were quality of life issues, the positive work

CEO Dave North, COO Jim Wiertelak

ethic of the people, and the supportive business environment the city provides."

To celebrate the company's move into new offices in 2001, North and Wiertelak named the company's conference rooms – 12 in all – after Memphis landmarks. Sedgwick CMS sponsored a contest among photography students at the Memphis College of Art to take original photographs for display in the company's conference facilities. Contest winners' photographs were purchased by Sedgwick CMS for $250 each. Today dozens of photographs of Memphis – circa 2001 – adorn the company's headquarters. "We made sure that all submitting students sold at least one photograph," Wiertelak explains, adding, "Many students made their first professional sale. Of course, some sold several and we have great photographs celebrating Memphis. Just like everything we do, we looked for a situation where everyone wins."

Sedgwick CMS Headquarters, 1100 Ridgeway Loop Road
Photography by Joe Murphy

Choices of Strategy

Sedgwick CMS is committed to continuing its momentum and industry leadership. The organization has constructed a solid business model for achieving consistently positive results by concentrating on three strategic elements:

Total Performance Management (TPM) – The objective of TPM is not only to meet, but to exceed clients' expectations by making outstanding client outcomes the principal reference point of work processes and training programs. TPM is an outcomes-oriented quality system based on key performance indicators designed to assure the alignment of colleague activities with client and corporate objectives.

Technology – Realizing that access to actionable information is critical in delivering quality claims services, Sedgwick CMS has set the pace for technology advances in the management of claims information, including convenient Web-based access to claims records and reporting functions. Its goal is to stay ahead of the pack. North noted, "We

Colleague training seminar

recently launched Project ATLAS, which teams colleagues from IT and operations to assure that we maintain our technology advantage over the long term, not just in claims information but in all of our operating systems."

Development of Colleagues – Sedgwick CMS is the only company in its industry, and also the only company headquartered in Tennessee, to have achieved certification as an Employer of Choice®. The company, realizing that the product it sells is the service provided by its colleagues, has established an integrated process of strategic recruitment, individual goal setting, performance counseling, training, colleague surveys, and colleague advancement. The firm continuously reviews its HR policies, evaluating them against Employer of Choice standards. Recent innovations have included Sedgwick CMS University's Claims College, an investment in the fast track development of outstanding claims professionals.

Bobby Davis, Cheryl Holmes, Milind Ganoo

Choices in Community Support

In keeping with its commitment to provide a positive environment for the company's colleagues, Sedgwick CMS supports civic and charitable organizations in which its colleagues and clients are personally involved. Sedgwick CMS contributes funds and colleagues' time to a variety of community groups in Memphis and other cities in which it has operations. Company giving and the office-based involvements of Sedgwick CMS colleagues tend to be concentrated in children's and women's health, youth activities and the arts.

Choices for the Future

The company is mindful that just as it has options in locations, business and employment practices, technologies and community philosophies, its clients and colleagues also have choices about working with Sedgwick CMS. "We are grateful for the choices made by our supportive clients and proud of the accomplishments of the colleagues who have elected to work with us," say North and Wiertelak. "We are also confident that our experience, values and focus on client outcomes will enable us to make educated choices in the future that will serve the best interests of everyone – our clients, colleagues, and other stakeholders."

Employer of Choice© Award

Smith & Nephew Orthopaedics

At Smith & Nephew Orthopaedics, innovation drives every aspect of the business, from the pioneering of ground-breaking orthopaedic trauma and joint reconstruction products to its strategic acquisitions of companies whose synergies with Smith & Nephew support its commitment to improved patient outcomes. A customer-focused organization built on the values of performance, innovation and trust, the Orthopaedics business has become the fastest-growing full-line orthopaedics company in the industry, accounting for 47 per cent of the $2.3 billion in annual consolidated Smith & Nephew sales.

A History of Firsts

Smith & Nephew's focus on innovation has resulted in a history of firsts in the orthopaedic industry, including the development of the world's first compression hip screw. The company also introduced the first U.S.-designed total hip, the first FDA-approved cementless hip, and one of the first American-invented total knees. All these breakthroughs occurred at Memphis-based Smith & Nephew Orthopaedics.

Smith & Nephew Orthopaedics has introduced new products that, according to Orthopaedics President David Illingworth, "have improved patient's lives and have the potential to revolutionize the face of Orthopaedics." These products include breakthrough material OXINIUM◊ oxidized zirconium, a unique wear-reducing technology employed in hip and knee implants and utilized in a whole family of products; SUPARTZ® a joint fluid therapy for pain management of the knee; and Crosslinked Polyethylene, a material that extends the life of hip implants by reducing the debris generated over time by wear. Other key products produced in Memphis by Smith & Nephew include EXOGEN◊ bone healing system, a unique ultrasound treatment to accelerate bone fracture healing, and TRIGEN nailing system that allows for badly broken bones to be repaired less invasively than with traditional methods.

Two additional Smith & Nephew products are having a major impact in the field of Orthopaedics: the SYNERGY hip and the TAYLOR SPATIAL FRAME◊ external fixation system. The SYNERGY hip allows surgeons the simplicity of a single set of surgical instruments that can be used with a variety of hip stems to more easily and accurately perform hip replacement procedures. The TAYLOR SPATIAL FRAME external fixator helps broken bones mend.

> *Today, innovation is still the driving force behind the Company's success. Globally, Smith & Nephew holds some 2400 patents (including patents pending) in its Orthopaedics, Endoscopy, and Wound Management businesses.*

Modest Beginnings

Smith & Nephew's history of innovation dates back almost one hundred and fifty years to its modest beginnings in a small chemist's shop in Hull, England. There, pharmacist T.J. Smith turned his passion for helping physicians provide better treatment to their patients into a well-respected hospital and pharmaceutical company serving clients throughout the United Kingdom. In 1896, Horatio Nelson Smith, the founder's nephew, entered into partnership with his uncle and the firm became known as T.J. Smith and Nephew.

The company, headquartered in London, expanded with the advent of World War I due primarily to the demand for wound dressings and other medical products; after the war, expansion continued to other countries, including the United States. Today, Smith & Nephew is one of the world's leading medical devices companies, specializing in Orthopaedics, Endoscopy and Advanced Wound Management. The company boasts established sales in 32 countries and employs more than 7,000 people worldwide. Smith & Nephew is listed on both the London and New York Stock Exchanges.

◊ Trademark of Smith & Nephew, Reg. U.S. Pat. & Tm.Off.
SUPARTZ® is a registered trademark of Seikagaku Corporation.

Sandra Johnson, 11-year employee, inspects and prepares a femoral component for sterilization.

Expansion to the United States

Smith & Nephew's 1986 acquisition of Richards Manufacturing Company (now Smith & Nephew Orthopaedics) significantly expanded its market penetration in the United States. Founded in Memphis in 1934 by J. Don Richards, an orthopaedic devices salesman, Richards had, over the years, evolved from a small surgical soft goods operation into a major orthopaedic trauma and joint reconstruction company. The synergy between Smith & Nephew and its newly acquired Orthopaedics business was obvious. Both, near the top of their fields, had a history of providing clinically-proven products to deliver more effective, less invasive, and more cost-efficient procedures to the medical community. By joining forces these two established companies could help improve the lives of even more people around the world.

Smith & Nephew Orthopaedics believes that its success as a leading provider of orthopaedic products is enhanced by its workforce. As senior vice president of Human Resources Elizabeth Bolgiano puts it, "Our people are the backbone of our organization and our link to our communities. It is truly exciting to know that, in addition to enhancing the quality of life of orthopaedic patients all over the world through our products, Smith & Nephew is able to improve the quality of life of those in our own area by giving our time and money."

Richard Scoggins, 15-year employee, prepares nearly 350 intermedullary nails a day in the anodization area.

The World is Our Community

Smith & Nephew makes significant contributions to quality of life around the globe and in the communities in which it operates. The company provides financial support to many non-profit health and human service organizations, as well as education, arts and civic groups. In addition to corporate dollars, Smith & Nephew has a strong volunteer culture that both supports and encourages employees to become involved in community work.

Locally, the United Way of the Mid-South is one of the largest beneficiaries of Smith & Nephew's corporate funding as well as its employees' donations, but many other non-profit groups benefit from Smith & Nephew's presence in the community. Examples include the Arthritis Foundation, the Church Health Center, The Campbell Foundation, The Greater Memphis Arts Council, and both the Memphis and Shelby County School Systems. In 2004, Smith & Nephew Orthopaedics helped establish and endow the J. R. Hyde Chair of Excellence in Rehabilitation Engineering at the University of Tennessee Health Science Center in Memphis.

Smith & Nephew's own Project Apollo, created and staffed by employee volunteers, is a charitable and humanitarian program that supports the work of surgeons, hospitals, and charitable organizations by providing medical products for use in a variety of settings from natural disasters like earthquakes to smaller medical missions providing ongoing care to the poor. This program also provides healthcare information, medical and technical consulting and medical textbooks to students in underdeveloped countries.

Improvement of the quality of life for all the worlds' people is a major focus of Smith & Nephew Orthopaedics, be it from the efforts of company employees to promote social responsibility or from the company's commitment to developing innovative products to help repair and heal the human body. Dave Illingworth sums it up very well, saying: "The Company creates innovative products whose performance has earned the trust of clinicians around the world. For over 70 years the Memphis-based Orthopaedics business has been a driving force in the medical device industry and in Memphis. We intend to expand and build on that reputation."

Smith & Nephew takes a proactive approach to employee health, Daphine Miller, 25-year employee, stops in the Wellness Center for a blood pressure check from Kathy McDenzie-Conley, RN, of Health Fitness Services.

St. Jude/ALSAC

It all started with a simple promise. More than 60 years ago, a struggling young entertainer with $7 in his pocket knelt in a church before a statue of St. Jude Thaddeus, the patron saint of hopeless causes. Danny Thomas asked the saint to "show me my way in life." Thomas pledged to build a shrine to the saint. When he became a nationally known entertainer, Thomas fulfilled his promise. The result is St. Jude Children's Research Hospital, the world's premier institution for the research and treatment of catastrophic childhood diseases.

More Than Childhood Cancer

St. Jude first made its name through advances in the treatment of childhood leukemia. But since its opening in 1962, the hospital has tackled other childhood killers, including genetic diseases such as sickle cell disease and osteogenesis imperfecta (brittle bone disease); infectious diseases such as tuberculosis and AIDS and numerous childhood cancers, including bone cancers, brain tumors and soft-tissue cancers.

Researchers at St. Jude have made amazing advances toward curing life-threatening childhood diseases. The hospital's therapy for children with acute lymphoblastic leukemia, the most common form of childhood cancer, revolutionized leukemia treatments worldwide. The survival rate has increased from 4 percent, when St. Jude opened, to 80 percent. Other previous killers such as Wilms tumor (a kidney cancer), retinoblastoma (a rare eye cancer) and Hodgkin disease (cancer of the lymph nodes) now have survival rates of more than 90 percent.

Basic and clinical research at St. Jude includes work in gene therapy, bone marrow transplant, chemotherapy, the biochemistry of normal and cancerous cells, radiation treatment, blood diseases, resistance to therapy, viruses, hereditary diseases, influenza and psychological effects of catastrophic illnesses. St. Jude is also a leader in pediatric AIDS research and has pioneered the development of a multi-envelope HIV vaccine designed to combat all the natural strains of HIV. The hospital conducts long-term biostatistical investigations on its patients and is the only pediatric research hospital to be awarded a National Cancer Institute cancer center support grant.

St. Jude is also the only pediatric research center to build an on-site facility to produce highly specialized medicines and vaccines that pharmaceutical companies do not produce due to lack of financial benefit.

Hospital Without Walls

At St. Jude, families never pay for treatments that are not covered by insurance, and families without insurance are never asked to pay. The hospital also covers the cost of lodging, food and travel for patients and their families.

Although St. Jude has about 4,300 patients undergoing treatment at any given time, the hospital only has 58 inpatient beds. To maintain as normal a life as possible for the children and families, patients are treated on an outpatient basis whenever possible. Hospitalization is only considered when all other options are exhausted.

Many St. Jude patients can receive care at local affiliates instead of traveling to Memphis. An extensive network of pediatric hematology-oncology clinics, hospitals and universities are also united to extend the mission of St. Jude.

Less than 30 percent of the world's children with cancer have access to modern treatments. Since its inception, St. Jude has sought to share its groundbreaking research and treatment with scientists and caregivers on a global scale. St. Jude has numerous collaborations with medical institutions in other countries. The hospital's scientific discoveries are freely and immediately shared with scientific and medical communities throughout the world. Teams of doctors come from every region of the world to study for months at a time and take St. Jude protocols back to their homelands.

When Danny Thomas founded St. Jude, the hospital consisted of a single building staffed with talented researchers and caregivers who dreamed of saving children's lives. Now, the numerous buildings of the St. Jude campus cover several blocks of downtown Memphis, and those early pioneers' dreams are coming true. One of the crown jewels of American pediatric medicine, St. Jude attracts patients, physicians and some of the brightest scientific minds in the world to Memphis. All of those people are united in one goal: Finding cures and saving children.

A simple promise. What a difference it has made for the children of the world.

Summerfield Associates, Inc.

Summerfield Associates, Inc. is a Memphis-based staffing, recruiting, and consulting company boasting local, regional and national clients of all sizes. Areas of specialization offered by Summerfield include information technology, human resources, accounting and finance, corporate attorneys, manufacturing, and sales and marketing.

However, company founder Dotty Summerfield-Giusti is quick to clarify that Summerfield Associates' areas of specialization are continuously evolving. "Our clients' needs and levels of service are constantly changing. We like to think of ourselves as 'client centric' – which means our areas of expertise are always expanding."

A Solid Relationship Business

Company founder
Dotty Summerfield-Giusti

Summerfield-Giusti explains that, from the beginning of each client relationship, a partnership is formed so that the recruitment and hiring processes operate as an integral function of the client's human resources department. She notes that, "Although many firms will tell you they are in the relationship business, with Summerfield Associates, it's much more than words. From the beginning, we have explained to staff, recruits, and clients that we cannot help them succeed without a total understanding of their business philosophies, their missions, and their individual corporate or personal cultures."

The firm is proud of its small size, which enables Summerfield Associates to change and adapt to the transforming needs of each client and the fluctuating economy. "We're unusual in that, unlike most traditional contingency search recruiting firms, we can react quickly and creatively to any change that arises. That ability makes us a much more efficient corporate partner to our clients," she added.

Recently Summerfield Associates partnered with two other firms to form The SPC Consortium, a unique blend of HR consulting, executive coaching and staffing services. With one firm, *The Point of Contact*, Summerfield Associates offers one of the most effective of the new services –*The Running Start*. She explained the new service; "After a placement is made, an interview is conducted with the hiring manager and a report is created for the manager that provides a smoother transition for the newly-hired employee."

The company's founder says that Summerfield's plan for success is to keep doing what they've been doing for years while, at the same time, being willing to do things differently as client preferences and economic changes dictate. Changing with the times is nothing new for Summerfield-Giusti. She remembers the days before computers were de rigueur. In fact, she recalls the exact day she learned the term "Information Technology." It was in the early 1980's. Working for a recruitment service company that specialized in placing administrative personnel, she was given a request from her boss for an "IT specialist." Summerfield-Giusti reveals, with a laugh, that she had no idea what an "IT specialist" did. When her boss explained that the IT job was related to computers, she admitted to her that she didn't know anything about them. Her boss responded that, as she was the employee with the mathematics background, she needed to learn. And learn she did.

Associations & Community

In 1986-87, Summerfield-Giusti served as the first female President and first vendor President for the local chapter of the Data Processing Management Association. She has also served as Director and Vice President for the Tennessee Association of Personnel Services, served on the Board of Directors of the National Association of Personnel Services for 10 years, chairing the National By-Laws and Ethics Committee, and served as Treasurer and Vice Chair of the Executive Board.

Committed to giving back to the community in which she prospers, Summerfield-Giusti currently sits on the Board of Directors for Playhouse on the Square/Circuit Playhouse, Make-A-Wish Foundation of the Mid-South, and volunteers as an educator and speaker for outplacement workshops throughout the city.

The professional staff at Summerfield Associates includes (l. to r.) Marla Ripperton, Kim Myers, Mark McCurdy, Dotty Summerfield-Giusti, and Patricia Bell. Janice Lee (not pictured). Photography by Uttam.

The Bodine Company

The Bodine Company is an electronics manufacturing company headquartered in Collierville, Tennessee. It was created in 1962 to build home intercoms, sound systems, burglar alarms and fire alarms. Today, it is a dominant player in the lighting industry. The Bodine Company designs and manufactures award-winning, innovative emergency and specialty lighting products for the national and international markets. Products are sold through manufacturer representatives, fixture manufacturers, distributors and private label accounts.

The company's current position in the industry is remarkable considering its very modest beginning (e.g., the company spent some of its early days in a revamped chicken coop). Then again, founders Dick and the late Jinnie Bodine were remarkable entrepreneurs. They started their business with a shoestring budget and the belief that they could build a company devoted not only to outstanding products and customer service but to outstanding community service. The Bodines succeeded.

The Bodine Company is best known for fluorescent emergency ballasts, but the first lighting product the company sold was the TRAN-BAL® inverter ballast, which allows a fluorescent light to run from a battery source. Dick and Jinnie sold this product to taxi drivers to light cab-top signs, as well as to the Apollo space program, Honeywell, the U.S. Department of Agriculture and Skylab. The Bodines were the first to make the TRAN-BAL inverter ballast commercially available.

Commitment to Technology Development

The Bodine Company excels in developing technologies that solve lighting problems. Many of its advanced fluorescent emergency ballasts serve as great examples. Its self-testing models increase the ease with which code-required testing is done. Its extended-temperature models allow emergency lighting to operate under cold, damp conditions. The company's newest products are no exception. They are definitely solution-driven technologies. These include the ARC Keeper®, the Odyssey™ LED (Light Emitting Diode) driver series and the FEBnet™ Fluorescent Emergency Ballast Network.

The ARC Keeper solves the problem of arc loss (i.e., lighting loss) for HID metal halide fixtures, which are commonly used in warehouse stores, hangars, auditoriums, indoor stadiums and other such areas. The Odyssey driver series makes it possible for LED fixtures to serve as emergency lighting. LED lighting is likely to surpass fluorescent and incandescent as the major lighting source for general illumination, so LED fixtures will play an increasingly significant role in emergency lighting. FEBnet allows users to manage entire emergency ballast networks from a single, centralized computer. Centralized management saves time and money in testing and maintenance.

Two of these products, FEBnet and the LED emergency driver, were first-place winners at Lightfair International in 2004. Lightfair is the premier annual lighting tradeshow in North America and features architectural and commercial lighting products.

FEBnet also received one of Lightfair's special recognition prizes, the Technical Innovation Award. The Technical Innovation Award is presented to the Lightfair New Product Showcase entry that "represents the best leap forward in lighting technology excellence."

The Bodine Company leadership: (L to R) Alexander Ertz, vice president, engineering; Richard "Dick" Bodine, company founder; David Crippen, chief executive officer; and Alpha Lyons, president

The chicken coop utilized by Bodine in the company's early days

The Bodine Company celebrating Bonus Day in 2004

Commitment to Customer Service

Part of the Bodine mission statement is "to be a competitive world supplier of electrical and electronic products and services by providing superior customer satisfaction." The Bodine Company is well regarded by its customers because they know that the company sincerely cares about the customer and the products it sells to the customer.

Emergency lighting, for example, a large portion of Bodine's business, is a critical, code-required element in commercial, institutional and educational facilities. There is no room for shortcuts or compromises when it comes to life safety.

The Bodine Company takes its responsibility to its customers and end-users very seriously. In fact, one of the reasons that Bodine, unlike many other manufacturers, does not manufacture its products abroad is quality control. Products are put together on site at the company's Collierville, Tennessee, facility, where management can walk the line and inspect any product or procedure at any time. Customers appreciate this hands-on approach, and when there is a power failure, so do end-users.

Bodine President Al Lyons understands the importance of good customer relations. "We believe that absolutely everything we do from answering the phone to building the product to shipping the product to customer follow-up is a part of our customer service program, and we

strive to make it the best. If product quality is not exceptional or if we give our customers less than 100% in any way, it's a failure on our part. Customers are our business. Without them there is no Bodine Company." Dick and Jinnie would agree.

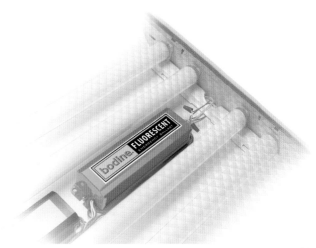

The Bodine Company provides innovative, dependable, unobtrusive emergency and specialty lighting solutions for commercial, industrial and institutional applications.

Commitment to Community

Richard "Dick" Bodine

"We believe our corporate responsibility extends beyond the company to the community," said Lyons. The Bodine Company is a generous contributor to various social, civic and educational programs in the Memphis area. "It's a company tradition and something we want to do."

Indeed, giving back to the community was engrained in The Bodine Company from the start. In 1972, for example, the Bodines established The Bodine School for students with language-based learning disabilities. The Bodine School was the fourth of its kind in the United States and a tribute to Dick and Jinnie's son, Rick, who had dyslexia. The school is located in Germantown, Tennessee, and continues to enrich the lives of many.

"The Bodines felt that their community and their employees were part of their family," said David Crippen, the company's chief executive officer. "And they treated them as such. I think that feeling of family, teamed with their commitment to product development, product quality and customer service, was key to Dick and Jinnie's success as entrepreneurs and to Bodine's success as a company.

"Our continued support is strong in education, sports, children's programs, the arts, medical research and health care for the poor," Crippen said. "The Bodine Company is proud to be a part of the community and support programs that benefit lives in the tri-state metropolitan area."

Virginia "Jinnie" Bodine

Time Warner, Mid-South Division

The Mid-South Division of Time Warner Cable is one of the leading divisions of the largest entertainment company in the world. Time Warner has long utilized the Memphis-area market to test innovative products and services – even before larger markets like New York or Los Angeles.

Memphis and cable television have always been linked, beginning in 1948 with the first written record of a single antenna being used to pick up a distant broadcast television signal and distribute it via coaxial cable to multiple television sets. Although the antenna and cables were in Tuckerman, Arkansas, the program being broadcast (an Ole Miss vs. University of Tennessee football game) originated from the new broadcast station in Memphis.

The Historical Perspective on Memphis Cable

Prior to the 1970's, cable television was available primarily in rural markets and consisted of programming from broadcast stations in larger markets, provided via community antennae; in other words, the programs were increasingly sophisticated versions of the 1948 football broadcast. In 1965, when William Farris and Henry Hancock applied for the first cable franchise in Memphis, the general consensus was that the two Memphis attorneys were taking a huge risk. However, in less than ten years, Farris and Hancock were operating a cable network of approximately 100 customer households in midtown Memphis, which led to the formation of Memphis CATV in partnership with Denver-based American Television & Communications (ATC) in 1976. ATC was owned by the entertainment company, Time Inc.

Original local owner Henry Hancock says, "When we see cable today with its sophisticated technology and its huge influence on our community and our culture, it's hard to remember what it was like back in the beginning. There were months when Bill and I paid the office rent and payroll from our own pockets and had to convince all our friends what a good idea it would be to sign up. I can still hear them telling me that no one would ever need more than three or four channels."

Cable network broadcasting as we know it today did not exist until the mid '70s, when the first satellite transmissions of major cable networks emerged: WTCG (now TBS) was launched by Ted Turner in Atlanta, HBO and CNN hit the air, and ESPN, arguably the riskiest of all cable ventures, began offering 24-hour sports programming. Communications specialists at the time were leery of these programming innovations as they failed to fit broadcasting's standard business model.

Innovations Introduced in Memphis

Cable networks and channels proliferated during the next two decades. Time, Inc. and Warner Bros. Entertainment merged and the new powerhouse, Time Warner, fully acquired the Memphis cable television system, offering 36 channels – a huge increase from the normal offering of 4 to 5 local stations. The introduction of fiber optic technology in 1995 served as the basis for a future of new digital services provided by Time Warner's Mid-South Division. Joe Williams, Communications Officer for the division explained that, "The advancements that fiber optics allowed us to make are almost infinite. All of the product introductions since the mid '90s are standing firmly on the platform provided by fiber optics technology. Not the least among them is Road Runner broadband Internet access, introduced in 1997. Memphis served as the beta test for pay-per-view programming and several other available services that fiber optics has afforded us. As a market we've always been in the forefront for product and service introductions."

Today, the Mid-South Division of Time Warner continues its innovative offerings to area customers. Currently providing over 300 channels, high definition, interactive and digital programming, digital video recording capabilities, pay and free on-demand programming, and broadband internet access, Time Warner's Mid-South Division provides more than 220,000 homes with state-of-the-art communications.

Time Warner Cable Tech Bucket Truck

The Storm of 2003 – Hurricane Elvis Provides Lessons

The early morning storm of July 22, 2003, took less than fifteen minutes to take down thousands of old-growth oak trees that knocked out power to more than 400,000 homes, and blocked streets, demolished houses, and flattened utility poles. The poles had to be replaced or repaired, with the order of repair being electricity, phone, and finally, cable.

"We learned some great lessons from the storm. Now, we have enhanced our abilities to handle calls in several ways. Many customers can utilize interactive programming to determine their community's status and our customer service personnel have access to much more information at their fingertips. All of this makes the customer service process decidedly more efficient," Williams explained.

Community Service is a Company Mandate

Time Warner has a company mandate to "provide a long-term positive impact on the community" it serves. The Mid-South Division of Time-Warner is a company leader in this area, providing exposure and support to local community civic and charitable institutions estimated at $2.6 million per year. The company participates in dozens of these organizations each year, but focuses primarily on those related to education and literacy.

For example, Time Warner sponsors the nation's largest corporate-sponsored literacy initiative, "Time To Read". With more than 5,300 participants at 100 locations throughout the Mid-South, the program has enabled thousands of people to improve their reading skills since it was started in 1990 by Time Warner Mid-South division retiree Nardine Aquadro. Utilizing publications produced by parent company Time Warner, Aquadro's fledgling program has grown to be larger than the next three largest Time Warner division initiatives combined. "Time to Read" was a Points of Light award winner in 1998. It provides in-kind services valued at $1.1 million per year in the Mid-South.

Time Warner Cable Call Center

The company also sponsors several annual events including the Time Warner Road Runner 5K for St. Jude, the Renaissance Gala to benefit LeMoyne-Owen College, and the Hope House Classic Golf Tournament. The benefit for Hope House was established in 1998 when then division president Dean Deyo challenged the management team to identify and aid a truly needy organization unique to the community. Hope House, the only facility of its kind in Tennessee, provides housing for children impacted by HIV/AIDS. In 1998, Hope House was not a United Way Agency and was struggling to survive. The Hope House Classic golf tournament raised $60,000 its first year, and now raises more than $100,000 annually for the charity. The Renaissance Gala has raised more than $700,000 for LeMoyne-Owen College.

Looking Forward

Products to be introduced in the near future include service-bundling offerings such as residential digital phone service and high definition digital video recording services. And the division will continue its many community service endeavors, pledging its material and human resources to the corporate goal of positively impacting the community it serves. Bob Barlow, Time Warner Mid-South Division president, says, "On our website we maintain that we are dedicated to innovation. This means that we will continue to be on the leading edge of product and service introduction for many years to come."

Save the Music Presentation

Amro Music

Amro Music is as defining a presence in the mid-south's music industry as the Mississippi River is in Memphis. The thriving 83-year-old store can lay claim to being one of the 100 largest music retailers nationwide, to having the fourth generation of Averwaters join the family business - and to having the likes of Elvis, B.B. King and Carl Perkins as customers.

Roots

Amro Music's roots date back to 1921 as a California dream. Aspiring pianist, Mil Averwater, and his friend, Frank Mormon, hopped a train from Cincinnati to Los Angeles. Their journey came to an unexpected end after a brief stopover in Memphis, however, when Averwater noticed a lack of piano instructors in town. Seizing the business opportunity, Averwater and Mormon opened a modest second-floor studio on Main Street.

Short on cash but long on ingenuity, Averwater advertised by simply opening the studio windows so passersby could hear the piano music drift down: When curious folks poked their heads in, many didn't leave without a multi-lesson package in hand. Business grew as the men added saxophone, banjo and guitar classes to their repertoire, capitalizing on the era's popular instruments.

While Mormon ultimately decided to return to Cincinnati, Averwater rolled with the punches of being a small-business owner. When jazz became popular, the classically trained musician developed a teaching method called "The Amro System of Popular Jazz" and wrote a how-to book that cemented his local reputation. During the Great Depression, he traded music lessons for eggs, chicken and milk. And when radio became popular, Averwater performed as a background musician for local stations.

This blend of music and business acumen continues to run in the Averwater veins, and the family tree bristles with business degrees and musical instruments. Mil's three children joined the family business, with son Bob becoming president. In turn, Bob's sons Chip and Pat eventually became president respectively.

The fourth-generation Averwater CJ, Chip's son, who recently completed his MBA and continues to gig at a local club, came on board at Amro full-time this year. Bob retired more than 20 years ago but still asks about the business every week. "I recently asked him if he wanted his office back, but he very smartly said no," Pat joked.

Staff members follow in the tradition of the store's mission statement, which is "to be recognizably the best." The bigger challenge comes in conveying the mission statement to customers, which includes band directors, students and parents alike.

Amro faces a particular challenge in that it works primarily with school districts residing within a 150-mile radius of Memphis. School music programs constitute 50 percent of Amro's business, and each road rep averaged about 43,800 miles last year.

Amro invests heavily in outreach and education. Amro maintains an informative Web site - in large part to help solidify the store's reputation for far-flung parents who research where they spend their money. Amro also believes passionately in educating and supporting young band directors.

Despite Amro's success, the Averwater family never rests on its collective laurels. Division performance and industry trends are constantly scrutinized. New ideas for events and offerings are regularly proposed and tried. Pat explained, "We never stop asking ourselves if there is a better way."

The Racquet Club of Memphis

The Racquet Club of Memphis, conveniently located in the center of the City, is a family-owned, private club that sets itself apart with its facility, its employees, its members, "one of the best" reputations in professional tennis, and its sense of community.

The facility is luxurious and broad in scope, from the tennis-viewing Executive Suites (the first in the world) to its own laundry. In 2003, The Racquet Club was voted by the United States Tennis Association as the Top Private Club Facility in the U.S.

The employees are professional, committed and loyal; more than half of the staff have been at the Club over 15 years.

The members are diverse and active – from tiny tots to seniors – more than 80% use the Club monthly.

The services are first-rate and versatile, from a la carte dining and family night buffets to business meetings and wedding receptions; from the nationally acclaimed Junior Development Program and a resident Pilates Center to a Fitness Center with more than 35 pieces of state-of-the-art equipment and eleven (11) personal trainers; from David Deviney Hairstyling, manicures and massages to top-of-the line sport and ladies' ready-to-wear merchandise in The Shop, twice voted "the best in the U.S."

Home of the Premier "International" Sporting Event in the Mid-South

The Regions Morgan Keegan Championships and the Cellular South Cup, held each February at the Club, is a great regional asset. For 30 years, The Racquet Club has hosted the biggest stars in tennis: Borg, Connors, Lendl, Agassi, Sampras, McEnroe, Edberg, Courier, and Roddick. Only the U.S. Open can match Memphis' number of year-end #1 players as its champions – Nine (9)!

The addition of the women's event in 2001 makes the event the only ATP (Association of Tennis Professionals) and WTA (Women's Tennis Association) combined indoor tennis tournament in the world.

Star
Andy Roddick

International Attention, the Best Tennis, Corporate Support, Making a Difference

With the prestigious Regions Morgan Keegan Championships and the Cellular South Cup, The Racquet Club of Memphis brings international attention to the city, the Region and St. Jude Children's Research Hospital. The tennis event generates an atmosphere both on and off the court that is unparalleled. One of only three major championships to be held in a private club (Monte Carlo and The All England Lawn Tennis and Croquet Club in Wimbledon), the setting is intimate for fans and players, and no other championship-level tennis event in the world brings the fans so close to the court.

"Memphis is the most friendly and intimate stop on the tour," says Andy Roddick. "The organizers (The Club's Tournament Team) do the very best job of conducting the tournament."

"We have a committed staff, averaging 15 years of service here, and several of the tournament volunteers have been with us more than 20 years," says Mac Winker, tournament owner.

The sense of community has never been more alive at The Racquet Club of Memphis, as it continues to support St. Jude's Children's Research Hospital. The Winkers and the Racquet Club employees are proud, as a small business, of generating impacting sponsor involvement of the more than $7 million contributed (1993-2004) to support the work done for children at St. Jude.

Barbara Bush with Mac Winker

Play It Again

Call Play It Again, Memphis at (901) 474-6462 and help make music education a reality for our youth. When you donate a new or used musical instrument to Play It Again, Memphis, you will receive your choice of a music concert, sporting event, or special production – courtesy of TicketMaster. Plan It Again, Memphis does just that by encouraging residents of Memphis and Shelby County to take used band instruments from their attics and closets and give them new homes in our schools.

Part of the Play It Again boosters (l to r): Tommie Pardue, Joe Utsey, Charlie Ryan, Chip Averwater, Jim Rout, Jim Holcomb, Jon Hornyak, Janice Wood, Onzie Horne

Today there continues to be talented children in our city and county schools who are eager for the opportunity to learn and play music, but cannot afford to buy band instruments.

Memphis City and Shelby County Schools need all types of band instruments to equip their music programs, but school budgets do not always provide for that.

Play It Again, Memphis was created with the objective of providing the instruments necessary to make music education a reality for every student.

Music enriches all of our lives – especially in Memphis, where our music history is legendary. The number of talented musicians in this area, their diversity, and their achievements are simply phenomenal.

Today there continues to be talented children in our city and county schools who are eager for the opportunity to learn and play music, but cannot afford to buy band instruments. And, unfortunately, they can't depend on their school's budget to meet the needs.

As the home of the Blues and birthplace of Rock and Roll, Memphis' place in American History demands we help the young children development their musical skills. We must commit to the musical talents of the future.

Once given to Play It Again, Memphis, the instruments are repaired through donated labor and then distributed to the deserving schools. An independent committee assess applications from music directors throughout the city and county to determine which schools are in greatest need of instruments. Music education means more than learning the notes to a song. Children enrolled in music education programs have a more rewarding schools experience. Studies show that music education impacts students' achievement scores and is directly correlated to the development of skills and abstract reasoning. Kids who might otherwise be at risk can be motivated to stay in school through music.

Success and entrepreneurship can come in small or large packages. Brother Juniper's College Inn is a home-grown and very successful restaurant near the University of Memphis. The Hard Rock Cafe, since its London origin in 1971, now has over 100 world-wide cafes plus hotels and casinos. The photograph shows Memphis' Hard Rock Cafe on Beale Street (top-by Robert W. Dye, bottom-by API Photographers, Inc.)

Corporate Profile Index

Acknowledgements

Special thanks to the following archives and individuals who supplied resource material and images for this project: Ed Frank and staff, Special Collections Department, University of Memphis Libraries; Dr. Jim Johnson and staff, Memphis Room, Memphis Library and Information Center; Bill Carrier, API Photographers, Inc.; Robert W. Dye; Memphis Archives; Arcadia Archives; Ken Neill & Frank Murtaugh, Memphis Magazine; Jackie Flaum, Memphis Symphony; Jim Perrin; Ray Darby; Junior Achievement; Pat Kerr Tigrett; John Hull Dobbs; Dottie Bonds, Kemmons Wilson, Inc.; Ann Brand, Boyle Investments; Willitt's Designs; Baker Donelson Bearman Caldwell & Berkowitz PC; Judy Baird, Saks, Inc.; Mary Jo Weakes, Hyde Family Foundation; Norma Egbert, Gaylord Entertainment; Angie Whitfield, Campbell Clinic Orthopaedics; Kathy Moye, Folgelman Properties; Jo Harshberger, SunTrust Bank.